CORBA FOR
REAL PROGRAMMERS

LIMITED WARRANTY AND DISCLAIMER OF LIABILITY

CORBA FOR
REAL PROGRAMMERS

REAZ HOQUE

Morgan Kaufmann

ACADEMIC PRESS, A HARCOURT SCIENCE AND TECHNOLOGY COMPANY

San Diego   San Francisco   New York   Boston
London   Sydney   Tokyo

ACADEMIC PRESS
A Harcourt Science and Technology Company
525 B Street, Suite 1900, San Diego, CA 92101-4495 USA
http://www.academicpress.com

Academic Press
24-48 Oval Road, London NW1 7DX United Kingdom
http://www.hbuk.co.uk/ap/

Morgan Kaufmann
340 Pine Street, Sixth Floor, San Francisco, CA 94104-3205 USA
http://www.mkp.com

Library of Congress Catalog Card Number: 99-60085
International Standard Book Number: 0-12-355590-6

Printed in the United States of America
99 00 01 02 03 IP 6 5 4 3 2 1

Contents

Contents

Contents

Dedication

Growing up was not easy for me. Like every one else, I had good times and bad. For the times when I needed the support, I could always turn to Diana Apa, Shampa Apa, Liana Apa, Sina Bhaia, and Iti. You will always remain a significant part of my life. My soul will always be with you regardless of where on earth I might be.

Preface

In today's computing world, prebuilt components play a major role. The reason? Components reduce development time: Companies reuse components that they can assemble quickly to produce high-end applications. Well-developed components can be glued together without much code having to be written.

This new paradigm of computing raises two questions: How can components communicate if they are not on the same computer; and how can components using various technologies be compatible? This is where CORBA comes in, by making communications among objects from different programming languages possible in a distributed environment. This is a very simple description of the role of CORBA. More about its role and importance can be found in the first chapter.

Why This Book

More and more companies today are using CORBA and making sure that their products are CORBA compliant. Indeed, CORBA has become *the architecture* for distributed computing. This popularity has encouraged publishers to publish books on the subject, as a quick search of online books sellers will show. In May 1998, IDG published my book, *CORBA 3*. That book and most of the books on the market show how CORBA can be used to develop enterprise-level applications.

Given the popularity of *CORBA 3*, I decided to write this book, which covers the development of CORBA-compliant applications. *CORBA for Real Programmers* will be the only reference guide you will need for all your CORBA development needs. It will not teach you how to program in CORBA, but will help you implement CORBA in your organization.

Who Should Read This Book

This book is not for those who are just learning CORBA, but is for those who already are doing CORBA-related development on a regular basis. For those who are unfamiliar with CORBA, I suggest a tutorial-based book such as *CORBA 3*.

CHAPTER 1

The Common Object Request Broker Architecture (CORBA)

1.1 Introduction

The need for a distributed architecture has existed perhaps 15 to 20 years now. The general problem such a system is designed to solve is the connection of the individual components of hardware and software so that they work together seamlessly in a cohesive framework. How best to do this was the focus of much effort over the years, some of it successful, some of it not. For the most part, however, custom solutions for a particular case worked best.

Only recently have off-the-shelf distributed solutions become available. In the last five years or so two have been specified, built, and used in commercial applications: the Distributed Computing Architecture (DCE) and the Common Object Request Broker Architecture (CORBA), the latter the subject of this book.

Quite possibly, the most important thing CORBA contributes to a distributed architecture development effort is architecture, language, and platform independence. Architecture independence allows a system to execute within and through different operating system platforms. CORBA achieves this by creating a layer that lies between the OS and the applications using it. Since the OS is thus tightly coupled to a hardware platform, components of CORBA can run on SPARCs, NT machines, Java Stations, and more.

CORBA delivers language independence through its use of the Interface Definition Language (IDL). IDL and its associated constructs can be translated, or *mapped*, into any language, thus freeing developers and architects to choose the best language for an implementation as opposed to being "locked" into a particular one.

CORBA delivers platform independence by the fact that it is itself an open specification. Therefore, any vendor can implement a CORBA system on the platform of its choosing. CORBA ORBs and their tools and compilers currently exist for, among others, Windows95, WindowsNT, Linux, HP/UX, Solaris, AIX, and real-time operating systems. They also work with SunPro compilers, GNU compilers, Microsoft and Borland compilers, integrated development environments, and the like.

Broadly, and perhaps most importantly, CORBA forces developers to "break down" component interfaces, which encourages more clear thought and thus better component design. Incidentally, it involves more people in the development effort, leading to a better understanding of how the system works.

1.2   N-Tier Systems

Tiering is best illustrated through a historical look at software engineering and how applications have been built. Real software engineering started with the mainframe—dumb terminals were hooked up to one central processing unit, and all software was based on that unit. Therefore, writing the software meant simply creating it on the mainframe, and all of the terminals then repeating what they saw there. As might be imagined, software development was easy for this type of system.

It wasn't until the next generation of software came out—client/server— that difficulties arose. The cause was the fundamental separation now introduced between two halves of a functioning system. One half was the user interface at the PC. The other, more important, half was the server-side: the functional units on a file server or other very fast computer that computed all the equations and retrieved all the data necessary for a particular application to work.

The software created in the first two generations showed both similarities and differences. One similarity was that an interface wasn't necessary for the user to get to information from the computational half of the system. Another was the database or data storage needed at the back half of the system for it to operate correctly. As for differences, in the first, mainframe, generation the application was stored on one computer and the dumb terminal acted as a simple interface to the system. In the second, client/server, generation one part of the application, the data, sat on a fast computer and the other part, the interface, sat on a separate PC.

The third and current generation of software engineering—and the subject of this book—is *N-tier systems*. Tiering builds on the client/server idea that processing is separate from the interface; however, it does not specify where the processing will take place. This means that processing can occur in any number of "services," such as actual database systems, authentication systems, or notification systems. The commonality is that all of the systems interact with the client. Tiering thus breaks down processing into functional areas that suit the needs of the end user. This is where CORBA comes in, as we shall see.

1.3   Distributed Systems

Distributed systems are the entire set of existing hardware and software that allow developers to build third-generation, N-tier, solutions. The basic idea behind them is that the tasks to be carried out by the system are broken down into separate, autonomous processes, and that each of these has its own process space. For example, in a distributed collaborative engineering system, several important areas must be considered:

- Notification among users
- Secure authentication of all users

- File uploading and profiling for users
- Different data repositories needed by users, such as a file meta-data system
- Live text, audio, and video on-demand management components
- Translation components to handle the different data formats needed by users
- Graphical user interfaces (GUIs) for different users
- "White pages" lookup of all users
- "Yellow pages" lookup of common services and other helpful system resources

One way to build such a system, the client/server method, would be to put all of this functionality in a main processing unit and break the interfaces out separately. Another, more attractive, way would be to make each component a separate economical process that could be used by any other process within and across systems. For this method to work, an agent that brokers requests between the disparate processes would be necessary— that is, an *object request broker*, known as an ORB.

With CORBA, developers can define interfaces to all of the components in the collaborative engineering example, register them, and then use them during system execution. Furthermore, those components are interchangeable in two ways. First, the interface is directly portable to another CORBA system, which means that the interface file, which is in ASCII format, can be moved to any other ORB system and run through the corresponding tool(s) to generate low-level "stubs" and "skeletons" (defined later) for the object services. Second, the level of compatibility is binary, meaning that actual compiled and linked binary object services are mobile within the same type of ORB environment. Thus, developers can build objects in the development environment and, using a development "white pages" naming service, simply reregister them in the production environment. There is no need to do another build.

1.4 The Object Management Group

CORBA was created by the Object Management Group (OMG). Founded in 1989 to promote object-oriented technology in software development, the OMG is an international consortium of over 800 member organizations ranging from large companies, such as Sun Microsystems, to small companies, such as Iona Technologies and Visigenic/Inprise Software Corporation.

The people directly responsible for the CORBA specification came from different backgrounds such as telecommunications and commercial software development. This diversity of talents made for a specification that would work for years to come, yet success did not come easily. There were many long nights of discussion and argument before each part of the specification fell into place. Indeed, some have said that CORBA was one of the fastest specifications to become reality given how many different groups contributed to it. A partial list of those groups follows:

- BNR Europe, Ltd.
- Defense Information Systems Agency
- Expersoft Corp.
- Fujitsu, Ltd.
- Genesis Development Corp.
- Gensym Corp.
- IBM
- ICL plc
- IONA Technologies, Ltd.
- Digital Equipment Corp.
- Hewlett-Packard
- Hyperdesk Corp.
- Micro Focus Ltd.
- MITRE Corp.
- NCR Corp.
- Novell USG

- Object Design, Inc.
- Objective Interface Systems, Inc.
- OC Systems, Inc.
- Open Group–Open Software Foundation
- Siemens Nixdorf Informationssysteme AG
- Sun Microsystems, Inc.
- SunSoft, Inc.
- Sybase, Inc.
- Visual Edge Software, Ltd.

The OMG can be contacted at the following addresses and phone numbers:

OMG Headquarters
492 Old Connecticut Path
Framingham, MA 01701
USA

Tel: (508) 820-4300
Fax: (508) 820-4303
Email: pubs@omg.org
Web: http://www.omg.org

Listed below are several concepts defined by the OMG that should further an understanding of CORBA technology. The concepts are grouped by object semantics categories.

- An *object* is an entity that provides a service to requesting clients.
- A *request* is an event that occurs at a particular time, generated by CORBA clients. It has four parts: an operation, a target, zero or more parameters, and an optional request context.
  - A *value* is anything that can be a legal parameter within a request context. An object reference is a "handle" to a CORBA object.
- Objects can be created or destroyed in response to certain types of client requests.
- A *type* is a special identifiable primitive that can be used in the CORBA context. Basic types consist of primitive bit values such as 16-bit, 32-bit,

and 64-bit signed and unsigned 2's complement integers. Constructed types consist of records, sequences, arrays, discriminated unions, and interfaces.

- An *interface* is a set of operations or methods that a client can invoke on an object.

- An *operation* is an identifiable construct that allows a service to be requested and identified by an operation identifier. This is not to be confused with *value*, defined above. An operation has a signature that describes the possible return results and request parameters.

- As in object-oriented languages, an interface may have *attributes*. However, instead of actual values, CORBA attributes are accessor and mutator functions only. Obviously, the actual value is independent of the definition. Because these functions, rather than the actual value, are defined, any language can be used to define them.

The CORBA specification is currently at revision 2.1. It is divided into the following four general areas:

CORBA — the inner workings of the specification. Its chief component is the Object Request Broker (ORB). Also important are the Interface and Implementation Repositories.

CORBA Services — the fundamental, self-functioning parts of the specification that assist the ORB during its operations.

CORBA Facilities — the group of service-type activities that function within the ORB itself.

Vertical Domain Functionalities — the parts of the specification that have a specific vertical market focus.

1.5   The ORB

The Object Request Broker (ORB) is the "heartbeat" of the CORBA system. A self-running autonomous process, it handles the various call-backs outlined in the CORBA 2.1 specification. The OMG defines four general ORB types:

Client and implementation resident. The ORB component and the client are "married," meaning that functions are very tightly coupled. Thus, the client stub might directly access a location rather than go through a location service.

Server-based. One of possibly several ORB servers routes requests and replies between clients and object service implementations. Obviously, there is a tight coupling between the servers, the machines they reside on, and the ORB itself.

System-based. The ORB functions are integrated with the operating system of the server computer, or otherwise very near it, in terms of functionality.

Library-based. Objects are shared, so the client cannot be allowed to ruin or otherwise damage the data in the service object(s) it interacts with.

1.5.1 Object Reference

As of this writing, and throughout CORBA versions 1.1 to 2.1, the infrastructure has been pass-by-reference; that is, the object services are passed as a value, much like a memory value, to the client. The service itself resides on the machine on which it was registered or otherwise implemented, but the reference makes it appear to be local to the requesting client. The client takes this referential value, or reference, into its memory and acts on it by invoking one or more operations. Over the last couple of years, the OMG has worked hard on the problem of pass-by-value.

In a pass-by-value infrastructure (a clever illustration of which is Java 1.1's "object serialization"), the client takes the entire object from the socket from which it is reading the response, loads it into its own memory, and then invokes directly on it. A pass-by-reference invocation must be translated or otherwise transferred between the client and the machine on which the actual object resides through the commonality of the reference. This is known as an *Interoperable Object Reference* (IOR) and is used throughout the specification and this text.

A look at the structure of an actual ORB shows at a high level the clients and object implementations, and the ORB carrying requests from one to the other. Down a level in execution are the stubs and skeletons, which can be either static (i.e., predefined) or dynamic (i.e., defined at runtime), and an object adapter between the ORB and the object implementation. We can envision the overall transport of the system as a pipe. From the transport pipe (IIOP), there would stem various objects, which are the services. If you add a layer to the pipe, that wraps the IIOP transport section, you can think of that as an ORB. IIOP is defined and discussed in further detail in the Inter-ORB communications section of this chapter. A client passes a request through either a dynamic invocation or an IDL stub. The object implementation receives the request through its object adapter, in the form of a static IDL skeleton or a dynamic skeleton.

CORBA does not dictate how the ORB will be implemented; rather, the ORB need only implement the interfaces specified. The interface to the ORB is organized according to the following three categories:

- Operations equivalent across all ORB implementations
- Operations particular to specific objects themselves
- Operations particular to styles of objects

The vendor of the particular ORB is free to decide how to implement these functionalities, which was a problem when CORBA 2.0 came out. The two leading implementations at that time, Iona's Orbix, and Sun Microsystems NEO, had trouble passing requests to each other over the Internet. Only after the two specifications had time to mature and stabilize could they exchange requests without translation, or "marshaling" difficulties.

The ORB tracks objects through its Interface and Implementation repositories. The Interface Repository tracks the defined interface between an object and its clients. The Implementation Repository tracks the location of the executable for that object and otherwise lets the ORB know how to start and stop it to maintain the life cycle service; we might think of it as the actual code that executes the particular methods of an object service.

Through the ORB, clients notice only the reference for a particular object service on which they can then invoke operations or methods to access the object's defined functions. The interface works in the executable form for a particular object service through of a language mapping, which is defined later.

The object reference differs from ORB to ORB. It is compiled to handle an object service within a singular ORB, so it will vary depending on the vendor's ORB implementation. The structure of an object implementation, although it can be confusing in practice, is easy to understand in theory: It maintains the state and methods, or execution mechanisms, of that stateful data.

We might think of the implementation as two halves. One half houses the object's actual state, through its attributes, and provides the methods or functions that utilize the stateful data attributes. The other half is the CORBA-specific information, which consists of the actual specified skeleton for the interface, as generated by the IDL tool that came with the CORBA implementation.

1.5.1.1   The ORB Interface
A portion of the CORBA specification defines operations that are specific to the ORB and implemented "native" to the process or daemon itself. These operations do not specifically depend on object adapters, as previously discussed.

One of the first operations defined is object–string conversion. This allows the ORB to take an object it "controls"—that is, it has an interface and implementation entry in the ORB's repositories—"stringify" it into an ASCII character string. Conversely, it provides a standard way for the ORB to convert a "stringified" reference back to an actual object reference that it knows and thus can invoke upon. The importance of this operation is apparent: ASCII strings are tremendously more portable than objects. Once in string form, an ORB can pass an object to almost any machine, over any network, and the object's integrity, as represented by that string, is maintained.

Another important defined functionality allows the ORB to obtain service information. Using it, the ORB can "report on," or return requests for, information on the services and facilities it supports. Also defined are *object reference operations*, which allow the ORB to determine an object interface, the operations the object serves, and how an operation is served in terms of its associated parameters and return values. The ORB allows duplication of an object reference. The reason for this is that the references themselves are implemented through the ORB system and so are dependent on it. Thus, a client cannot store a reference and, without going through the ORB, cannot know what it translated into (it is possible to implement the CORBA object–string conversions on the client as well, but it still does no good). Finally, there are nil object reference operations and equivalence checking operations.

An ORB can probe for objects that do not exist but are still registered, which is useful in bounds checking and exception handling. The ORB can do referential identity operations and obtain and operate on "policies" associated with objects.

1.5.1.2 The Interface and Implementation Repositories

The Interface Repository provides secure, stateful, persistent memory for the interface definitions. As might be imagined, its own interface is specified in IDL terms. For the repository to function properly, the ORB must be able to interact with the actual object interface definitions, either through static access to the actual code stubs and building on that access with a "parsing" routine, or through runtime access provided via interface-based or other objects.

The Implementation Repository can be thought of as paired with the Interface Repository. Once the ORB has found the interface for a given object in the Interface Repository, it searches the Implementation Repository for that object's implementation. Together, the two repositories allow cleaner integration of the ORB and the object it services in terms of the object's life cycle (handled by the Life Cycle service, described later) by allowing the ORB to start and stop the object through operating system execution calls.

Obviously, both the interface implementation components of the ORB are implementation specific. That is to say, different vendors will build them differently in their own ORB systems.

1.6 Defining a Distributed Interface

CORBA's most important component is the mechanism for defining an interface to a component or service—the Interface Definition Language (IDL). Using IDL, a developer can define the interface in a standard ASCII format and generate stubs and skeletons for that description.

1.6.1 IDL

The Interface Definition Language is the handshake, or "contract" that exists between clients and the associated object services. At a high level it looks like any other programming language. In reality, however, it specifies an object-oriented (OO) interface to a service object for both the object implementation and the client. IDL has been said to look like C but have all of the power and functionality of C++.

The two most important parts of an IDL description are the interface defined and its associated parameters, which include return types for particular functions or methods as well as the actual parameters used within those functions or methods. In this way the data types that *pass through* the interface can be captured and utilized. IDL follows the lexical rules of C++, but presents more keywords to associate distributed operations. It can be run through a C++ preprocessor and in fact supports a direct subset of the ANSI C++ specification. IDL also supports conventions for block and in-line comments.

Within CORBA 2.1, the IDL is specified as an Extended Backus-Naur Format. Chapter 2 covers the grammar in detail. For now, it is enough to know what the IDL is and why it is so important to the CORBA specification.

After the IDL description for a given module, or set of modules, is written, a (vendor-specific) tool can be utilized to generate client-side stubs server-side skeletons (which are described in detail in the next subsection) through a specified mapping of IDL constructs and conventions to a particular language. Currently, mappings exist for, among others, C++, C, Fortran, Java, Cobol, and Smalltalk. The mapping is a part of the CORBA specification, so that a developer can look there for how a particular language implements the IDL. This is literally how CORBA delivers on its promise of language independence—by allowing a vendor to define an interface and use any language of its choosing to implement it.

One of the most important aspects of the IDL is that it supports single *and* multiple inheritance. This is legal only because each interface can be specified as a direct base interface of a derived interface no more than once, which means that multiple inheritance can be supported without creating turmoil for vendors in implementing it.

1.6.2   Stubs and Skeletons

The stubs and skeletons are the tools that come with a particular ORB on the basis of an IDL description. They are the low-level code that are compiled and used to pass the actual data specified in IDL for a given object. The stub is the client side; the skeleton, the server side.

When stubs and skeletons are generated from an IDL description, usually certain libraries, headers, or some other means of combining a vendor's source code or libraries with the stub or skeleton are introduced. Once generated, the associated stubs and skeletons are otherwise linked, or compiled, with the dynamic library or object portion of the vendor's library to make the cohesive solution work.

When compiled or linked properly, the stub forms the client-side invocation mechanism—the low-level networking code (including the marshaling and unmarshaling of the actual transmitted data bytes) that the client uses to pass messages to an ORB and otherwise invoke upon a server-side object service. The skeleton, the opposite of the stub, is coupled to the service object. It determines how the object receives and processes requests from ORBs or client-side objects.

1.7   InterORB Communications

The second most important piece of the CORBA infrastructure is the specification by which ORBs communicate. This specification resides atop TCP/IP, which is the de facto networking standard for most systems today. As mentioned earlier, it took a while for interORB communications to work because of the freedom vendors had to implement an ORB system as they saw fit. Obviously, at a bit and byte level there is some flexibility in interpretation, and this would holds true for actual binary code generated by a compiler. For instance, if a CORBA specification is for an IEEE 64-bit floating-point number, one compiler might compile this as a 32-bit value; another, as a 64-bit value.

These days most ORBs are very good at interoperability. This is good for developers because it allows them to choose the ORB system they think is best for a particular task. For example, one ORB might prove superior in fault tolerance, and so would be best in telecommunications applications. Another might promote rapid development, and so would be better than others for generating front ends to commercial vertical market products. The beauty of this is that components from both these systems can be used interchangeably later.

The OMG defines interoperability in terms of domains and bridges. Reference domains describe how an ORB references an object; connectivity and security domains respectively cover network topology and security concerns. A bridge, on the other hand, simply creates a means of translation between two distinct protocols—for instance, between the Distributed Computing Environment (DCE) and TCP/IP.

The Interoperable Object Reference (IOR) permits communication between and across ORBs. As it turns out, the IOR is a key element in low-level interoperations. Using it, an ORB need not understand an object intrinsically but only know how to refer to it and invoke operations on it. The IOR is created in the bridging between reference domains and supports only one tagged profile per protocol.

Inline bridging is internal to an ORB and translates "live" between the ORB's reference domain(s) and other ORBs. Request-level bridging links the ORB to an outside object that does the translations; that object passes the references as results back to the ORB. Interfaces to bridges can be either static, that is, generated by static IDL, or dynamic, that is, and discovered at runtime via the Dynamic Skeleton Interface (DSI) and Dynamic Invocation Interface (DII) (discussed later in this chapter).

Communication between ORB systems, whether or not they are built by the same vendor, is specified according to the interORB protocols outlined below.

1.7.1   GIOP

The Generic InterORB Protocol (GIOP) is the base protocol (in terms of messages) for official interORB communication. This can include vendor-specific proprietary communication, so GIOP must be able to map to *any* connection-oriented medium. It is meant to be cheap, scalable, simple to understand, general in scope, and widely usable by vendors for implementation.

The OMG specifies three parts to GIOP:

* The Common Data Representation (CDR)
* The various GIOP message formats (seven in all)
* The message transport assumptions

The CDR is essentially a low-level transfer syntax that maps between OMG IDL types and low-level raw data types for use between network agents and processes. It consists of the following:

* Variable byte ordering (as in big- and little-endian).
* Aligned primitive types (for more efficiency in aligning memory).
* A complete OMG-specified IDL mapping (therefore supporting *all* OMG IDL data types).

Table 1.1 lists the seven base GIOP message types. Along with these,

Table 1.1   GIOP Message Types

Message	Type Originator	Value (enum)
Request	Client	0
Reply	Server	1
CancelRequest	Client	2
LocateRequest	Client	3
LocateReply	Server	4
CloseConnection	Server	5
MessageError	Both	6

GIOP makes the following message transport assumptions:

- The transport is connection oriented.
- The transport is reliable.
- The transport can be viewed as a byte stream.
- The transport provides reasonable notification of a bad connection and the associated loss of connection.
- The transport's connection model can be mapped to the general TCP/IP connection model.

The similarity between the CORBA generic protocol and the Internet's TCP/IP stack is clear, which is, in part, why the mapping of GIOP to the Internet and TCP/IP is referred to as the Internet InterORB Protocol (IIOP).

1.7.2 IIOP

If we think of IIOP, we see that its lowest level is the physical link layer, where the actual physical connections such as Ethernet connections, CSU/DSUs, token rings, and fiber (FDDI), reside. The next layer up is the "post-office box." This is where the physical connections and entities are given two addresses: a hard-coded address that uniquely identifies a device among all other similar devices—for example, a MAC address on an Ethernet card; and a network address that uniquely identifies a device, or the machine it hosts, among all other entities within a network—for example, an IP address on the Internet.

The next layer in the stack is where stream-based reliable delivery of packets takes place. This is the Transmission Control Protocol (TCP), which ensures that no data integrity will be lost over the life of the packet stream while in transit (i.e., through routers, switches, and hubs). Finally, the highest layer is IIOP, which ties everything together: stream-based reliable delivery, accessible and addressable across the Internet on any physical device that supports it, of the GIOP's seven message types. This is the definition of IIOP—the Internet itself becomes the "backbone" ORB.

1.7.3   ESIOP

For all nonnative TCPs, vendors may devise an Environment Specific InterORB Protocol (ESIOP). An ESIOP provides a half-bridge to the ORB, which the vendor completes to provide IIOP to the same ORB. In this way the ORB can talk through a proprietary system to its own objects and services, but still can be invoked upon by other ORBs through the Internet.

Two camps are emerging with respect to ESIOP in today's markets. One camp believes that IP should be the "base-level" protocol and that all other protocols should build on it. The other believes that a problem should be broken down in terms of the network that connects the disparate parts and all the other pieces that make the solution (GUI, logical units, and so forth).

CORBA addresses the concerns of both camps. It provides a base topology that is very much TCP/IP-centric with most of the stipulations discussed above bound on it. However, it also allows developers to build their own protocols into the topology by mapping those protocols to the seven GIOP message types.

One environment-specific protocol provided by CORBA is the Open Foundation's Distributed Computing Environment (DCE) architecture. The OMG actually provides the specification for this adaptation, but it proves to be a very good example of what an ESIOP is, and how one could do about specifying one before building it. DCE is built on the Remote Procedure Call (RPC) mechanism. (Actually, it extends secure-RPC, thus building more dependability into the model.) It is not socket and/or port driven, as a TCP/IP application is. In adapting DCE to CORBA, the OMG made sure that DCE would support all of the interoperability issues outlined above, including synchronous message passing within the GIOP.

DCE has its own ORB, which uses a Common Inter-ORB Protocol (CIOP) that is specified as a set of secure-RPC messages. DCE also supports the GIOP-based CDR. Although DCE and IP are two of the most popular network transports in use today, GIOP is not restricted to them. Other vendors have mapped the GIOP to other transports, such as real-time network systems.

1.7.4   Invocation on a Distributed Object

Object services are provided to requesting clients via a handle, or reference, to a service. The client invokes on an object service through the following sequence of events:

1. The client performs lookup and contacts the ORB.
2. The client asks the ORB for a "white pages" reference to a particular object service.
3. The ORB performs lookup and locates the requested service through the Implementation Repository.
4. If the service is not running, the ORB utilizes the Life Cycle service to start the service object.
5. The ORB passes a tested "live" reference of the service object back to the client.
6. The client, having received a reference to the service object requested, invokes a method on it.

Note that the method invoked on the reference has been specified in IDL.

In CORBA there are two ways a client can invoke on the service object reference. One way is via the Static Invocation Interface—using the IDL specification above, a low-level interface is generated for the client that can be compiled with the client's implementation. The other way is the Dynamic Invocation Interface—the client performs a lookup through the ORB on a particular service, discovers the interface to that service at runtime, and acts on it.

1.7.4.1   Static Invocation Interface (SII)

The SII follows the convention that the interface between actual objects and the ORB is static, as in statically linked and loaded into memory. It uses an IDL conversion or translation tool to convert IDL descriptions into directly generated code. That code is in turn compiled and linked with its implementation and used to communicate to requesting clients.

Obviously, static invocation is both simpler to understand and simpler to implement than dynamic invocation. Thus, it is no surprise that it happened first and became stable first. The issue for developers in deciding whether to use a static or dynamic interface comes down to choice between latency and flexibility.

Dynamic interface mechanisms allow a great deal of flexibility. All a developer needs to know is the type of method to be invoked, and its associated data. SII, on the other hand, allows *no* flexibility! Once the interface is defined, compiled, and linked, it is set in stone until the process is redone. However, since the ORB knows so much about the interface, once it registers that service object in its Interface and Implementation repositories, it can add more information about it and therefore speed things up when the interface methods are called.

1.7.4.2   *Dynamic Invocation Interface (DII)*

The Dynamic Invocation Interface allows a more complex and flexible, "live" method for invoking on an object service. This is an alternative to using a stub generated from an IDL description, whereby the client issues the request at runtime and the ORB takes the raw information from the client and turns it into an actual request on the object service.

When issuing a request through DII, the client utilizes a structure, called a `NamedValue`, that allows the raw data to be passed to the ORB in a specific, identifiable fashion. The ORB can then channel the request to the proper object or component. A request consists of an object reference, an operation, and a basic listing of the parameters needed by the operation. The CORBA exception `WrongTransaction` is thrown whenever a match cannot be made by the ORB between the dynamic information and an actual call. The parameters can be subjected to runtime type checking, if necessary.

As with most of the features and functionalities specified by the OMG in CORBA, DII is specified as unique IDL. Developers should become accustomed to IDL as the "definition" language of CORBA and make themselves familiar with defining interfaces to components used in a development solution. The IDL and detailed description of DII are the subjects of Chapter 2.

1.7.5 Object Adapters

Object adapters, a core component of CORBA, are the lowest level of ORB system implementation available from the OMG. They provide the following functionalities:

- Generating and interpreting object references
- Invoking methods or otherwise calling functions on the particular object they are a part of
- Providing security within the context of these actions
- Activating or otherwise instantiating and deactivating or freeing objects from memory
- Mapping object references to their corresponding object implementations
- Registering implementations with the correct Naming service component of an ORB system

In these ways the object adapter controls both the ORB's services and their interactions with the corresponding object service implementation.

Any developer can see how important this is to the specification. Further, it is easier to note that it has been a long standardization process for this particular part of the specification could and does have a detrimental impact on the implementations of the adapters. Therefore, vendors have extended their implementations to meet their needs and thus have built up their own counter-dependencies.

1.7.5.1 The Basic Object Adapter

The Basic Object Adapter (BOA) is the base-level handle that the ORB uses to communicate with its object services. It applies to adapters most commonly used in normal CORBA ORB operations. At a high level, the BOA allows objects and their corresponding methods to be declared in one of three ways:

- Each implementation is a separate program.
- A separate program (or process) can be started for each method of a service object.

- A separate program (or process) can be stated for each whole object.
- A shared program (or process) can be stated for all instances of an object type.

As with the other parts of CORBA, the IDL defines the interface. To avoid ambiguity, however, parts of the BOA differ among language mappings, and are so noted by OMG.

The BOA performs the following functions:

- Generating and interpreting object references
- Authenticating a principal process making a call
- Activating and deactivating an implementation
- Activating and deactivating individual objects
- Invoking methods through the (generated) skeletons

The BOA supports can be one *or more* object implementations, which means that how a service object is activated is left up to the vendor. To the developer using the object service—that is, from the requesting client's standpoint, the object looks like one entity. On the back-side, however, there may be many dynamic modules, or code fragments, being loaded and unloaded depending on the requests coming in.

The following shows, step by step, how the BOA is implemented and what it does during its lifetime:

1. An incoming request comes in via the ORB for a particular object service.
2. The BOA activates the object implementation that it is responsible for. The implementation then notifies the BOA that it has initialized and is ready to start handling requests.
3. The object implementation is available—that is, loaded into RAM— and can now be invoked upon. The BOA registers that implementation with the appropriate ORB services (e.g., Naming).
4. The BOA activates the object through its BOA itself, meaning that it skips the above steps and goes straight through the skeleton to the object.

5. The BOA calls any method and invokes it on the object through its skeleton.

6. The object may need to invoke a service of the BOA, such as (re)activation and deactivation or further object creation.

One of the more haunting problems facing the OMG was that the Basic Object Adapter (BOA) was not completely specified. This led to many implementation difficulties for commercial organizations and their ORBs.

1.7.5.2 The Portable Object Adapter (POA)

Since the BOA specification was so vague to begin with, there is no way to interpret these proprietary implementations as thwarting the "openness" of CORBA, or some such. Further, the ORB systems have had a chance to mature now, and thus, it would be very difficult to otherwise change the BOA specification around at this point to "extend" it. Once standardized, the POA will deal with the issues of incompatibility arising from the numerous proprietary BOAs in service. It accomplishes two things:

- Removal of the BOA specification from all current CORBA literature, since the OMG will not be supporting the specification any longer. Vendors will be free to support their proprietary BOAs, however.

- Creating a new portable BOA, or POA, so that new adapters will be much more portable.

The POA will be more specific in its implementation of the interface and services of the object adapter. It also will increase the adapter's functionality in response to CORBA users' suggestions. The POA will not derive or extend the BOA for the same controversial reasons as mentioned above.

1.8   Common Services

The following paragraphs cover the main services that have been specified in CORBA. Services that are in the RFP stage or in the process of being specified or voted upon will be ignored here. Readers can find the most up-to-date information on these at http://www.omg.org.

Obviously, the goal of each service is to capitalize on the service interface and make it type specific. The service specifications assume that a clean 2.1 implementation of the basic ORB operations (called ORBOS) is in place, meaning that the ORB adapters, the stub and skeleton generation processes, DII/DSI, and so forth, have been built to specification. This is an important assumption because the service implementations rely on fast message passing and clean object references for the component objects and services involved in each transaction. Also important are the IDL's powerful multiple inheritance and subtyping.

One of the first of these that were specified was the Naming Service. This service was one of the most important, because it actually allowed the ORBs to function properly. From there, the OMG quickly furnished the Event Service specification. There have been several more, and these are covered in more detail below.

1.8.1   Naming

The naming service can be thought of as a "white pages" for CORBA, which an ORB contacts to locate a specific object service by name. The Naming service does not provide the category of object reference to requesting clients. That is the job of the ORB itself.

The naming service uses *bindings* and *contexts* to *bind* a particular name to an object within a given *context*. That is to say, there can be no "absolute name" for a given object. If there were, all ORBs would have to conform to one specification, in which the algorithm to generate names for all objects would be the same across all ORBs. This algorithm would somehow have to guarantee that the name was absolute and would probably operate off time principles, in the way GUIIDs are generated for COM objects.

The OMG defines name binding as creating an associated name for an object in a given context. It defines name resolving as associating an object name already created with the actual representation. The latter process is very closely coupled with the stringification operations mentioned earlier.

Sun Microsystems has solved the problem of naming contexts with *namespaces*. These are file–system-based spaces (no surprise, considering that Sun invented NFS), providing a good separation between objects registered with the same ORB. As always, the interface is the only part of the process that is strongly typed and so needs to be strict. Because the implementation is independent, the choice of namespaces versus object databases is up to the vendor.

OMG specified context nesting so that the Naming service could maintain extensibility and inheritance properties. Nesting is made possible through naming graphs. These are directed with nodes and labeled edges, the nodes being the (nestable) naming contexts. The entire name is built up of components. A simple name has a single component; a compound name has multiple components.

The name component breaks down into identifier and kind attributes. The kind attribute is descriptive, whereas the identifier is unique to a particular component within a particular context. These values are specified at a low level; it is up to the implementation to determine any higher-level uses.

The OMG also defined a Names library, where object and service names can be stored as pseudo-objects. This allows much faster and simpler manipulation of object names by an ORB and other service objects. The Names library is especially useful when, for example, a name of an object or service is passed as a parameter to another method. Moreover, it establishes a common, fast mechanism by which all ORBs can interoperate with the names and handles/references of various objects.

A "directory assistance" analogy might help to explain how the Naming service works. A client interested in making a request of an object or service asks the ORB to look up the particular object or service in its phone book ("white pages"). The ORB asks its secretary, the Naming service, to check the phone book, which is divided into alphabetical sections, or naming graphs, and find the particular object. The Naming service then tells the ORB the object's unique handle, or phone number, which the ORB passes back to the requesting client.

Theoretically, once the client has the unique handle, it can issue a request on it. To do so, it contacts the ORB with the handle, or phone number, and the ORB checks the handle's Interface Repository to see if it knows the requestor and is willing to accept a call. It also looks at the handle's map of switchable phone circuits in its Implementation Repository to see if a connection can be made. If so, the ORB makes the "call" and hands over the circuit to the requesting client.

1.8.2   Event

Before going into the specifics of the Event service, it is important to review how requests and actions are handled in CORBA "out of the box," that is, without Event or another service. The main point here is that CORBA functions synchronously, so that when clients request services and references to other objects, they wait, or "hang," until they get a correct response from the ORB.

This situation is both good and bad. On the good side is fault tolerance. The ORB ensures reliable delivery of requests from clients to services and reliable response. In a distributed network system, there is safety in synchronous connections.

The bad side is that the Event service does not help at all in massively networked systems, or in systems that otherwise pass many messages in day-to-day operations. It would not be fair to call this fault a lack of scalability, because it is possible to scale CORBA out of the box. Take as an example a war simulation. If many clients try to interact with servers of some sort, the latency between operations can fall below expectations. If all of those clients try to interact with a distributed "location" service object, each time any of them move, they issue a request and wait to receive a response through the ORB of that request. Clearly, this can become a menacing situation rather quickly.

Another failing of an asynchronous service reveals itself in exception handling—that is, when a synchronous request of a service object or component returns incorrect values or parameters. In this case the ORB and other processes might be kept waiting and then handle an exception of some sort, perhaps because data was passed incorrectly by value or specified incorrectly to begin with. In such a case, an asynchronous request of some sort would be beneficial, depending on the data and speed intensity of the operations.

Regardless of its positives and negatives, the Event service occupies a special place in CORBA. Its primary role is separating the communication between objects into two roles:

- The *supplier,* which creates event-based data.
- The *consumer,* which receives and processes the event-based data generated by the suppliers.

These roles are played according to one of two possible models:

- The *push* model, in which the supplier controls the events and how they are sent. The supplier in effect uses a "broadcast" mechanism that sends the event to be acted on only to the consumers that *need* to act on this event type.
- The *pull* model, in which the consumers "tap" the supplier when they need to request a specific event.

The actual event data is either *generic* or *typed.* Generic event data is passed through a common event object that can be processed by all components and objects involved in the event-based operations for the given "suite" or collection of objects. With typed event data each event has its own data object that is passed to another object within the suite. Obviously, the object must have its interface defined in the IDL. Note that the actual data for the event is passed via parameters, which can be defined by the developer.

An *event channel* is a special CORBA object that can be both supplier and consumer of event-based data, and can asynchronously communicate it to and from groups of interested objects. The interface for the event channel object is defined in the IDL, and the object handles normal CORBA requests. Its scalability is not specified, which means that the object can be task specific or it can be generalized to a workgroup or even an enterprise. The system architect must use good design judgment in determining the scalability of an event channel.

Event channels define how events are propagated between suppliers and consumers. They also define other intricate matters, such as the quality of service expected of the interested client objects. The event channel is a legitimate middleman of sorts for the objects involved in the asynchronous communication of events. It is in use by many CORBA applications today and will continue to play a strong role in asynchronous systems.

In its description of the Event service, the OMG adopted the following key design principles:

- The events and their associated data work in a distributed space and thus do not depend on any global or centralized information authority.
- The Event service allows for multiple consumers and multiple suppliers (as outlined above) in the distribution and processing of event data.
- Consumers can either request or receive event data, based on sound design principles.
- The consumer and supplier objects support standard IDL and do not require special processing or intervention by other unnamed (proprietary) objects to operate correctly.
- A supplier can have a one-to-many interface to many consumers.
- Suppliers and consumers need not know the exact handle or identity of any of their opposite objects; they support a level of "typed anonymity."
- Multiple levels of service quality are supported.
- The Event service is not bound in any way to a particular platform; the best illustration of this is a system that supports threading operations versus one that does not.

1.8.3 Persistent Object

The Persistent Object service provides IDL-based interfaces for persistent storage of CORBA component and object service data. Its job is to serve other object services, not to provide a service itself to requesting clients. In this way, the OMG defines two sides of the equation when it comes to objects and state:

- The *dynamic* state is the state the object uses during its actual execution; it is stored in volatile RAM.

- The *persistent* state is the state the object uses to re-create as best it can the last known dynamic state; it should be stored somewhere other than in volatile RAM.

The underlying object maintains itself persistently, but may require the Persistent Object service to do some or all of the work. Also, the ingrained facilities of the ORB provide the Persistent Object service with useful tools, such as object-to-string and string-to-object conversion. The Persistent Object service may or may not utilize these functions, depending on whether the IDL interfaces are maintained.

The vendor that implements this service decides how it stores, or has stored for it, any persistent states. Thus, the vendor may implement the state storage facility as a file-based, a relational database, or object-based system. There are obvious drawbacks and benefits to each of these data "engine" methods.

The Persistent Object Service plays a valuable role in the CORBA system by helping to shape the entire framework for distributed operation; many objects and components use it. This service is broken down into several components and interfaces to achieve persistence. Chief among these are object-oriented (OO) concepts because they allow for self-discovery and proper abstraction of data and access methods.

As defined by the OMG, the major components of the Persistent Object service are

- *Persistent Identifier* (PID)—a "key" that locates an object in a particular data storage mechanism. It is ANSI-string based.

- *Persistent Object* (PO)—the actual object being maintained as persistent. Outside (client) objects control its persistent state.

- *Persistent Object Manager* (POM)—the component that provides the OMG-specified IDL-based persistent operations on the PO. POs are usually grouped to a single POM, which handles their high-level operations.

- *Persistent Data Service* (PDS)—a mid-level object that sits between a datastore and a protocol. Its primary function is to serve a singular PO.
- *Protocol* — the means by which to get data in and out of a PO.
- *Datastore* — the means by which to store a PO's data persistently without having to know exactly where it is executing in RAM.

By plugging these components together, the Persistent Object service provides distributed persistence to objects as necessary.

1.8.4 Life Cycle

The Life Cycle service is the most important service implementation in CORBA. Indeed, it is implemented apart from, instead of incorporated into, object adapters and the like so that *clients* can control these critical operations on objects and object services. The core of an object's existence within CORBA is defined by this service, which consists of

- Creating an object
- Deleting an object
- Copying objects
- Moving an object from one place (memory) to another

One way to understand the Life Cycle service is to consider first the difficulties in controlling memory and other resources across computer systems. In a fully distributed system, client and service objects can be on the same machine or on different machines, but they must perform as though unaware of this fact. That means that requests, data, and operations passed from one process to another must be independent of the machine they are from and the machine they are acting upon.

Obviously, this cannot happen on an "out-of-the-box" computer. Rather, the CORBA software, through the Life Cycle service, provides the continuity between objects interacting on that system. This is because, for an object to be available to a client in the system, it must have been, or be, created. When operations are finished, it is very possible that the object created to handle them will need to be destroyed. How the requesting client object makes such a request, given that it probably lies on a different machine from the one the service object it is interacting with is on, is the heart of the problem.

The Life Cycle service handles the remote dispatching of critical processes. After it receives a request, the ORB interacts with the Life Cycle service, perhaps asking it to start the object service for which the request is intended. If a machine reboots on a network, the object services that reside on that machine need to be accounted for. The Life Cycle service keeps the object services "alive." If the ORB can't reach it, then it starts executing again.

So much for the creation and destruction of objects. Much more complex is copying an object from one place to another. Again, the problem lies in the fact that the machine responsible for allocating the memory into which a new object is to be copied might very well be different from the originating machine.

More important, the Life Cycle services handle operations for graphs of objects, which are groups of objects intrinsically related so as to represent a singular, complex set of data. Put more simply, they are objects that contain other objects. Life Cycle service handles the subordinate objects in a graph, such as whether and how to copy them.

1.8.5 Concurrency

As its name suggests, the Concurrency service handles concurrent "hits" on the same object, which can be either actual computations or message-passing operations. This service deals with both transactional and nontransactional operational modes. With a transactional mechanism, a "rollback" can be employed with which Concurrency interacts in performing its locking operations for concurrent access (see "Transaction Service" below for more details).

Concurrency's primary job is to serialize multiple requests from clients to an object or service. That is, it takes a possibly pseudo-concurrent application, perhaps through the use of multiple processors and/or threads, and breaks each request down discretely, so as to singularize it. The benefit is that developers never know about any of this and thus can implement their programs without concern for concurrency issues.

Concurrency operates in terms of *clients* and *resources*, allowing many clients to utilize a singular resource (many-to-one). It is up to the developer to define exactly what the interface of each side is and what the limitations of and the expectations for resources are to requesting clients. With transactional concurrent clients, the OMG does not define a transaction. That is left to the Transaction service, outlined below.

Resources are controlled through special *locks*, which levels of access to various concurrent resources. Multiple locks on an object are collected into *sets*, and the service creates the association between a given set and the object to which it is bound. This allows for different levels of granularity to be achieved with the objects. The lock model, and the duration of the locking mode are included in the specification.

1.8.6 Externalization

Externalization service defines the protocols and implementation for either externalizing or internalizing a CORBA object service. In essence, it "dumps" an object's contents into a readable stream—a concept that many readers will recognize from the Java programming language. Externalization standardizes "object dumping." However, CORBA does not prohibit a vendor from implementing its own ways and means of storing and retrieving objects externally.

Externalization is related to the Relationship service and runs alongside the Life Cycle service. It handles the definitions of how to copy objects. Its protocol is defined in three areas:

- The *requesting client* — how the client processes an object externally or internally, specified as a *stream* interface.
- An *object* — how an interface processes its own state from an externalized means.
- The *stream* — how the stream encodes and decodes an object to be externalized, as well as the corresponding graph of objects that must maintain referential integrity.

There is no real difficulty in externalizing one object. The externalization service simply follows the OMG specification for protocols and state storage and pipes the object out. But what if there is another object "nested" (has-a) within that object? How can both nesting and nested objects be stored in a neutral (specified) format and, at the same time, the state of the pointers that form the relationship between the two be maintained?

One solution is to create an "object graph" as a way to organize the set of objects that make up the object to be externalized. Within this graph a directed leg is drawn between each "held" object and the "holding" object—that is, the one to be externalized. Objects not in the holding object but that need a reference can be indicated with, say, a dashed line. This is not a perfect solution—we can imagine how complicated things will become as more and more objects are added to the graph. Nevertheless, this is one way to determine the state of all objects that are related to the initial instance.

The interfaces for the externalization service (as specified) can be summarized in terms of the following objects: `Stream`, `StreamFactory`, `FileStreamFactory`, `Streamable`, `StreamableFactory`, `StreamIO`, `Node`, `Relationship`, and `Role`.

1.8.7   Relationship

According to true object modeling concepts, an object more often than not does not exist by itself, but is connected to other objects through *relationships*, which can be illustrated through a graph or some other means. The Relationship service standardizes these relationships. The OMG knows full well that vendors have their own ways of encoding relationships among objects in their CORBA implementation. However, if they support the Relationship service, they must implement the storage and retrieval of relationship information as the Relationship service dictates.

The OMG characterizes relationships in terms of several environmental factors:

- *Type*. The entities within a given relationship are typed, as is the relationship itself. This holds true for any number of entities and any number of relationships.

- *Role.* The roles of all entities in a given relationship are combined to form a singular relationship role.
- *Degree.* The number of roles in an entity is a unique factor in defining a relationship.
- *Cardinality.* The number of relationships allowed within a given role on a particular object can be defined as one-to-one, one-to-many, many-to-many, and so forth.
- *Relationship Semantics.* The semantics can be useful in defining operations and attributes.

The objects defined by the Relationship service are *relationship* and *role*. All entities and their relationships are explicitly defined and represented. Much of the relationship integrity between objects in a CORBA system is utilized by CORBA's Interoperable Object Reference (IOR). The Relationship service sits on top of the IOR and deals with more complex relationships such as those that are multidirectional, those that allow third-party manipulation, traversals supported for graphs of related objects, and relationships and roles that can be extended with attributes and behavior.

The OMG defines several levels of the Relationship service, as follows:

Level 1 — Base relationships, where the relationship and role interfaces define a basic relationship service. A role represents an object in a relationship.

Level 2 — Graphs of related objects, where a graph of objects that interconnect and represent one compound object can be used and manipulated.

Level 3 — Specific relationships, where containment and references can be represented as discrete binary relationships.

1.8.8 Transaction

The Transaction service is very important, indeed, as shown by its heavy use in the industry today. At a high level, a transaction is a discrete event that occurs in relation to time which can be either *committed* or *rolled back*. A committed transaction merely turns a one-step process into a two-step process. Thus, a transaction is not treated as finished until it is committed. If a transaction is made and for some reason cannot be committed, it is rolled back. In other words, all of the logic and changes of state within the system are returned to what they were, as if the transaction had never taken place.

Transactions are best utilized in fault-tolerant or otherwise very reliable operations, such as banking, telecommunications, and satellite systems. They become nontrivial when the access to data or objects become concurrent or shared. The OMG defines a transaction as:

- *Atomic*. The OMG defines this as the ability to be rolled back in case of failure or error.
- *Consistent*. Once the transaction takes place, certain of its properties are preserved.
- *Isolated in time*. Transactions appear to execute serially, and any intermittent states they take on are unknown to the (CORBA) processes interacting with them.
- *Durable*. Their effects are preserved indefinitely.

There is no scope to the number of objects or requests specified by the OMG. Therefore, any given transaction can consist of multiple objects and requests. The OMG does specify that the application of the Transaction service be covered by the following entities:

- A *transactional client* (TC)—a process that can request operations on any transactional objects.
- A *transactional object* (TO)—an object whose behavior is directly affected by a transaction. This typically includes persistent data that can be modified by the other objects within the transaction.
- A *recoverable object* — a transactional object that can recover its own states if necessary. The TOs can have other recoverable objects implement this and thus not have any state information associated with them.
- A *transactional server* — a set of objects whose behavior is affected by a transaction.
- A *recoverable server* — a set of objects at least one of which is recoverable.

The Transaction service supports *flat* and *nested* distributed transaction models. A flat transaction model permits only a top-level transaction that cannot have any children. This specification follows the X/Open Distributed

Transaction Processing XA Specification. A nested transaction model allows transactions that are embedded in other transactions.

A transaction is considered terminated when it issues either a commit or a rollback directive. Termination is usually invoked by the transaction's requesting client. Transaction integrity is imposed via a "checked" transaction behavior that is also specified in the X/Open DTP specification. The ORB maintains a thread that is context sensitive to the transaction taking place. This contextual awareness is portable and can be sent from the ORB to an object.

The OMG defined the Transaction service to satisfy the following functional and design requirements:

- It must be able to support multiple, discrete transaction models. Since there is no "final" specification for a transaction process or process framework implementation, no restrictions are imposed.

- It must support evolutionary deployment. This means that the existing object infrastructure needs to be containable within new objects over time and as they mature.

- It must support transaction model interoperability. This is mainly for developers who want to incorporate a procedural model into this OO model or otherwise utilize a procedural model to accomplish a transaction. The Transaction service must support both individual models and those working together to accomplish the same goals.

- It must support network interoperability. Developers can utilize ORB objects and implementations from several vendors if necessary.

- It must support flexible transaction propagation control. The Transaction service supports system (implicit) as well as application-level (explicit) propagation of events associated with a transaction. The clients and associated transaction objects must be able to propagate events associated with a transaction.

- It must support transaction processing (TP) monitors. This allows transactions to be executed concurrently, and the client, server, and transaction processes to be separate.

- It must be able to exploit OO technology, meaning that the specification thinks of transactions as objects, and thus they have inheritance, encapsulation of data, and polymorphic properties.

- It must be inexpensive to implement. The OMG specifies cost savings for clients, ORB vendors, and Transaction service providers.
- It must be portable—obviously, since it is a part of CORBA.
- It must avoid IDL variation between transactional and nontransactional interface implementations.
- It must support both single and multithreaded implementations.
- It must provide a variety of implementation choices. This allows vendors to exploit and advance the technology while complying with the specification.

1.8.9   Query

The Query service is a specific implementation of query-type operations on discrete sets of CORBA objects. The queries themselves are based on predicate operations and can return object sets—either those selected from a source set whose objects satisfy a given predicate, or those produced by an external evaluator based on its own evaluation of a predicate.

The complexity of the Query service is in the randomness of the objects it serves. Basically any object can invoke a query on any object sets. The request can be random and can be related to another CORBA service. The query evaluators can be nested and federated; that is, they can be collected for different purposes over their life cycle and can be incorporated into queries at any time.

The query service supports SQL Query (92), the de facto standard query language used with relational databases; OQL, the Object Query Language, used similarly to SQL with object databases (which are becoming more popular in today's applications); and OQL-Basic (93).

Two structures are possible for the Query service:

- *Collections*, defined in terms of collection and iterator interfaces.
- *Query framework*, in which the QueryLanguageType interface is employed to provide more flexibility.

1.8.10 Licensing

The Licensing service helps users of ORB systems manage and control the many types of software licenses that can be found within a single instance. It also helps vendors prevent illegal access to their products. Licensing is intended as well to help unravel the complexity of licensing distributed software as opposed to the classical singular-instance variety.

The OMG recommends sound business policies regarding any licensing service. These are the rules and procedures of software use within a CORBA framework installation. Licensing supports the classic and newer forms of licensing, such as concurrent or "floating" licenses, and it is set to be scalable to almost any application context.

A key aspect of the licensing service is its handling of legacy systems, since such systems must be "wrapped" and licensed accordingly. Five components come into play: a producer client, a COS license service manager, a COS producer license service, a producer policy, and a licensing system. First, a producer client issues a request to the COS license service manager. Next, the manager interacts with the COS producer client, who issues a request to the licensing system. The licensing system, which contains the actual licenses, then interacts with the producer policies. Lastly, the COS producer license service issues a request to the producer client.

The key attributes of the Licensing service are

- *Time* — such as when a request was made, how long a license can last, and if it is still valid.
- A *value mapping* — consisting of a unit quantity used in policies and allocative and consumptive qualities.
- A *consumer* — containing the assignment of reservation.
- A *licensing policy* — consisting of, but not limited to, time windows, values, use of a set of related objects, postage meter, and gas meter (see the COS Service Specification for more details).

There are also several appendixes that outline various helpful tips, suggestions for data points for use within the model, asynchronous vs. synchronous events, and so forth.

1.8.11   Property

The Property service is specified to help customize and build on the fundamentals of CORBA. Because the IDL interface describes objects, methods, and attributes, but does not describe state, two objects can be essentially the same within this context if they both implement the same IDL interface descriptions correctly. In actuality, however, these objects could be intrinsically very different.

Basically, the property service deals with this problem, by storing typed, named values that are dynamically related to an object instance. The service is specified in terms of the following interfaces:

- `PropertySet` supports the operations of defining, destroying, enumerating, and checking if a particular property exists.
- `PropertySetDef` supports the operations associated with obtaining `PropertySet` constraints and obtaining or manipulating property modes.
- `PropertiesIterator` allows clients more fine-grained control of the enumeration of properties.
- `PropertyNamesIterator` allows clients more fine-grained control over the names of properties.
- `PropertySetFactory` allows the creation of `PropertySets`.
- `PropertySetDefFactory` allows the creation of `PropertySetDefs`.

1.8.12   Time

The Time service, used only in conjunction with other services, enables client objects to request the current time along with an error estimate about that value. It also provides the order in which events "occurred." This service can generate time-based events founded on timers and alarms and can compute the interval between two events.

Time representation is very important. Thus, to maintain the highest possible degree of openness, the OMG decided to use the X/Open DCE Time Service specification. Another important element is synchronization.

The Time service is specified first as consisting of the object definitions defined in the IDL for maintaining and synchronizing time.

1.8.13   Security

The Security service is one of the most commercially viable services on the distributed market today. In fact, many companies invest in CORBA systems primarily to handle security in a Web environment. The OMG defines security in terms of confidentiality, integrity, accountability, and availability. Obviously, the security threat only intensifies in a distributed system such as CORBA.

The OMG summarizes the features and functions of the security service as follows:

- *Principal identification and authentication.* A principal is any independent user processes or objects that interact within the context of the system.
- *Authorization and access control* to objects, decided on a principal-by-principal basis.
- *Security auditing* within the context of the Security service. This means that all transactions and/or processes that interact with the service can be logged to a file or data repository.
- *Secure communication* between objects. This is especially important because transmission between objects usually occurs on top of several layers of nonsecure network protocols and/or devices (links).
- *No repudiation* of actions and events that occur between the objects the security service interacts with.
- *Administration* of the Security service through the use of security policies and the like.

Security policies come in different flavors. For example, an access control policy might utilize access control lists (ACLs), identity information, role information, and so forth. Audit policies also can be flexible, as can security functionality profiles, which are where national or international government criteria are defined and used.

Fully object-oriented, the Security service is also application portable as well as interoperable. Its interoperability extends between and across ORBs, secure systems, distributed domains, realms, and systems that support different security technologies. Service performance overhead should not be unacceptable vis-à-vis encryption, ciphers, keys, and the like.

Site or otherwise specific security concerns are also supported by the Security service. These can be regulatory requirements or specific compliance evaluation criteria (e.g., multilevel security needs for government agencies). Even with this built-in support, however, there is still difficulty meeting user expectations. For that reason, the Security service is very scalable in its levels of security as well as flexible in the types of security it can support.

The Security service specification is broken down into four sections. First is the main security functionality, which has two levels: Level 1, application-level security, in which the entities themselves are limited in their ability to enforce security themselves, and Level 2, which provides more security features and functions, and allows applications to control the level of security at object invocation.

The second part of the specification deals with security options, that is, nonrepudiation of evidence and a system of "checks and balances."

The third part treats security replaceability, or how ORBs can work with different security models. An example is ORB services replaceability, which is handled through "interceptor" interfaces, so that the ORB does not have to include the security implementation itself.

Another example is security replaceability, which is where the Security service runs completely independently of the ORB. As might be imagined, this is more complicated than it sounds, because security operations require certain levels of encryption, authentication, and verification that cover ORB requests, data, and operations. An implementation in which the ORB and the security service are close together would be much less difficult to accomplish. In this case, the ORB would not use interceptors, and both the ORB and security service would co-exist, and maintain their own interfaces separately.

The final part of the specification is secure interoperability, for which two alternatives are given. One, standard secure interoperability, is where the ORB creates and maintains the security information via the IOR, and passes information around via standard GIOP/IIOP with the security enhancements protocol (SECIOP). The other, the standard plus DCE-CIOP, adds more security between ORBs through the DCE security services (DCE-CIOP).

The interfaces, defined in IDL, are administrative, implementors, a security reference model, a security architecture, application developers, and interoperability.

1.8.14   Trading

If the Naming service can be thought of as "white pages," the Trader service can be thought of as "yellow pages." In other words, *specific* object relative to an ORB deployment is located by the Naming service, whereas a *type* of object is located by the Trader service. You could think of it in terms of announcing a specific functionality, and in reciprocal matching what is available to a type of function.

At a high level, an object contacts the Trader service (or Trader) and announces its type. The Trader notes the object's type and stores this exported information along with where and who the object is. Later, a requesting client object contacts the Trader, asking if the Trader knows of a particular type of object through an import operation. The Trader then locates that type of object and connects the requesting client to it.

The OMG is aware that in widespread use these services will proliferate quickly, requiring the Trader service and its associated trader objects to be further partitioned. This partitioning might be around communities of objects. The Trader service must be able to support diversity and scalability, obviously because of the many types of services and announcements a vendor will build into an object.

Traders can be "linked" together to exchange information about their announced clients. This linking is very useful in providing services across different ORB deployments, either in-house (within an enterprise) or out-of-house (across multiple businesses, enterprises, campuses, etc.).

To summarize, the exporter announces types of services to the Trader, either providing these services itself or making its announcement on behalf of another object or service. The importer uses the Trader to search for the services of the specific type it is interested in. The service types themselves are interfaces that define a computational signature and zero or more named property types. These attributes and methods are not otherwise specified through the traceable signature.

1.8.15   Object Collection

Object Collection is an important utilitylike service specification for CORBA—more like Query and Relationship than the stand-alone services that act autonomously such as Naming and Trader.

Usually a data type that is to contain a set of objects is rigid—for example a binary tree structure that only stores integer values. In this way, the system logic can determine how to search for a particular object and how to store it in relation to the objects already stored. Collections are special data types that can contain random objects. They differ in that how their stored objects are searched is not specified. Obviously, a method exists, or there would be significant memory leaks and no one would be able to locate particular objects; however, it is basically unknown to the developer, who merely puts things in the collection and searches things out of it.

The setup of this service falls into the following categories:

- The *collection interfaces* and *factories* represent the entities a requesting client needs at certain times. The requesting client matches the interface or factory to its needs before issuing the request.
- The *interator* interfaces are created by the client to iterate over the elements of a collection, usually in searching operations.
- The *function* interfaces are user defined for user-specific needs. They are passed into a collection when it is created to add or otherwise extend its functionality with this particular feature.

Much of the Object Collection specification is based on what the OMG refers to as "the nature of a collection." That is to say, the Collection service collects and searches collections, having little or nothing to do with the "nature of objects" within them. Thus, the logic and functionality of the service concern themselves only with these "collective" operations.

An important property of a collection is the ordering of its elements—for a set to be "ordered," it must provide a "previous" and "next" functionality. Not all collections are ordered, however. In a key collection any element can be accessed via a key mechanism. In an element quality collection a test for equality is performed on the objects it contains in a search for one in particular. The uniqueness of an element ensures that there will be no duplicate entry for a particular value.

The properties of a collection are mapped into interfaces and can be combined through multiple inheritance. The inheritance hierarchy is abstract. Any interface that can be considered restrictive in the access it offers to requesting objects is known as a restrictive access collection. Such collections include, among others, stacks offering only a push and pop metaphor and queues restricted to FIFO or FILO.

Each collection is created in its own factory. In this way, as with other parts of the CORBA specification, the creation of the "components" or "object services" can be clean and reliable. The mapping between factories and the corresponding collection is one-to-one. That is to say that if there are several types of collections defined, then there are an equal amount of factories that can create those corresponding collections.

It is the OMG's belief that iterator entities are not as trivial as they seem. For that reason it created an entire hierarchy of iterators defined for each type of collection that actually represent multiple levels within the collection. These iterators must be manageable throughout a framework, which makes them more expensive to allocate and deallocate in terms of RAM and processing time.

1.9   Future Directions

Because its tools are not yet in widespread use, CORBA can still be considered relatively youthful. On paper the specification is about eight years old, but it has taken the actual software some time to catch up with the paper, and so it seems younger. In particular, CORBA's interoperability features have not been tested in a mission critical environment. As of this writing, only implementations with many of the same ORBs (e.g., Orbix) are known to be in use.

The CORBA specification is in fact a large set of smaller specifications, which the OMG has been adding to and maintaining at an almost feverish pace. There is still much to do, but for the most part the specification as a whole is stable and in use in a variety of applications. Telecom and satellite applications are two fields in which CORBA is in wide use today. As for other applications in which it could be beneficial, the possibilities are endless. A few are described in the following paragraphs.

1.9.1   Java and Beans-Mania

One of the biggest promoters of "netcentric" software solutions, other than the World Wide Web (WWW), is Sun Microsystems. Before Java, Java Beans, and everything else Java, Sun was heavily involved in the CORBA process and still is. Not surprisingly, one of its most significant CORBA systems was "Distributed Objects Everywhere" or "DOE." With the advent of competing systems and vendors, Sun quickly turned a research project into a commercial product, and DOE became NEO.

Unfortunately, NEO lost out to competing products, but it was useful as a proof of concept. A side product, called "Java Objects Everywhere" or "JOE," gave way to a Java–IIOP mapping and CORBA classes included with the Java 1.2beta development kit (Note "beta!"). What is important here is that mapping from IDL to Java does exist and is stable. Furthermore, CORBA classes can be used today in simple Java applications.

A user of any Java technology can capitalize on CORBA through the use of IIOP sockets. The JDK 1.2beta provides these sockets, which are just like the TCP sockets that have been available since the first release. They are easy to use and provide a way to stream input/output from and to applications directly to and from CORBA-enabled processes.

CORBA and Java feed off each other. Consider the preliminary specification for CORBA "Beans," which will allow for dynamic, runtime discovery of methods and attributes similar to what Java Beans provide now. This kind of mutual development will continue as a way to accommodate the demands of the market.

1.9.2 Diversification and Proliferation

One of the most important areas in which CORBA is expected to expand is the use of newly created object services. As prices for ORB systems continue to decline, and more companies invest in CORBA, more developers will build previously unheard of objects, services, and components geared to different vendors. This diversification and proliferation of distributed object services will not diminish any time soon.

This leads to an interesting point. It is important to note that as you are thinking about how to build an application, or are otherwise procuring software for an application, don't hesitate to look around for components and objects that are already off-the-shelf (C/GOTS). There is always the possibility that one of them will solve particular problems within the context of your system. There are new components, and objects coming out every day.

The OMG promotes diversification and proliferation through its vertical–market-focused specifications. One of particular interest is the Common Business Object Facilities (CBOF), designed for vertical commercial business applications, such as financial institutions. Proposed IDL will define an account entity and how it interacts with banker objects, customer objects, and so forth.

Obviously, the standard CORBA services will figure in this scenario as well. For instance, the Naming service will locate particular objects for "white pages" functionality. The Trader service will locate objects of a particular type, for instance, banker objects, new account creation objects, and the like, for requesting clients. The Transaction service will handle any transactions that require the payment or transfer of money. And the Security service will provide secure encryption between critical contact points within the framework, especially for databases. The ORB will register all of these components in its Interface and Implementation repositories and allow communications over the Web through IIOP.

This is a good example of the trend toward "assembling" systems instead of building them from scratch. The overarching principle is having at hand a complete "toolbox" of functionality and choosing components from it as the situation and problem dictate. Obviously, much custom code will still be created, but that code can be added to the toolbox for use in the next system in an ongoing process of system building.

CHAPTER 2

OMG IDL
Syntax and
Semantics

OMG IDL specifies interfaces that the object implementations provide and the client objects invoke. An OMG IDL interface offers the information required to develop the clients that use the interface's operations. An interface definition written in OMG IDL completely defines the interface and fully specifies each operation's parameters.

The OMG Interface Definition Language (IDL) describes the interfaces that client objects call and that object implementations provide. The clients themselves are written not in OMG IDL, which is a purely descriptive language, but in languages for which mappings from OMG IDL concepts have been defined. Thus, the "strength" of the language determines how much the client will be able to use the OMG IDL facilities. For example, an OMG IDL exception might be mapped to a structure in a language that has no notion of exceptions (which does not mean that a language cannot take full advantage of the OMG IDL is in any way weak).

OMG IDL obeys the same lexical rules as in C++, although it introduces new keywords to support distribution concepts, and provides full support for standard C++ preprocessing features. Moreover, the OMG IDL specification can track relevant changes to C++ introduced by the

ANSI standardization effort. Its grammar is a subset of the proposed ANSI C++ standard, with additional constructs to support the operation invocation mechanism. OMG IDL is a declarative language—it supports C++ syntax for constant, type, and operation declarations, but it does not include any algorithmic structures or variables.

The source file containing interface specifications written in OMG IDL must have an `.idl` extension. All OMG IDL type definitions are present in `orb.idl` and available in every ORB implementation.

The OMG IDL grammar uses a syntax notation similar to the Extended Backus-Naur Format (EBNF). Table 2.1 lists the EBNF symbols and their meaning.

2.1 Lexical Conventions

The lexical conventions of OMG IDL are adapted from *The Annotated C++ Reference Manual*. This section explains the tokens defined in an OMG IDL specification and describes comments, identifiers, keywords, and the integer, character, floating-point constants, and string literals.

Table 2.1 IDL EBNF

Symbol	Meaning
::=	Is defined to be
|	Alternatively
<text>	Nonterminal
"text"	Literal
*	Preceding syntactic unit can be repeated zero or more times
+	Preceding syntactic unit can be repeated one or more times
{}	Enclosed syntactic units are grouped as a single syntactic unit
[]	Enclosed syntactic unit is optional and may occur zero or one times

An OMG IDL specification logically consists of one or more files, which are conceptually translated in several phases. The first phase, preprocessing, performs file inclusion and macro substitution, generating a file called a translation unit. Preprocessing is controlled by directives introduced by lines with # as the first character other than white space. The result of preprocessing is a sequence of tokens, which makes up the translation unit.

OMG IDL uses the ISO Latin-1 (8859.1) character set, which comprises alphabetic, digit, graphic, and formatting characters and the space (blank) character. The set includes the 26 letters of the Latin alphabet (with upper- and lowercase equivalencies) as well as the diacritical marks—grave and acute accent (Àà, Éé), circumflex (Êê), tilde (Ññ, Ãã), cedilla (Çç), diaresis or umlaut (Üü), oblique stroke (Øø), and ring above (Åå); the dipthong (æ); and the German sharp *s* (ß). Table 2.2 lists these alphabetic characters. The 10 numerical digits are, of course 0123456789, as shown in Table 2.3. Tables 2.4 and 2.5 respectively list the graphic and formatting characters.

Table 2.2   Alphabetic Characters

Character	Description	Character	Description
Aa	Upper-/Lowercase A	Àà	Upper-/Lowercase A with grave accent
Bb	Upper-/Lowercase B	Áá	Upper-/Lowercase A with acute accent
Cc	Upper-/Lowercase C	Ââ	Upper-/Lowercase A with circumflex
Dd	Upper-/Lowercase D	Ãã	Upper-/Lowercase A with tilde
Ee	Upper-/Lowercase E	Ää	Upper-/Lowercase A with diaeresis
Ff	Upper-/Lowercase F	Åå	Upper-/Lowercase A with ring above
Gg	Upper-/Lowercase G	Ææ	Upper-/Lowercase dipthong A-E
Hh	Upper-/Lowercase H	Çç	Upper-/Lowercase C with cedilla

Table 2.2   Alphabetic Characters   (Continued)

Character	Description	Character	Description
Ii	Upper-/Lowercase I	Èè	Upper-/Lowercase E with grave accent
Jj	Upper-/Lowercase J	Éé	Upper-/Lowercase E with acute accent
Kk	Upper-/Lowercase K	Êê	Upper-/Lowercase E with circumflex accent
Ll	Upper-/Lowercase L	Ëë	Upper-/Lowercase E with diaeresis
Mm	Upper-/Lowercase M	Ìì	Upper-/Lowercase I with grave accent
Nn	Upper-/Lowercase N	Íí	Upper-/Lowercase I with acute accent
Oo	Upper-/Lowercase O	Îî	Upper-/Lowercase I with circumflex
Pp	Upper-/Lowercase P	Ïï	Upper-/Lowercase I with diaeresis
Qq	Upper-/Lowercase Q	Ññ	Upper-/Lowercase N with tilde
Rr	Upper-/Lowercase R	Òò	Upper-/Lowercase O with grave accent
Ss	Upper-/Lowercase S	Óó	Upper-/Lowercase O with acute accent
Tt	Upper-/Lowercase T	Ôô	Upper-/Lowercase O with circumflex
Uu	Upper-/Lowercase U	Õõ	Upper-/Lowercase O with tilde
Vv	Upper-/Lowercase V	Öö	Upper-/Lowercase O with diaeresis
Ww	Upper-/Lowercase W	Øø	Upper-/Lowercase O with oblique stroke
Xx	Upper-/Lowercase X	Ùù	Upper-/Lowercase U with grave accent
Yy	Upper-/Lowercase Y	Úú	Upper-/Lowercase U with acute accent

Table 2.2   Alphabetic Characters   (Continued)

Character	Description	Character	Description
Zz	Upper-/Lowercase Z	Ûû	Upper-/Lowercase U with circumflex
		Üü	Upper-/Lowercase U with diaeresis
		ß	Lowercase German sharp S
		ÿ	Lowercase Y with diaeresis

Table 2.3   Decimal Characters

0 1 2 3 4 5 6 7 8 9

Table 2.4   Graphic Characters

Character	Description	Character	Description
!	Exclamation point	¡	Inverted exclamation point
"	Double quote	¢	Cent
#	Number	£	Pound
$	Dollar	¤	Currency
%	Percent	¥	Yen
&	Ampersand	¦	Broken bar
'	Apostrophe	§	Section/paragraph
(	Left parenthesis	¨	Diaeresis
)	Right parenthesis	©	Copyright
*	Asterisk	ª	Feminine ordinal
+	Plus	«	Left angle quotation mark
,	Comma	¬	Not
-	Hyphen-minus sign	-	Soft hyphen
.	Period-full stop	®	Registered trade mark
/	Solidus	¯	Macron
:	Colon	°	Ring above, degree

Table 2.4   Graphic Characters   (Continued)

Character	Description	Character	Description
;	Semicolon	±	Plus-minus
<	Less than sign	2	Superscript 2
=	Equals sign	3	Superscript 3
>	Greater than sign	´	Acute
?	Question mark	µ	Micro
@	Commercial *at*	¶	Pilcrow
[	Left square bracket	•	Middle dot
\	Reverse solidus	¸	Cedilla
]	Right square bracket	1	Superscript 1
^	Circumflex	º	Masculine ordinal
_	Low line- underscore	»	Right angle quotation mark
'	Grave	¼	Vulgar fraction ¼
{	Left curly bracket	½	Vulgar fraction ½
|	Vertical line	¾	Vulgar fraction ¾
}	Right curly bracket	¿	Inverted question mark
~	Tilde	×	Multiplication sign
		÷	Division

Table 2.5   Formatting Characters

Description	Abbreviation	ISO 646 Octal Value
Alert	BEL	007
Backspace	BS	010
Horizontal tab	HT	011
Newline	NL LF	012
Vertical tab	VT	013
Form feed	FF	014
Carriage return	CR	015

2.1.1 Tokens

The five types of tokens are identifiers, keywords, literals, operators, and other separators. Blanks, horizontal and vertical tabs, newlines, formfeeds, and comments (collectively referred to as "white space"), as described in the comments section, are ignored unless they separate tokens. Some white space is required to separate otherwise adjacent identifiers, keywords, and constants.

If the input stream has been parsed into tokens up to a given character, the next token is taken to be the longest string of characters that could possibly result in another token.

2.1.2 Comments

As in C++, comments are of two types. The first type is similar to traditional C language comments that start and end with the /* and */ characters, respectively. Nesting of comments is not allowed. The second type is more like C++ comments. The comment characters //, /*, and */ have no special meaning within a // comment and are treated like other characters. Similarly, the comment characters // and /* have no special meaning within a /* comment. Comments may contain alphabetic, digit, graphic, space, horizontal tab, vertical tab, formfeed, and newline characters.

2.1.3 Identifiers

An identifier is made up of an arbitrarily long sequence of alphabetic, digit, and underscore (_) characters. Important here is that the first character must be alphabetic, and all characters are significant.

Identifiers that differ only in case collide and yield a compilation error. An identifier for a definition must be consistent with respect to case throughout a specification.

A comparison of two identifiers to see if they collide requires the following conditions:

- Upper- and lowercase letters are treated as the same letter. Table 2.2 defined case equivalencies.
- Equivalencies between digraphs and pairs of letters are *not* taken into account (e.g., *ae* and *AE* are not considered equivalent). Nor are equivalencies between accented and nonaccented letters (e.g., *Á* and *A* are not considered equivalent).
- All characters are significant.

There is only one namespace for OMG IDL identifiers. The same identifier used for a constant and an interface, for example, produces a compilation error.

2.1.4 Keywords

The identifiers listed in Table 2.6 are reserved for use as keywords only. The rules for keywords are the same as those for identifiers. They must be written as shown in Table 2.6—for example, writing `Readonly` instead of `readonly` produces a compilation error. The keyword `Object` can be used as a type specifier.

Table 2.6 Keywords

Any	double	interface	readonly	unsigned
Attribute	enum	long	Sequence	union
Boolean	exception	module	Short	void
Case	FALSE	Object	String	wchar
Char	fixed	octet	Struct	wstring
Const	float	oneway	Switch	
Context	in	out	TRUE	
Default	inout	raises	Typedef	

The characters given here are used as punctuation:

Table 2.7 Punctuation characters

;	{	}	:	,	=	+	-	(	)	<	>	[	]
`	"	\	|	^	&	*	/	%	~				

The preprocessor also uses the tokens #, ##, !, | |, and &&.

2.1.5 Literals

2.1.5.1 Integer Literals

Unless it begins with a 0, an integer literal consisting of a sequence of digits is taken to be decimal (base ten). A sequence of digits starting with a 0 is considered an octal integer (base eight), but the digits 8 and 9 are not octals. A sequence of digits preceded by 0x or 0X is taken as a hexadecimal integer (base sixteen). The hexadecimal digits include *a* or *A* through *f* or *F* with decimal values 10 through 15, respectively. For example, the number 10 can be written 10, 012, or 0XA in the decimal, octal, or hexadecimal formats, respectively.

2.1.5.2 Character Literals

A character literal is made up of one or more characters enclosed in single quotes, as in 'a'. Character literals have type char.

A character is an 8-bit quantity with a numerical value between 0 and 255 (decimal). The value of a space, alphabetic, digit, or graphic character literal is the numerical value of the character as defined in the ISO Latin-1 (8859.1) character set standard, discussed above. The value of a null is 0. The value of a formatting character literal is the numerical value of the character as defined in the ISO 646 standard (as shown in Table 2.5). All other characters are implementation dependent, and their meaning can vary from implementation to implementation.

The Nongraphic characters are represented by escape sequences as defined in Table 2.8.

Table 2.8   NonGraphic Characters

Description	Escape Sequence
Newline	\n
Horizontal tab	\t
Vertical tab	\v
Backspace	\b
Carriage return	\r
Formfeed	\f
Alert	\a
Backslash	\\
Question mark	\?
Single quote	\'
Double quote	\"
Octal number	\ooo
Hexadecimal number	\xhh

The two hexadecimal digits in the escape character \xhh specify the value of the desired character. The same applies to the one, two, or three octal digits in the escape \ooo. The first character that is not an octal or hexadecimal digit terminates a sequence of octal or hexadecimal digits, respectively. The value of a character constant is implementation dependent if it exceeds that of the largest char.

Wide-character and wide-string literals are specified exactly as character and string literals are. All character and string literals, both wide and nonwide, may be specified (portably) using only the characters found in the ISO 8859-1 character set; that is, interface names, operation names, type names, and so forth, are so limited.

2.1.5.3   Floating-Point Literals

A floating-point literal comprises an integer part, a decimal point, a fraction part, an *e* or *E*, and an optionally signed integer exponent. Both integer and fraction parts consist of a sequence of decimal (base ten) digits. Either part (but not both) may be missing, as may either the decimal point or the *e* (or *E*) and the exponent (but not both).

2.1.5.4 String Literals

A string literal is a sequence of characters surrounded by double quotes. Adjacent string literals are concatenated, but characters in concatenated strings are kept distinct. For example, \xA B contains the two characters \xA and B, and becomes \xAB after concatenation.

The size of the literal string is the number of character literals enclosed by quotes after concatenation. Within a string a double quote character (") must be preceded by \. A string literal may not contain \0.

2.1.5.5 Fixed-Point Literals

A fixed-point decimal literal consists of an integer part, a decimal point, a fraction part and a *d* or *D*. Both integer and fraction parts comprise a sequence of decimal (base 10) digits. Either part (but not both) may be missing; the decimal point (but neither *d* nor *D*) may be missing.

2.1.6 Preprocessing

The OMG IDL's preprocessing, which is based on ANSI C++ preprocessing, provides macro substitution, conditional compilation, and source file inclusion. In addition, directives are provided to control line numbering in diagnostics and for symbolic debugging, to generate a diagnostic message with a given token sequence, and to perform implementation-dependent actions. Also available are certain predefined names. These facilities are conceptually handled by a preprocessor, which may or may not be implemented as a separate process.

For communication with the preprocessor, the lines, also called "directives," are prefixed with #. White space is allowed before the #. These lines are syntax independent of the rest of OMG IDL; they may appear anywhere and their effects last (independent of the OMG–IDL scoping rules) until the end of the translation unit. The textual location of OMG–IDL-specific pragmas may be semantically constrained.

A preprocessing directive (or any line) can be continued on the next line in a source file when a backslash character \ is placed immediately before the newline at the end of the line. The preprocessor effects the continuation by deleting the backslash and the newline before the input sequence is divided into tokens. A backslash character cannot be the last character in a source file.

A preprocessing token is an OMG IDL token; a file name, as in a #include directive; or any single character other than white space that does not match another preprocessing token. The primary use of the preprocessing facilities is to include definitions from other OMG IDL specifications. Text in files included with a #include directive is treated as if it appeared in the including file.

2.2   OMG IDL Grammar

```
(1) <specification>              ::= <definition>+
(2) <definition>                 ::= <type_dcl> ";"
                                 | <const_dcl> ";"
                                 | <except_dcl> ";"
                                 | <interface> ";"
                                 | <module> ";"
(3) <module>                     ::= "module" <identifier>
                                     "{" <definition> +"}"
(4) <interface>                  ::= <interface_dcl>
                                 | <forward_dcl>
(5) <interface_dcl>              ::= <interface_header>
                                     "{" <interface_body> "}"
(6) <forward_dcl>                ::= "interface" <identifier>
(7) <interface_header>           ::= "interface" <identifier>
                                     [ <inheritance_spec> ]
(8) <interface_body>             ::= <export> *
(9) <export>                     ::= <type_dcl> ";"
                                 | <const_dcl> ";"
                                 | <except_dcl> ";"
                                 | <attr_dcl> ";"
                                 | <op_dcl> ";"
(10) <inheritance_spec>          ::= ":" <scoped_name>
                                     { "," <scoped_name> } *
(11) <scoped_name>               ::= <identifier>
                                 | "::" <identifier>
                                 | <scoped_name> "::" <identifier>
```

```
(12) <const_dcl>              ::= "const" <const_type>
                                  <identifier> "=" <const_exp>
(13) <const_type>            ::= <integer_type>
                              | <char_type>
                              | <wide_char_type>
                              | <boolean_type>
                              | <floating_pt_type>
                              | <string_type>
                              | <wide_string_type>
                              | <fixed_pt_const_type>
                              | <scoped_name>
(14) <const_exp>             ::= <or_expr>
(15) <or_expr>               ::= <xor_expr>
                              | <or_expr> "|" <xor_expr>
(16) <xor_expr>              ::= <and_expr>
                              | <xor_expr> "^" <and_expr>
(17) <and_expr>              ::= <shift_expr>
                              | <and_expr> "&" <shift_expr>
(18) <shift_expr>            ::= <add_expr>
                              | <shift_expr> ">>" <add_expr>
                              | <shift_expr> "<<" <add_expr>
(19) <add_expr>              ::= <mult_expr>
                              | <add_expr> "+" <mult_expr>
                              | <add_expr> "-" <mult_expr>
(20) <mult_expr>             ::= <unary_expr>
                              | <mult_expr> "*" <unary_expr>
                              | <mult_expr> "/" <unary_expr>
                              | <mult_expr> "%" <unary_expr>
(21) <unary_expr>            ::= <unary_operator> <primary_expr>
                              | <primary_expr>
(22) <unary_operator>        ::= "-"
                              |"+"
                              |"~"
(23) <primary_expr>          ::= <scoped_name>
                              | <literal>
                              | "(" <const_exp> ")"
(24) <literal>               ::= <integer_literal>
                              | <string_literal>
                              | <wide_string_literal>
                              | <character_literal>
                              | <wide_character_literal>
                              | <fixed_pt_literal>
                              | <floating_pt_literal>
                              | <boolean_literal>
(25) <boolean_literal>       ::= "TRUE"
                              |   "FALSE"
(26) <positive_int_const>    ::= <const_exp>
```

```
(27) <type_dcl>                ::= "typedef" <type_declarator>
                                 | <struct_type>
                                 | <union_type>
                                 | <enum_type>
                                 | "native" <simple_declarator>
(28) <type_declarator>         ::= <type_spec> <declarators>
(29) <type_spec>               ::= <simple_type_spec>
                                 | <constr_type_spec>
(30) <simple_type_spec>        ::= <base_type_spec>
                                 | <template_type_spec>
                                 | <scoped_name>
(31) <base_type_spec>          ::= <floating_pt_type>
                                 | <integer_type>
                                 | <char_type>
                                 | <wide_char_type>
                                 | <boolean_type>
                                 | <octet_type>
                                 |<any_type>
                                 | <object_type>
(32) <template_type_spec>      ::= <sequence_type>
                                 | <string_type>
                                 | <wide_string_type>
                                 | <fixed_pt_type>
(33) <constr_type_spec>        ::= <struct_type>
                                 | <union_type>
                                 | <enum_type>
(34) <declarators>             ::= <declarator>
                                    { "," <declarator> } *
(35) <declarator>              ::= <simple_declarator>
                                 | <complex_declarator>
(36) <simple_declarator>       ::= <identifier>
(37) <complex_declarator>      ::= <array_declarator>
(38) <floating_pt_type>        ::= "float"
                                 | "double"
                                 | "long" "double"
(39) <integer_type>            ::= <signed_int>
                                 | <unsigned_int>
(40) <signed_int>              ::= <signed_short_int>
                                 | <signed_long_int>
                                 | <signed_longlong_int>
(41) <signed_short_int>        ::= "short"
(42) <signed_long_int>         ::= "long"
(43) <signed_longlong_int>     ::= "long" "long"
(44) <unsigned_int>            ::= <unsigned_short_int>
                                 | <unsigned_long_int>
                                 | <unsigned_longlong_int>
(45) <unsigned_short_int>      ::= "unsigned" "short"
```

```
(46) <unsigned_long_int>     ::= "unsigned" "long"
(47) <unsigned_longlong_int> ::= "unsigned" "long" "long"
(48) <char_type>             ::= "char"
(49) <wide_char_type>        ::= "wchar"
(50) <boolean_type>          ::= "boolean"
(51) <octet_type>            ::= "octet"
(52) <any_type>              ::= "any"
(53) <object_type>           ::= "Object"
(54) <struct_type>           ::= "struct" <identifier>
                                  "{" <member_list> "}"
(55) <member_list>           ::= <member>+
(56) <member>                ::= <type_spec> <declarators> ";"
(57) <union_type>            ::= "union" <identifier>
                                  "switch" "("<switch_type_spec>
                                  ")" "{" <switch_body>"}"
(58) <switch_type_spec>      ::= <integer_type>
                               | <char_type>
                               | <boolean_type>
                               | <enum_type>
                               | <scoped_name>
(59) <switch_body>           ::= <case>+
(60) <case>                  ::= <case_label>+<element_spec> ";"
(61) <case_label>            ::= "case" <const_exp> ":"
                               | "default" ":"
(62) <element_spec>          ::= <type_spec> <declarator>
(63) <enum_type>             ::= "enum" <identifier>
                                  "{" <enumerator> { ","
                                      <enumerator> } * "}"
(64) <enumerator>            ::= <identifier>
(65) <sequence_type>         ::= "sequence" "<"
                                  simple_type_spec> ","
                                  <positive_int_const> ">"
                               | "sequence" "<"
                                  <simple_type_spec> ">"
(66) <string_type>           ::= "string" "<"
                                  positive_int_const> ">"
                               | "string"
(67) <wide_string_type>      ::= "wstring" "<"
                                  <positive_int_const> ">"
                               | "wstring"
(68) <array_declarator>      ::= <identifier> <fixed_array_size>+
(69) <fixed_array_size>      ::= "[" <positive_int_const> "]"
(70) <attr_dcl>              ::= [ "readonly" ] "attribute"
                                  <param_type_spec>
                                  <simple_declarator> {
                                  "," <simple_declarator> }*
```

```
(71) <except_dcl>          ::= "exception" <identifier>
                               "{" <member>* "}"
(72) <op_dcl>              ::= [ <op_attribute> ]
                               <op_type_spec> <identi-fier>
                               <parameter_dcls>
                               [ <raises_expr> ]
                               [<context_expr> ]
(73) <op_attribute>        ::= "oneway"
(74) <op_type_spec>         ::= <param_type_spec>
                             | "void"
(75) <parameter_dcls>      ::= "(" <param_dcl> {
                               "," <param_dcl> } * ")"
                             | "(" ")"
(76) <param_dcl>           ::= <param_attribute>
                               <param_type_spec>
                               <simple_declarator>
(77) <param_attribute>     ::= "in"
                             | "out"
                             | "inout"
(78) <raises_expr>         ::= "raises" "(" <scoped_name> {
                               "," <scoped_name> } * ")"
(79) <context_expr>        ::= "context" "("
                               <string_literal> { ","
                               <string_literal> } * ")"
(80) <param_type_spec>     ::= <base_type_spec>
                             | <string_type>
                             | <wide_string_type>
                             | <fixed_pt_type>
                             | <scoped_name>
(81) <fixed_pt_type>       ::= "fixed" "<"
                             <positive_int_const> ","
                             <integer_literal> ">"
(82) <fixed_pt_const_type>  ::= "fixed"
```

2.3   OMG IDL Specification

An OMG IDL specification contains one or more type definitions, constant definitions, exceptions definitions, or module definitions. The syntax is:

```
<specification>            ::=<definition>

<definition>               ::=<type_dcl> ;"
                             | <const_dcl> ";"
```

```
| <except_dcl> ";"
| <interface> ";"
| <module> ";"
```

Constant, type, and module definitions will be described later in the chapter.

2.3.1   Module Declaration

The module definition uses the following syntax:

```
<module>                    ::="module" <identifier>
                               "{" <definition> +"}"
```

2.3.2   Interface Declaration

The interface definition uses this syntax:

```
<interface>                 ::= <interface_dcl>
                            | <forward_dcl>
<interface_dcl>             ::= <interface_header>
                               "{" <interface_body> "}"
<forward_dcl>               ::= "interface" <identifier>
<interface_header>           ::= "interface" <identifier>
                               [<inheritance_spec> ]
<interface_body>            ::= <export> *
<export>                    ::= <type_dcl> ";"
                            | <const_dcl> ";"
                            | <except_dcl> ";"
                            | <attr_dcl> ";"
                            | <op_dcl> ";"
```

2.3.2.1   Interface Header

The interface header is made up of the interface name and the optional inheritance specification. The interface name must be preceded by the keyword interface and consists of an interface identifier. The inheritance specification is described in the next section.

The <identifier> that names an interface is a legal type name, which may be used anywhere an <identifier> is grammatically legal, subject to the semantic constraints described in the following sections. Since the identifier can only hold references to an object, the meaning of a parameter or structure member that is an interface type is as a *reference* to an object supporting that interface. This interface references are language dependent.

2.3.2.2 Inheritance Specification
The syntax for inheritance is as follows:

```
<inheritance_spec>        ::= ":" <scoped_name>
                                {"," <scoped_name>}*
<scoped_name>             ::= <identifier>
                          | "::" <identifier>
                          | <scoped_name> "::" <identifier>
```

Each <scoped_name> in an <inheritance_spec> must denote a previously defined interface.

2.3.2.3 Interface Body
The interface body is made up of five kinds of declaration:

- *Constant* — specifies the constants that the interface exports.
- *Type* — specifies the type definitions that the interface exports.
- *Exception* — specifies the exception structures that the interface exports.
- *Attribute* — specifies the associated attributes that the interface exports.
- *Operation* — specifies the operations that the interface exports and the format of each, including name, type of data returned, types of all operation parameters, any legal exceptions that may be returned as a result of an invocation, and contextual information that may affect method dispatch.

The IDL syntax permits empty declarations, that is, those that do not have declarations.

Some implementations may require that interface-specific pragmas precede the interface body.

2.3.2.4 Forward Declaration
Declaring the name of an interface, without defining it, is called forward declaration; this allows the definition of interfaces that refer to each other. The syntax consists simply of the keyword interface followed by an

<identifier> that names the interface. The actual definition must follow later in the specification. The IDL syntax allows multiple forward declarations of the same interface name.

2.4 Inheritance

Interfaces allow inheritance, making it possible to derive one interface, the *derived interface*, from another, the *base interface*. The derived interface inherits the interfaces of the base class, and it can declare new elements (constants, types, attributes, exceptions, and operations). In addition, the elements of the base class can be redefined in the derived interface. Name resolution requires the :: operator, which permits reference to a name that has been redefined in the derived interface.

All keywords defined in CORBA are treated as though defined within a module named *CORBA*. However, OMG IDL keywords, such as *Object*, must not be preceded by the CORBA:: prefix. Other interface names, for example, *TypeCode* are not OMG IDL keywords, so they must be referred to by their fully scoped names (e.g., CORBA::TypeCode) within an OMG IDL specification.

The interface is called a direct base or an indirect base depending on its mention in the <inheritance_spec>. An interface mentioned in the <inheritance_spec> is called a direct base. An interface not mentioned in the direct base, but is a base interface of one of the interfaces in the <inheritance_spec> is called an indirect base.

If an interface is derived from more than one base interface, it is called a *multiple interface*. The order of derivation of these classes is not important. An interface may not be specified as a direct base interface of a derived interface more than once, but it can be an indirect base interface multiple times.

```
interface A { ... }
interface B: A { ... }
interface C: A { ... }
interface D: B, C { ... }
```

If an element name is shared among base interfaces, it is illegal for the derived interface to use it unambiguously. In such cases the element should be accessed via the scope resolution operator or by qualifying a name with its interface name using <scoped_name>.

References to constants, types, and exceptions are bound to an interface when it is defined. This guarantees that the syntax and semantics of an interface do not change when it is a base interface for a derived interface.

```
const long lval = 10;

interface A {
    typedef float coord[lval]):
    void func (in coord s); // s has 10 floats
};

interface B {
    const long lval = 20;
};

interface C: B, A {}// what is func()'s signature?
```

Interface inheritance causes all identifiers in the closure of the inheritance tree to be imported into the current naming scope. A type name, constant name, enumeration value name, or exception name from an enclosing scope can be redefined in the current scope; only when an attempt is made to access an ambiguous name without qualification does a compilation error result.

Operation names are used at runtime by both stub and dynamic interfaces. For that reason, all operations that might apply to a particular object must have unique names. This requirement prohibits redefining an operation name in the derived interface as well as inheriting two operations with the same name.

2.5   Constant Declaration

This section describes the syntax and semantics for a constant declaration.

2.5.1 Syntax

```
<const_dcl>                ::= "const" <const_type>
                               <identifier> "="
                               <const_exp>
<const_type>               ::= <integer_type>
                           | <char_type>
                           | <boolean_type>
                           | <floating_pt_type>
                           | <string_type>
                           | <scoped_name>
<const_exp>                ::= <or_expr>
<or_expr>                  ::= <xor_expr>
                           | <or_expr> "|" <xor_expr>
<xor_expr>                 ::= <and_expr>
                           | <xor_expr> "^" <and_expr>
<and_expr>                 ::= <shift_expr>
                           | <and_expr> "&" <shift_expr>
<shift_expr>               ::= <add_expr>
                           | <shift_expr> ">>" <add_expr>
                           | <shift_expr> "<<" <add_expr>
<add_expr>                 ::= <mult_expr>
                           | <add_expr> "+" <mult_expr>
                           | <add_expr> "-" <mult_expr>
<mult_expr>                ::= <unary_expr>
                           | <mult_expr> "*" <unary_expr>
                           | <mult_expr> "/" <unary_expr>
                           | <mult_expr> "%" <unary_expr>
<unary_expr>               ::= <unary_operator>
                               <primary_expr>
                           | <primary_expr>
<unary_operator>           ::= "-"
                           | "+"
                           | "~"
<primary_expr>             ::= <scoped_name>
                           | <literal>
                           | "(" <const_exp> ")"
<literal>                  ::= <integer_literal>
                           | <string_literal>
                           | <character_literal>
                           | <floating_pt_literal>
                           | <boolean_literal>
<boolean_literal>          ::= "TRUE"
                           | "FALSE"
<positive_int_const>       ::= <const_exp>
```

2.5.2 Semantics

The `<scoped_name>` in the `<const_type>` production must be a previously defined name of an `<integer_type>`, `<char_type>`, `<wide_char_type>`, `<boolean_type>`, `<floating_pt_type>`, `<fixed_pt_const_type>`, `<string_type>`, or `<wide_string_type>` constant.

An infix operator can combine the same types, but an error results when two different types are mixed. Infix operators are applicable only to integer, float, and fixed types.

Where the type of an integer constant is `long` or `unsigned long`, each subexpression of the associated constant expression is treated as an `unsigned long` by default or as a signed `long` for negated literals or negative integer constants. An error results if any subexpression values exceed the precision of the assigned type or if a final expression value exceeds the position of the target type.

If the type of an integer constant is `long long` or `unsigned long`, each subexpression of the constant subexpression is treated as an `unsigned long long` by default or as a signed `long long` for negated literals or negative integer constants.

If the type of a floating-point constant is `double`, each subexpression of the associated constant expression is treated as a `double`. If the type of a floating-point constant is `long double`, each subexpression of the associated constant expression is treated as a `long double`.

A fixed-point literal has the apparent number of total and factional digits, except that leading and trailing zeroes, including the nonsignificant zeros before the decimal point, are factored out. For example, `0123456.7890d` is considered `fixed<9,3>`, and `5000.00` is considered `fixed<1,-3>`. Prefix operators do not affect the precision; a prefix + is optional and does not change the result. The upper bounds on the number of digits and scale of an infix expression, `fixed<d1,s1> op  fixed<d2,s2>`, are shown in Table 2.9.

A quotient may have an arbitrary number of decimal places, denoted by scale of s_{inf}. The computation proceeds pairwise, with actual rules of left-to-right

Table 2.9   Operator Results

Op	Result: fixed<d,s>
+	`fixed<max(d1-s1,d2-s2) + max(s1,s2) + 1, max(s1,s2)>`
-	`fixed<max(d1-s1,d2-s2) + max(s1,s2) + 1, max(s1,s2)>`
*	`fixed<d1+d2, s1+s2>`
/	`fixed<(d1-s1+s2) + s inf , s inf >`

association, operator precedence, and parenthesis. If a computation between a pair of fixed-point literals generates more than 31 significant digits, a 31-digit result is retained as follows:

```
fixed<d,s> => fixed<31, 31-d+s>
```

Leading and trailing zeros are not considered significant and are discarded. The result of the computation then proceeds as one literal operand of the next pair of fixed-point literals to be computed.

Unary (+ –) and binary (* / + –) operators are applicable in floating-point and fixed-point operations. The unary (+ – ~) and binary (* / % + – << >> & | ^) operators are applicable in integer expression.

The ~ unary operator indicates that the bit-complement of the expression to which it is applied should be generated. The values are 2's complement numbers and are calculated as follows:

`long`	`Long -(value + 1)`
`unsigned long`	`Unsigned long (2**32-1) - value`
`long long`	`Long long -(value + 1)`
`unsigned long long`	`Unsigned long (2**64-1) - value`

The binary operator % yields the remainder from the division of the first expression by the second. If the second operand of the % is 0, the result is undefined. Otherwise,

```
(x/y)*y + x%y
```

is equal to x. If both operands are nonnegative, the remainder is nonnegative, else the sign of the remainder is implementation dependent.

The << binary operator indicates that the value of the left by operand should be shifted to the left by the number of bits specified by the right operand. The vacated bits are filled by a zero. The right operand must be in the range 0 <= right operand < 64.

The >> binary operator is similar to the << operator except that the value of the left operand should shift to the right by the number of bits specified by the right operand. Again, a 0 fills the vacated bits, and the same range applies to the right operand.

The & binary operator indicates that the logical, bitwise AND of the left and the right operands should be generated. The ∣ binary operator indicates that the logical, bitwise OR of the left and the right operands should be generated. The ∧ binary operator performs the logical, bitwise EXCLUSIVE-OR of the left and right operands.

`<positive_int_const>` must evaluate to a positive integer value.

2.6   Type Declaration

OMG IDL provides a C-like declaration that associates an identifier with a type using the keyword `typedef`. A name is also associated with a data type using the `struct`, `union`, `enum`, and `native` declarations. Here is the syntax:

```
<type_dcl>                 ::= "typedef" <type_declarator>
                           | <struct_type>
                           | <union_type>
                           | <enum_type>
                           | "native" <simple_declarator>
<type_declarator>          ::= <type_spec> <declarators>
```

For type declarations, OMG IDL defines a set of type specifiers to represent typed values. The syntax is as follows:

```
<type_spec>                ::= <simple_type_spec>
                           | <constr_type_spec>
```

```
<simple_type_spec>          ::= <base_type_spec>
                            | <template_type_spec>
                            | <scoped_name>
<base_type_spec>            ::= <floating_pt_type>
                            | <integer_type>
                            | <char_type>
                            | <wide_char_type>
                            | <boolean_type>
                            | <octet_type>
                            |<any_type>
<template_type_spec>        ::=<sequence_type>
                            | <string_type>
                            | <wide_string_type>
                            | <fixed_pt_type>
<constr_type_spec>          ::= <struct_type>
                            | <union_type>
                            | <enum_type>
<declarators>               ::= <declarator>
                               { "," <declarator> } *
<declarator>                ::= <simple_declarator>
                            | <complex_declarator>
<simple_declarator>         ::= <identifier>
<complex_declarator>        ::= <array_declarator>
```

The <scoped_name> in <simple_type_spec> must be a previously defined type. As seen above, OMG IDL type specifiers consist of scalar data types and type constructors. They can be used in operation declarations to assign data types to operation parameters. The coming section describes basic and constructed type specifiers.

2.6.1   Basic Types

The syntax of the supported basic types is as follows:

```
<floating_pt_type>          ::= "float"
                            | "double"
                            | "long" "double"
<integer_type>              ::= <signed_int>
                            | <unsigned_int>
<signed_int>                ::= <signed_long_int>
                            | <signed_short_int>
                            | <signed_longlong_int>
<signed_long_int>           ::= "long"
<signed_short_int>          ::= "short"
```

```
<signed_longlong_int>           ::= "long" "long"
<unsigned_int>                  ::= <unsigned_long_int>
                                | <unsigned_short_int>
                                | <unsigned_longlong_int>
<unsigned_long_int>             ::= "unsigned" "long"
<unsigned_short_int>            ::= "unsigned" "short"
<unsigned_longlong_int>         ::= "unsigned" "long" "long"
<char_type>                     ::= "char"
<wide_char_type>                ::= "wchar"
<boolean_type>                  ::= "boolean"
<octet_type>                    ::= "octet"
<any_type>                      ::= "any"
```

Each OMG IDL data type converts to a native data type via the appropriate language mapping. Conversion errors can occur during the mapping. For example, the invocation mechanism may throw an exception if the client attempts to convert an illegal value. The standard exceptions, which are signaled in such cases, are defined later.

2.6.1.1   Integer

OMG IDL integer types are `short`, `unsigned short`, `long`, `unsigned long`, `long long`, and `unsigned long long`, representing integer values in the range given:

Short	$-2^{15}..2^{15}-1$
Long	$-2^{31}..2^{31}-1$
Long long	$-2^{63}..2^{63}-1$
Unsigned short	$0..2^{16}-1$
Unsigned long	$0..2^{32}-1$
Unsigned long long	$0..2^{64}-1$

2.6.1.2   Floating-Point

OMG IDL floating-point types are `float`, `double`, and `long double`. `float` represents IEEE single-precision floating-point numbers; `double` represents IEEE double-precision floating-point numbers; and `long double` represents an IEEE double-extended floating-point number, which has an exponent at least 15 bits long and a signed fraction at least 64 bits long. For detailed specification see the *IEEE Standard for Binary Floating-Point Arithmetic*, ANSI/IEEE Standard 754-1985.

2.6.1.3 Char

OMG IDL defines a `char` data type as an 8-bit quantity that encodes a single-byte character from any byte-oriented code set, or, when used in an array, that encodes a multibyte character from a multibyte code set. In other words, an implementation may use any code set internally for encoding character data, though conversion to another form may be required for transmission.

The ISO 8859-1 (Latin1) standard character set defines the meaning and representation of the graphic characters used in OMG IDL. The meaning and representation of the null and formatting characters are their numerical values as defined in the ASCII (ISO 646) standard. The meaning and representation of all other characters are implementation dependent.

During transmission, characters may be converted to other appropriate forms as required by a particular language binding. Such conversions may change the representation of a character but maintain its meaning. For example, a character may be converted to and from the appropriate representation in international character sets.

2.6.1.4 Wide Char

OMG IDL defines a `wchar` data type, which encodes wide characters from any character set. As with character data, an implementation may use any code set internally for encoding wide characters, although, again, conversion to another form may be required for transmission. The size of `wchar` is implementation dependent.

2.6.1.5 Boolean

The `boolean` data type denotes a data item that can take only one of the values TRUE and FALSE.

2.6.1.6 Octet

The `octet` type is an 8-bit quantity that is guaranteed not to undergo any conversion when transmitted by the communication system.

2.6.1.7   Any

The any type permits the specification of values that can express any OMG IDL type.

2.6.2   Constructed Types

The constructed types are

```
<constr_type_spec>         ::= <struct_type>
                           | <union_type>
                           | <enum_type>
```

Although the IDL syntax allows recursive constructed types, only recursion through the sequence template type is permitted. For example, the following is legal:

```
struct foo {
    long value;
    sequence<foo> chain;
}
```

2.6.2.1   Structures

The structure syntax is

```
<struct_type>              ::= "struct" <identifier>
                               "{" <member_list> "}"
<member_list>              ::= <member>+
<member>                   ::= <type_spec> <declarators> ";"
```

The <identifier> in <struct_type> defines a new legal type. Structure types may also be named with a typedef declaration.

Name-scoping rules require unique member declarators in a particular structure. The value of struct is the value of all of the structure's members.

2.6.2.2   Discriminated Unions

The discriminated union syntax is

```
<union_type>               ::= "union" <identifier>
                               "switch"
                               "("<switch_type_spec> ")"
                               "{" <switch_body> "}"
<switch_type_spec>         ::= <integer_type>
                           | <char_type>
```

```
                          | <boolean_type>
                          | <enum_type>
                          | <scoped_name>
<switch_body>             ::= <case>+
<case>                    ::= <case_label><element_spec> ";"
<case_label>              ::= "case" <const_exp> ":"
                          | "default" ":"
<element_spec>            ::= <type_spec> <declarator>
```

OMG IDL unions are a cross between the C `union` and `switch` statements. They must be discriminated, which means that the union header must specify a typed tag field that determines the union member to be uses for the current instance of a call. The `<identifier>` following the `union` keyword defines a new legal type. Union types also may be named with a `typedef` declaration. The `<const_exp>` in a `<case_label>` must be consistent with the `<switch_type_spec>`. A `default` case can appear at most once. The `<scoped_name>` in the `<switch_type_spec>` production must be a previously defined `integer`, `char`, `boolean`, or `enum` type.

Case labels must match or be automatically castable to the defined type of the discriminator. The matching rules are shown in Table 2.10.

Table 2.10 Case Label Matching

Discriminator Type	Match
long	Any integer value in the range of `long`
Long long	Any integer value in the range of `long long`
short	Any integer value in the range of `short`
Unsigned long	Any integer value in the range of `unsigned long`
Unsigned long long	Any integer value in the range of `unsigned long long`
Unsigned short	Any integer value in the range of `unsigned short`
char	`Char`
wchar	`Wchar`
Boolean	`TRUE` or `FALSE`
Enum	Any enumerator for the discriminator enum type

Name-scoping rules require that the element in a particular union be unique. If the `<switch_type_spec>` is an `<enum_type>`, the identifier for the enumeration is in the scope of the union; thus, it must be distinct from the element declarators.

Not all possible values of the union discriminator must be listed in the `<switch_body>`. The value of a union is the value of the discriminator together with one of the following:

- The value of the element associated with a `case` statement, if the discriminator value was explicitly listed in that `case` statement.
- The value of the element associated with the default `case` label, if a default `case` label was specified.
- No additional value.

Access to the discriminator and the related element is language-mapping dependent.

2.6.2.3 *Enumerations*

Enumerated types are made up of ordered lists of identifiers. The syntax for the enumerators is

```
<enum_type>              ::= "enum" <identifier> "{"
                             <enumerator> { ","
                             <enumerator> } * "}"
<enumerator >            ::= <identifier>
```

A maximum of 2^{32} identifiers may be specified in an enumeration; for that reason, the enumerated names must be mapped to a native data type capable of representing a maximally sized enumeration. The order in which the identifiers are named in the specification of an enumeration defines their relative order.

Any language mapping that permits two enumerators to be compared or that defines successor/predecessor functions on enumerators must conform to this ordering relation. The `<identifier>` following the enum keyword defines a new legal type. Enumerated types may also be named by a `typedef` declaration.

2.6.3 Template Types

The syntax for template types is

```
<template_type_spec>      ::= <sequence_type>
                          | <string_type>
                          | <wide_string_type>
                          | <fixed_pt_type>
```

2.6.3.1 Sequence
The syntax for a sequence is

```
<sequence_type>           ::= "sequence"
                              "<" <simple_type_spec> ","
                              <positive_int_const> ">"
                          | "sequence"
                              "<" <simple_type_spec> ">"
```

A sequence is a one-dimensional array with a maximum size (fixed at compile time) and length (determined at runtime). OMG IDL defines the sequence type as sequence.

The second parameter in a sequence declaration indicates the sequence's maximum size. If a positive integer constant is specified as the maximum, the sequence is termed *bounded*. Prior to the passing of a bounded sequence as a function argument (or as a field in a structure or union), the sequence length must be set, as language-mapping dependent. By the time a sequence result from an operation invocation is received, the sequence length will have been set, also as language-mapping dependent.

If a sequence has no maximum size specified, it is considered *unbounded*. Prior to the passing of such a sequence as a function argument (or as a field in a structure or union), its length, its maximum size, and the address of a buffer to hold it must be set as language-mapping dependent. After receipt of such a sequence result from an operation invocation, the length of the returned sequence will have been set, also as language-mapping dependent. A sequence type may be used as the type parameter for another sequence type. For example, the following:

```
typedef sequence< sequence<long> > John;
```

declares John to be of type "unbounded sequence of unbounded sequence of long." Note that for nested sequence declarations, white space must separate the two > tokens ending the declaration so that they are not parsed as a single >> token.

2.6.3.2   String

The syntax for a string type is

```
<string_type>                    ::= "string"
                                     "<" <positive_int_const> ">"
                                 | "string"
```

OMG IDL defines the string type string as consisting of all possible 8-bit quantities except null, similarly to a sequence of char. As with sequences of any type, prior to the passing of a string as a function argument (or as a field in a structure or union), the string length must be set as language-mapping dependent. The argument to the string declaration is the maximum size. If a positive-integer maximum is specified, the string is bounded; if no maximum size is specified, it is unbounded.

Strings are considered as a separate type because many languages have special built-in functions or standard library functions for string manipulation. A separate string type may permit optimal handling of strings compared to what can be done with sequences of general types.

2.6.3.3   Wide-Char String

The wstring data type represents a null-terminated sequence of wchar. It is analogous to string, except that the latter's element type is char.

2.6.3.4   Fixed

The fixed data type represents a fixed-point decimal number of up to 31 significant digits. The scale factor is normally a nonnegative integer less than or equal to the total number of digits; however, some languages and environments may be able to accommodate types that have a negative scale or a scale greater than the number of digits.

2.6.4 Complex Declarator

2.6.4.1 *Arrays*

OMG IDL defines multidimensional, fixed-size arrays. An array requires that an implicit size for each dimension be given at array creation so that the overall array size is available at compilation.

The syntax for arrays is

```
<array_declarator>       ::=<identifier> <fixed_array_size>
<fixed_array_size>       ::="[" <positive_int_const> "]"
```

When an array is passed as a parameter in an operation invocation, all of its elements are transmitted. The implementation of array indices is language-mapping specific, so passing an array index as a parameter may yield incorrect results.

2.6.4.2 *Native Types*

OMG IDL provides a declaration by which object adapters can define a new, opaque type whose representation is specified by the adapter's language mapping. The syntax is

```
<type_dcl>               ::= "native" <simple_declarator>
<simple_declarator>      ::= <identifier>
```

A native type is similar to an IDL basic type. Its possible values, and the means for constructing and manipulating them, are language-mapping dependent.

A native type may be used to define operation parameters and results. However, its values need not be permitted in remote invocations, either directly or as components of a constructed type. In fact, any attempt to do so may raise the MARSHAL standard exception. It is recommended that native types be mapped to equivalent type names in each programming language, subject to the language's normal mapping rules for type names. For example, in a hypothetical object adapter IDL module,

```
module HypotheticalObjectAdapter {
    native Servant;
```

```
interface HOA {
    Object activate_object(in Servant x);
};
```

the IDL type `Servant` would map to `HypotheticalObjectAdapter::Servant` in C++ and the `activate_object` operation would map to the following C++ member function signature:

```
CORBA::Object_ptr activate_object(
HypotheticalObjectAdapter::Servant x);
```

The definition of the C++ type `HypotheticalObjectAdapter::Servant` would be provided as part of the C++ mapping for the `Hypothetical-ObjectAdapter` module.

2.7   Exception Declaration

Exceptions, declared via `struct`-like data structures, are returned when an exception occurs as a result of a client request. The syntax is as follows:

```
<except_dcl>             ::="exception" <identifier>
                            "{" <member>* "}"
```

An OMG IDL identifier, an exception type identifier, and the type of the associated return value (as specified by the `<member>` in its declaration) characterize each exception. If an exception is returned in response to a request, the value of the exception identifier is accessible to the programmer for determining what the problem is.

If an exception is declared with members, a programmer can access the values of those members. If no members are specified, no additional information is available. A set of standard exceptions is defined corresponding to standard runtime errors that may occur during request execution request.

2.8 *Operation Declaration*

Operation declarations in OMG IDL are similar to C function declarations. The syntax is

```
<op_dcl>            ::= [ <op_attribute> ]
                        <op_type_spec> <identifier>
                        <parameter_dcls>
                        [ <raises_expr> ]
                        [ <context_expr> ]
<op_type_spec>      ::=<param_type_spec>
                    | "void"
```

An operation declaration consists of

- An optional operation attribute specifying which invocation semantics the communication system should provide.

- The type of the operation's return result, which may be any type that can be defined in OMG IDL. Operations that do not return a result must specify void.

- An identifier that names the operation in the scope of the interface in which it is defined.

- A parameter list specifying zero or more parameter declarations for the operation.

- An optional raises expression indicating the exceptions to an invocation of this operation.

- An optional context expression indicating which elements of the request context may be consulted the operation's implementation method.

Some implementations and/or language mappings may require operation-specific pragmas immediately preceding the affected operation declaration.

2.8.1 Operation Attribute

The optional operation attribute specifies the semantics necessary for invocations of a particular operation. Its syntax is as follows:

```
<op_attribute>      ::="oneway"
```

When a client invokes an operation with the oneway attribute, the semantics are *best-effort*, which does not guarantee delivery of the call, but only that the operation will be invoked at most once. An operation with the oneway attribute cannot contain any output parameters and must specify a void return type. Moreover, it may not include a raises expression (although such an operation might raise a standard exception). If an <op_attribute> is not specified, the semantics are *at-most-once* if an exception is raised and *exactly-once* if the operation invocation returns successfully.

2.8.2   Parameter Declarations

Parameter declarations in OMG IDL operation declarations have the following syntax:

```
<parameter_dcls>           ::="(" <param_dcl>
                                { "," <param_dcl> } * ")"
                           | "(" ")"
<param_dcl>                ::=<param_attribute>
                                <param_type_spec>
                                <simple_declarator>
<param_attribute>          ::="in"
                           | "out"
                           | "inout"
<param_type_spec>          ::=<base_type_spec>
                           | <string_type>
                           | <scoped_name>
```

A parameter declaration must have a directional attribute that tells the client's and server's communication services the direction in which the parameter is to be passed. The directional attributes are

- in—client to server
- out—server to client
- inout—both directions

An implementation must *not* attempt to modify an in parameter, as the attempt itself is language-mapping specific, and its effect is undefined. If an exception is raised as a result of an invocation, the values of the return result and any `out` and `inout` parameters are likewise undefined. When an unbounded string or sequence is passed as an `inout` parameter, the returned value cannot be longer than the input value.

2.8.2.1   Raises Expressions

A `raises` expression specifies which exceptions may be raised by an invocation. The syntax for its specification is as follows:

```
<raises_expr>          ::="raises"
                          "(" <scoped_name>
                          { "," <scoped_name> } *")"
```

A `<scoped_name>` in the `raises` expression must be a previously defined exception. In addition any of a standard set of exceptions may be signaled by the ORB, but these are *not* listed in a `raises` expression.

The absence of a `raises` expression on an operation means that there are no operation-specific exceptions. Invocations are still liable to receive a standard exception.

2.8.2.2   Context Expressions

A `context` expression specifies which elements of the client's context may the outcome of a request by the object. Its syntax is as follows:

```
<context_expr>         ::="context" "("
                          <string_literal> {
                          "," <string_literal> } *")"
```

The runtime system guarantees to make any value associated with each `<string_literal>` in the client's context available to the object implementation when the request is delivered. The ORB and/or object can use information in this *request context* during request resolution and performance. Without a context expression there is no request context for this operation. Each `string_literal` is an arbitrarily long sequence of alphabetic, digit, period (`.`), underscore (`_`), and asterisk (`*`) characters. The first character must be alphabetic, and an asterisk may be used only as the last character. Some implementations use the period to partition the namespace.

2.9   Attribute Declaration

An interface can have attributes as well as operations which are defined as part of the interface. An attribute declaration is logically equivalent to declaring a pair of accessor functions: one to retrieve the value of the attribute and one to set it. The syntax for `attribute` declaration is

```
<attr_dcl>                ::=[ "readonly" ] "attribute"
                              <param_type_spec>
                              <simple_declarator>
                              { "," <simple_declarator> }*
```

The optional `readonly` keyword indicates a single assessor function, retrieve value. Consider the following example:

```
interface foo {
    enum material_t {rubber, glass};
    struct position_t {
        float x, y;
    };
    attribute float radius;
    attribute material_t material;
    readonly attribute position_t position;
    ...
};
```

The attribute declarations are equivalent to the following pseudo-specification fragment:

```
...
float _get_radius ();
void _set_radius (in float r);
material_t _get_material ();
void _set_material (in material_t m);
position_t _get_position ();
...
```

The actual accessor function names are language-mapping specific (C, C++, and Java mappings are described in separate chapters). The attribute name is subject to OMG IDL's name-scoping rules, so the accessor function names are guaranteed *not* to collide with any OMG IDL legal operation names. Attribute operations return errors through standard exceptions. Also, they are inherited. An attribute name *cannot* be redefined to be a different type.

2.10   *CORBA Module*

To prevent CORBA-defined names from clashing with those in programming languages and other software systems, they are treated as though defined within a module named CORBA. However, in an OMG IDL specification, keywords such as `Object` must not be preceded by a `CORBA::` prefix. Other interface names, such as `TypeCode`, are not OMG IDL keywords, so they must be referred to by their fully scoped names (e.g., `CORBA::TypeCode`).

2.11   *Names and Scoping*

An entire OMG IDL file forms a naming scope, and module, interface, structure, union, operation, and exception definitions form nested scopes. Also scoped are identifiers for the type, constant, enumeration value, exception, interface, attribute, and operation definitions.

An identifier can be defined only once in a scope, but can be redefined in nested scopes. An identifier declaring a module is considered defined by its first occurrence in a scope; subsequent occurrences within the same scope reopen the module, allowing definitions to be added to it.

Because of possible restrictions imposed by future language bindings, OMG IDL identifiers are case insensitive; that is, two identifiers, one upper- and one lowercase, are considered the same. However, all references to a definition must use the same case as in the defining occurrence, which allows natural mappings to case-sensitive languages.

Type names defined in a scope are available for immediate use within that scope.

An unqualified name can be used within a particular scope; it will be resolved by successive searching in farther out enclosing scopes. Once an unqualified name is used in a current or enclosing scope, it cannot be redefined. Such a redefinition yields a compilation error.

A qualified name (one of the form `<scoped-name>::<identifier>`) is resolved by first resolving the qualifier `<scoped-name>` to a scope S and then locating the definition of `<identifier>` within S. The identifier must be directly defined in S or (if S is an interface) inherited into it. The `<identifier>` is not searched for in enclosing scopes.

When a qualified name begins with `::`, the resolution process starts with the file scope and locates subsequent identifiers in the qualified name by the rule described in the previous paragraph.

2.11.1 Global Names

Every OMG IDL definition in a file has a global name in that file. The global name for a definition is constructed as follows.

Prior to the scanning of a file containing an OMG IDL specification, both the name of the current root and that of the current scope are empty (`""`). Whenever a `module` keyword is encountered, the string `::` and the associated identifier are appended to the name of the current root, and when termination of the `module` is detected, the trailing `::` and identifier are deleted. Likewise, whenever an `interface`, `struct`, `union`, or `exception` keyword is encountered, the string `::` and the associated identifier are appended to the name of the current scope, and deleted upon detection of these keywords' termination. A new, unnamed scope is entered when the parameters of an operation declaration are processed, which allows the parameter names to duplicate other identifiers. When parameter processing has been completed, the unnamed scope is exited.

The global name of an OMG IDL definition is the concatenation of the current root, the current scope, a `::`, and the `identifier`, which is the local name for that definition. Note that the global name in an OMG IDL files corresponds to an absolute `ScopedName` in the Interface Repository.

Inheritance produces shadow copies of the inherited identifiers; that is, it introduces names into the derived interface that are considered semantically the same as the originals. Two shadow copies of the same original introduce a single name into the derived interface and do not conflict.

Inheritance introduces multiple global OMG IDL names for the inherited identifiers. Consider the following example:

```
interface A {
      exception E {
      long L;
   };
   void f() raises(E);
};

interface B: A {
   void g() raises(E);
};
```

Here, the exception is known by the global names `::A::E` and `::B::E`. Ambiguity can arise in specifications because of the nested naming scopes. For example:

```
interface A {
   typedef string<128> string_t;
};

interface B {
   typedef string<256> string_t;
};

interface C: A, B {
   attribute string_t Title;/* AMBIGUOUS!!! */
};
```

The attribute declaration in C is ambiguous, since the compiler does not know which `string_t` is desired. Ambiguous declarations yield compilation errors.

2.12   *OMG IDL and C++*

The OMG IDL grammar attempts to conform to the C++ syntax, but is somewhat more restrictive, as the following rules show:

- A function return type is mandatory.
- A name must be supplied with each formal parameter to an operation declaration.
- A parameter list consisting of the single token `void` is *not* permitted as a synonym for an empty parameter list.
- Tags are required for structures, discriminated unions, and enumerations.
- Integer types cannot be defined as simply `int` or `unsigned`; they must be declared explicitly as `short` or `long`.
- `char` cannot be qualified by `signed` or `unsigned` keywords.

2.13   Standard Exceptions

The standard exceptions may be returned as a result of any operation invocation, regardless of the interface specification. They may not be listed in `raises` expressions. To limit the complexity of standard-exception handling, the set of standard exceptions should be kept to a tractable size. This constraint forces the definition of equivalence classes of exceptions rather than the enumeration many similar ones. For example, an invocation can fail at many points because of an inability to allocate dynamic memory. Rather than different exceptions for all the ways that memory allocation can fail (during marshaling, unmarshaling, in the client, in the object implementation, when allocating network packets, etc.), a single overall exception for the failure is defined. Each standard exception includes a minor code designating the subcategory of the exception; the assignment of values to the minor codes is left to each ORB implementation.

Each standard exception also includes a `completion_status` code, which takes one of the values {COMPLETED_YES, COMPLETED_NO, COMPLETED_MAYBE}. These have the meanings given in the code that follows. Not all system exceptions are listed, both because future versions of this specification may define additional ones and because ORB implementations may raise nonstandard System exceptions.

```
#define ex_body {unsigned long minor; completion_status completed;}
enum completion_status {COMPLETED_YES, COMPLETED_NO, COMPLETED_MAYBE};
enum exception_type {NO_EXCEPTION, USER_EXCEPTION, SYSTEM_EXCEPTION};
exception UNKNOWN ex_body; // the unknown exception
exception BAD_PARAM ex_body; // an invalid parameter was
// passed
exception NO_MEMORY ex_body; // dynamic memory allocation
// failure
exception IMP_LIMIT ex_body; // violated implementation limit
exception COMM_FAILURE ex_body; // communication failure
exception INV_OBJREF ex_body; // invalid object reference
exception NO_PERMISSION ex_body; // no permission for
                                 //attempted op.
exception INTERNAL ex_body; // ORB internal error
exception MARSHAL ex_body; // error marshaling param/result
exception INITIALIZE ex_body; // ORB initialization failure
exception NO_IMPLEMENT ex_body; // operation implementation
                                // unavailable
exception BAD_TYPECODE ex_body; // bad typecode
exception BAD_OPERATION ex_body; // invalid operation
exception NO_RESOURCES ex_body; // insufficient resources for req.
exception NO_RESPONSE ex_body; // response to req. not yet
// available
exception PERSIST_STORE ex_body; // persistent storage failure
exception BAD_INV_ORDER ex_body; // routine invocations out of order
```

COMPLETED_YES (The implementation completed processing before the exception was raised.)

COMPLETED_NO (The implementation was not initiated before the exception was raised.)

COMPLETED_MAYBE (The status of implementation completion is indeterminate.)

```
exception TRANSIENT ex_body; //transient failure - reissue
              //request
exception FREE_MEM ex_body; //cannot free memory
exception INV_IDENT ex_body; //invalid identifier syntax
exception INV_FLAG ex_body; //invalid flag was specified
exception INTF_REPOS ex_body; //error accessing interface
                              //repository
exception BAD_CONTEXT ex_body; //error processing context
                               //object
exception OBJ_ADAPTER ex_body; //failure detected by
                               // object adapter
exception DATA_CONVERSION ex_body; // data conversion error
exception OBJECT_NOT_EXIST ex_body; //non-existent object,
                                    //delete reference
exception TRANSACTION_REQUIRED ex_body; //transaction
                                        //required
exception TRANSACTION_ROLLEDBACK ex_body; // transaction
                                  // rolled back
exception INVALID_TRANSACTION ex_body; //invalid transaction
```

2.13.1 Object Nonexistence

The OBJECT_NOT_EXIST exception is raised to an invocation on a deleted object. It is an authoritative "hard" fault report, and any client receiving it is allowed (even expected) to delete all copies of this object reference and to perform other appropriate "final recovery" procedures.

Bridges forward this exception to clients, destroying any records they may hold (for example, proxy objects used in reference translation). Clients can in turn purge any of their own data structures.

2.13.2 Transaction Exceptions

The TRANSACTION_REQUIRED exception indicates that the request carries a null transaction instead of the required active transaction.

The TRANSACTION_ROLLEDBACK exception indicates that the transaction associated with the request has been rolled back or marked to roll back. Thus, the requested operation either cannot be performed or is not performed because further computation on its behalf would be fruitless.

The INVALID_TRANSACTION exception indicates that the request carries an invalid transaction context. For example, an error might have occurred during an attempt to register a resource.

CHAPTER 3

CORBA to COM and COM to CORBA: Mappings

The two different object models discussed in this chapter are COM (Component Object Model), from Microsoft Corporation, and CORBA (Common Object Request Broker Architecture), from OMG (Object Management Group).

The COM model represents Microsoft's effort to establish an object environment focusing on the component as the reliable and atomic entity. The demand of the computing world today is to minimize the effort required in software development and at the same time provide a ubiquitous operating environment. The demand for flexibility in development tools and coordination between the results are of highest priority. With this in mind, COM addresses the problem of binary object interoperability by providing well-defined interfacing mechanisms that can be applied from various programming languages. In its early days confined to the Microsoft operating environment but being developed on other platforms like the different flavors of UNIX, on different IBM platforms, etc. CORBA is the work of the OMG, a consortium of many software-development companies. The goals of OMG, creators of CORBA, were to bring out an object model that would unify software development within multiple environments and domains, so that, for example, applications for the healthcare industry and applications for the airline industry would follow the same model. The model is kept identical but different domains apply them differently.

These efforts are directed in an excellent manner to unify the software developing communities of different domains. The commonalties between these different application domains would be retained in a common object kernel. The object models differ on their base philosophies, but the underlying idea is the same.

Since unification is the ultimate horizon of both COM and CORBA, it makes perfect sense for them to map onto each other. In other words, one would certainly expect to have a mapping from CORBA to COM and vice-versa. This chapter is an attempt to accomplish this glorified effort.

We will start our discussion by first looking at the mappings from CORBA to COM and then at those from COM to CORBA. This will provide us a much clearer understanding than if the mappings are studied individually.

The following mappings are covered:

- Data type
- Interface
- Operations
- Attributes
- Inheritance
- Interface Repository

3.1   Data Type Mapping

We will start by analyzing the mapping of various data types from CORBA to COM and vice-versa. IDL is a general-purpose interface definition language. It is used to define interfaces in CORBA as well as COM. Although in COM the actual language is called MIDL, a derivative of DCE

IDL. Current versions of Windows are purely 32-bit, but the earlier versions were 16-bit. As a matter of fact, Windows95 was the first operating environment that allowed both 16-bit and 32-bit applications to co-exist harmoniously. The mapping from CORBA to COM for Win 32 uses MIDL but neither MIDL nor Microsoft RPC exists Win 16, which thus uses ODL (Object Definition Language). As we shall see throughout the chapter, much of the mapping between COM and CORBA is one-to-one. Only certain portions of the model need conversion; however, these areas require caution to avoid any data loss between the two. Also, MIDL and/or ODL are used to represent COM purely on the basis of their recognition in the COM domain. Indeed, no hard-and-fast rule requires either to be the only target for the mapping from CORBA to COM. A developer could easily create a new mapped model for this, but the intricacies of doing so must be addressed. We start our analysis with a look at the basic data types supported by the two models, which are listed in Table 3.1.

Table 3.1   OMG IDL to MIDL Intrinsic Data Type Mappings

OMG IDL	Microsoft IDL	Microsoft ODL	Description
short	short	short	Signed integer with range of $-2^{15} \ldots +2^{15} - 1$
long	long	long	Signed integer with range of $-2^{31} \ldots +2^{31} - 1$
unsigned short	unsigned short	unsigned short	Unsigned integer with a range of $0 \ldots 2^{16} - 1$
unsigned long	unsigned long	unsigned long	Unsigned integer with a range of $0 \ldots 2^{32} - 1$
float	float	float	IEEE single-precision floating point number
double	double	double	IEEE double-precision floating point number
char	char	char	8-bit quantity limited to the ISO Latin-1 character set

Table 3.1   OMG IDL to MIDL Intrinsic Data Type Mappings   (Continued)

OMG IDL	Microsoft IDL	Microsoft ODL	Description
`boolean`	`boolean`	`boolean`	8-bit quantity which is limited to 1 and 0
`octet`	`byte`	`unsigned char`	8-bit opaque data type, guaranteed to not undergo any conversion during transfer between systems

Source: OMG

3.1.1   Mapping for Constants

The keyword `const` states that a variable cannot change its value, which is fixed. It has a one-to-one mapping from OMG IDL to Microsoft's IDL and Microsoft's ODL. No conversion is needed from OMG IDL to Microsoft's IDL (henceforth referred to simply as "MIDL") or Microsoft's ODL (henceforth referred to simply as "ODL").

Table 3.2 shows the mappings for keywords. As just mentioned, the mapping for all `const`s is one-to-one, except that OMG IDL allows `float` and `double` to be constant. This would cause an error in converting from OMG IDL to MIDL or ODL. The mapping does not deal with error handling, so it is up to the developer to design a suitable conversion or

Table 3.2   Constants Mapping

OMG IDL	Microsoft IDL and ODL
`const short`	`const short`
`const long`	`const long`
`const unsigned short`	`const unsigned short`
`const unsigned long`	`const unsigned long`
`const char`	`const char`
`const boolean`	`const boolean`
`const float`	`??`
`const double`	`??`

error-handling mechanism. Note that such a situation would never arise in conversions from MIDL or ODL to OMG IDL because `const float` or `const double` is an invalid syntax in both domains.

3.1.2   Mapping of Enumerators

The mapping of the enumerators from CORBA to COM and vice-versa is somewhat complex. Enumerators, as the name suggests, allow the programmer to enumerate on a certain allowable range of values, which is provided within the definition. For programming ease the enumerators are declarative, but for the system they have basic numeric values, which are generally as simple as integer values. Some programming languages need explicit values tagged to the enumerator, and others maintain the order of enumerators on the basis of their defined position. This same variation is visible between CORBA and COM: CORBA enumerators do not have explicit tagged values whereas IDL and ODL do. For example:

```
// OMG IDL
enum val {A, B, C};
```

The OMG IDL enumerator `val` can take in values `A` or `B` or `C`. The values are determined by the incremental order of their definition, with `A` being the lowest and `C` being the highest. When converted to IDL or ODL the above example becomes:

```
// Equivalent Microsoft IDL or ODL
typedef [v1_enum] enum tagval {A=0, B, C} val;
```

Within the enumeration list an explicit value of `0` is assigned to `A` with `B` being greater than `A` and `C` being greater than `B` and the order is maintained. The keyword `v1_enum` is specific to Microsoft IDL. It indicates a 32-bit enumeration value, which Microsoft recommends for increasing the data marshaling and unmarshaling efficiency when such enumerators are embedded in structures and unions. In CORBA a maximum of 2^{32} identifiers may be specified, whereas IDL and ODL specify only 2^{16}. Hence, there are chances of truncation or data loss in conversion and so care should be taken. The conversion from IDL and ODL to OMG IDL is much easier than the other way around because these risks do not exist.

When IDL or ODL is mapped to OMG IDL, the explicit value assigned to the enumeration is not considered important for conversion. However, the order of the elements in the enumeration list is extremely important and is maintained in the converted OMG IDL format.

3.1.3   Mapping of String Types

A string is a collection of characters terminated by a NULL—a special character used as a string terminator. This definition of a string is highly generic and applicable in most programming environments—CORBA accepts it and respects it accordingly. Conventional characters are 8 bits wide, but with the advent of Unicode, wide characters have become important. IDL and ODL use a number of different data types for 8-bit character and wide-character strings.

Table 3.3 shows the mapping of OMG IDL string data types to their equivalents in IDL and ODL. Note that for a Unicode string in Microsoft the data type LPTSTR is required. Also, the flags used during compilation determine whether the variable has the capacity to hold Unicode values of only 8-bit characters.

Table 3.4 shows data type mapping from IDL and ODL to OMG IDL. Note the data type BSTR, which exists only in ODL, on a Win 16 platform, and maps to OMG IDL string data types. OMG IDL uses it for Unicode and non-Unicode strings. When a BSTR is passed from a COM to a CORBA client, a data conversion is necessary on the CORBA side. This conversion is in the form of an exception called E_DATA_CONVERSION.

Table 3.3   OMG IDL to Microsoft IDL/ODL Strings Mapping

OMG IDL	Microsoft IDL	Microsoft ODL	Description
String	LPSTR, char*	LPSTR	Null terminated 8-bit character string
	LPTSTR	LPTSTR	Null terminated 8-bit or Unicode string (depends upon compiler flags used)

Source: OMG

Table 3.4   Mapping of String Data Types from Microsoft IDL/ODL to OMG IDL

Microsoft IDL	Microsoft ODL	OMG IDL	Description
LPSTR, char *	LPSTR	string	Null terminated 8-bit character string
LPTSTR	LPTSTR	string	Null terminated 8-bit character string (or Unicode string)
	BSTR (on Win16)	string	Null terminated 8-bit character string

Source: OMG

OMG IDL supports two string forms, bounded and unbounded. The bounded string has its maximum length specified, which indicates the string's boundary. The unbounded string has no specified bounds.

3.1.4   Mapping of Unbounded String Types

The mapping of unbounded string from OMG IDL to Microsoft IDL and ODL goes as follows. An unbounded string, defined in OMG IDL as

```
// OMG IDL
typedef string ubn_string;
```

which maps to IDL or ODL as

```
// Microsoft IDL or ODL
typedef [string, unique] char * ubn_string;
```

An unbounded string from OMG IDL is mapped to a unique pointer to a one-dimensional character array. The array is not of fixed size. Its size is determined at the runtime. The size of the array at runtime is determined by a terminating null character. The mapping from IDL or ODL to OMG IDL is just the reverse of this; that is, a unique pointer to a one-dimensional character array, whose size is determined at runtime, maps to an OMG IDL unbounded string.

3.1.5   Mapping of Bounded String Types

Bounded string mapping from OMG IDL to IDL or ODL is slightly different from unbounded string mapping. First, a definition of a bounded string in OMG IDL:

```
// OMG IDL
const long NUM = 10;
typedef string <NUM> bn_string;
```

The above code snippet shows a definition of a bounded string in OMG IDL. The maximum number of characters the string can hold is defined as 10. (This is just an illustration. The reader can define the maximum length of the string to be whatever length is desired.) This OMG IDL definition will be mapped to Microsoft IDL or ODL as follows:

```
// Microsoft ODL or ODL
const long NUM = 10;
typedef [string, unique] char (* bn_string) [NUM];
```

The above declaration states that bn_string is a unique character pointer to a one-dimensional array of maximum length 10. The actual number of characters present in this pointer can be less than 10, but cannot be more than 10. The string is null terminated.

As noted, CORBA does not differentiate between Unicode and non-Unicode strings, that is, OMG IDL does not provide different data types for declaring Unicode and non-Unicode string variables. However, IDL and ODL do have separate data types and so a mapping from IDL and ODL to OMG IDL is necessary.

3.1.6   Mapping of Unicode Unbounded String Types

The declaration of a Unicode unbounded string variable in IDL or ODL is

```
// Microsoft IDL or ODL
typedef [string, unique] LPTSTR     u_ubn_string;
```

The keyword LPTSTR represents a Unicode character pointer. Thus, the declaration states that u_ubn_string is a unique stringified Unicode pointer to a one-dimensional character array, whose size is determined at runtime and does not have a specified maximum bound. This declaration maps to the following OMG IDL definition:

```
// OMG IDL
typedef wstring u_ubn_string;
```

The mapping is simple. The implementation is responsible for converting the Unicode format to the ANSI string format and vice versa.

3.1.7 Mapping of Unicode Bounded String Types

The mapping of Unicode bounded string types in IDL or ODL is no different from that for ANSI string types. Here is an IDL or ODL declaration for a Unicode bounded string variable:

```
// Microsoft IDL or ODL
const long NUM = 10;
typedef [string, unique]  TCHAR  (* u_bn_string) [NUM];
```

This maps to the OMG IDL declaration:

```
// OMG IDL
const long NUM = 10;
typedef wstring<NUM> u_bn_string;
```

As we see, the OMG IDL definition is identical to a bounded ANSI string mapping, except that `wstring` replaces `string`. Note that the conversion from the Unicode to the ANSI format is the responsibility of the implementation. (Readers familiar with the template declarations in C++ will also note that this type of bounded string declaration in OMG IDL is similar to templates in C++.)

3.1.8 Mapping for Struct Types

Structure is a user defined, customized data accumulation construct. Programmers can prepare structures that could consist of any type of data. It is an ordered set of values that are stored and retrieved, to and from the system, in unison. OMG IDL provides a way to define structures and it uses the keyword `struct` for this purpose. The declaration of a structure variable in OMG ODL is as follows:

```
// OMG IDL
typedef  ...  T0;
typedef  ...  T1;
typedef  ...  T2;
...
typedef  ...  Tn;
struct Moushumi
{
  T0  m0;
  T1  m1;
  T2  m2;
```

```
...
Tn   mN;
};
```

The code snippet above shows a structure variable declaration in OMG IDL. `Moushumi` is a variable of type `struct`. The squiggle brackets, { and }, shows the bounds of the structure or they represent the structure content. The structure consists of a name and value placeholder pair. `T0`, `T1`, `T2`... `Tn` are the various data types used within the structure. This OMG IDL when mapped to Microsoft's IDL or ODL will look like the following

```
// Microsoft IDL or ODL
typedef  ...   T0;
typedef  ...   T1;
typedef  ...   T2;
...
typedef  ... Tn;
typedef struct
{
   T0   m0;
   T1   m1;
   T2   m2;

   ...
   Tn   mN;
} Moushumi;
```

As shown, the mappings to IDL or ODL differ, slightly, only in the structure definition.

The mapping back to OMG IDL is simply the reverse of the process and need not be illustrated.

3.1.9   Mapping of Union Types

OMG IDL unions are complex and hence slightly difficult to understand. The union construct in an OMG IDL is encapsulated and discriminated. The discriminator must be encapsulated within the union itself and the discriminator can only be of the types `long`, `short`, `unsigned long`, `unsigned short`, `char`, `boolean`, or `enum`. Here is a union declaration in OMG IDL:

```
// OMG IDL
enum U_RakhaDisc
{
```

```
  dChar,
  dBoolean,
  dShort,
  dLong,
  dFloat,
  dDouble
};
union u_val
switch( U_RakhaDisc )
{
  case dChar:    char c;
  case dBoolean: boolean b;
  case dShort:   short s;
  case dLong:    long l;
  case dFloat:   float f;
  case dDouble:  double d;
  default: octet v[8];
};
```

We see that the discriminator is defined as `U_RakhaDisc` and that it
contains constant data types such as `char`, `boolean`, `short`, `long`, `float`,
and `double`. The union definition consists of a `switch` statement, which
selects the appropriate data type and value. The statement has one default
clause—no more are allowed. The only reason the discriminators are
limited to a standard set understood by the base system is that automatic
casting can be done to the desired data type. No room is provided for
custom marshaling from one format to another.

When mapped to encapsulated IDL, the above OMG IDL code becomes

```
// Microsoft IDL
typedef enum
{
  dChar,
  dBoolean,
  dShort,
  dLong,
  dFloat,
  dDouble
} U_RakhaDisc;
typedef union switch( U_RakhaDisc val_type )
{
  case dChar:    char c;
  case dBoolean: boolean b;
  case dShort:   short s;
```

```
  case dLong:    long l;
  case dFloat:   float f;
  case dDouble:  double d;
  default: byte v[8];
} u_val;
```

The Microsoft IDL code snippet shown above is mapped from the OMG IDL code. There are a few differences between the two definitions. One is that in the OMG IDL default clause, octet is the default type, whereas in Microsoft IDL it is byte. Earlier in the chapter we saw that an octet from OMG IDL always maps to a byte in Microsoft IDL.

IDL unions are discriminated, but need not always be encapsulated. In a nonencapsulated union the discriminator can be passed as a parameter. Thus, another difference between IDL and OMG IDL is that the IDL discriminator is not limited to constant expressions. A look at some source code of union declarations should elucidate how the mapping of unions to OMG IDL differs between encapsulated and nonencapsulated IDL.

3.1.10   Mapping for Encapsulated Unions

```
// Microsoft IDL
typedef enum
{
  dChar,
  dBoolean,
  dShort,
  dLong,
  dFloat,
  dDouble
} U_RakhaDisc;
typedef union switch( U_RakhaDisc _d)
{
  case dChar:    char c;
  case dBoolean: boolean b;
  case dShort:   short s;
  case dLong:    long l;
  case dFloat:   float f;
  case dDouble:  double d;
  default: byte v[8];
} val_type;
```

This Microsoft encapsulated discriminated union maps to the following OMG IDL definition:

```
// OMG IDL
enum U_RakhaDisc
{
  dChar,
  dBoolean,
  dShort,
  dLong,
  dFloat,
  dDouble
};
union val_val
switch( U_RakhaDisc )
{
  case dChar:    char c;
  case dBoolean: boolean b;
  case dShort:   short s;
  case dLong:    long l;
  case dFloat:   float f;
  case dDouble:  double d;
  default: octet v[8];
};
```

The encapsulated discriminated mapping from IDL to OMG IDL is a mirror image of the mapping from OMG IDL to IDL. The difference is observed only in the mapping of nonencapsulated unions between the two models.

3.1.11 Mapping for Nonencapsulated Unions

Microsoft IDL nonencapsulated unions are mapped to any in OMG IDL. The actual any type is determined at runtime and accordingly converted. Here is the nonencapsulated union definition in IDL:

```
// Microsoft IDL
typedef [switch_type( short )] union
tagUNION_OF_CHAR_AND_ARITHMETIC
{
  [case(0)] char c;
  [case(1)] short s;
  [case(2)] long l;
  [case(3)] float f;
```

```
    [case(4)] double d;
    [default] byte v[8];
} UNION_OF_CHAR_AND_ARITHMETIC;
```

This declaration will be converted into the OMG IDL statement below. Notice that no explicit discriminators are encapsulated in the IDL declaration. Selection of the actual type and value is based on a `switch`-like construct.

```
// OMG IDL
typedef any UNION_OF_CHAR_AND_ARITHMETIC;
```

The OMG IDL mapping is a single-line declaration. The actual value to which this `any` maps is determined at runtime, which is why discrimination is needed. Without it the system would require custom marshaling features and hooks to attach them. This would make the system mappings even more complex because the custom marshaling features also would have to be mapped from one platform to another.

The ODL unions are not discriminated and hence need custom marshaling for all interfaces in which they are used. For this specific reason, little can be said about mapping from ODL to OMG IDL.

3.1.12   Mapping for Sequence Types

`Sequence` is a collection placeholder data type that holds like data types. It is a one-dimensional array with two characteristics: an optional maximum size fixed at compile time and a runtime determined length. The data type that a sequence holds, and hence its length, is fixed at runtime. Once again, a sequence is bounded when its maximum size is specified and unbounded otherwise. A `sequence` data type is available only in OMG IDL, so we will look at a mapping from that model to IDL and ODL.

3.1.12.1   Mapping for Unbounded Sequence Types
Here is an unbounded sequence definition in OMG ODL:

```
// OMG IDL
typedef  …  T;
typedef sequence<T> UnSequence;
```

which maps to IDL and ODL as

```
// Microsoft IDL or ODL
typedef  …  U;
typedef struct
{
  unsigned long cbMaxSize;
  unsigned long cbLengthUsed;
  [size_is(cbMaxSize), length_is(cbLengthUsed), unique]
    U * pValue;
} UnSequence;
```

The type defined in the OMG IDL script is T, which maps to IDL or ODL type U. Note that these two types can be identical, as many are between OMG IDL and IDL or ODL. Different symbols are used here for the sake of generality.

The unbounded sequence type from OMG IDL maps to a unique pointer of an equivalently mapped type in IDL or ODL. The structure definition in the IDL or ODL mapping has a variable for holding the maximum size of the sequence and one for holding the length of the type forming the sequence. This variable is mapped into a pointer, because the sequence is unbounded in the OMG IDL declaration. Either the IDL or the ODL definition provides the appropriate maximum size and length for the uniquely defined pointer.

3.1.12.2 *Mapping of Bounded Sequence Types*

Bounded sequences can grow to the maximum bound defined for them. Here is the OMG IDL definition of a bounded sequence:

```
// OMG IDL
const long N = 10;
typedef …  T;
typedef sequence<T,N> Bsequence;
```

And here is the mapping of the bounded sequence to IDL or ODL:

```
// Microsoft IDL or ODL
const long N = 10;
typedef …  U;
typedef struct
{
  unsigned long cbMaxSize;
  unsigned long cbLengthUsed;
  [length_is(cbLengthUsed)] U Value[N];
} Bsequence;
```

The OMG IDL code snippet shows a sequence of type T and a maximum size of 10. This sequence variable is called Bsequence. Type T maps to IDL or ODL type U, which has an array size of 10, as specified in the OMG IDL. The maximum size of the array is fixed and the length is determined at compilation.

3.1.13   Mapping for Array Types

An Array is a data type that can act as a placeholder for a like data type. Both the data type and the array size have to be known at compilation or they are fixed.

OMG IDL allows users to define fixed length multidimensional arrays. So do IDL and ODL. The mappings from OMG IDL to IDL and ODL and vice versa are one-to-one and have no special requirements. However, the array's data maps according to its own rules. For example, this code shows an OMG IDL array declaration.

```
// OMG IDL
const long N = 10;
typedef …   T;
typedef T array_of_Type_T[N];
```

The declared array is of type T and of fixed length N. The value of N is set to be 10 and hence the array can hold data of type T in that amount. When mapped to IDL or ODL this declaration looks like the following:

```
// Microsoft IDL or ODL
const long N = 10;
typedef … U;
typedef  U  array_of_Type_U[N];
```

Here, the mapping is one-to-one, and we see that T maps to U (they do not have to be different). If the data type is a basic one such as long, short, float, or double, the mapping can be fairly straightforward as these types occur in both domains. If they differ, as octet in OMG IDL differs from byte in IDL or ODL, mapping is necessary.

The mapping of IDL or ODL fixed-sized multidimensional arrays to OMG IDL is simply the reverse of the mapping just described, so we will not discuss it here.

3.1.14 Mapping of Nonfixed Arrays

IDL and ODL support varying arrays and conformant varying arrays, defined as arrays whose size and bounds are determined at runtime. OMG IDL does not support either of these, so they are mapped into OMG IDL sequences. Here is an example of IDL's nonfixed-length array:

```
// Microsoft IDL
typedef short BTYPE[];
typedef char CTYPE[*];
```

The code shows two nonfixed array-size definitions: BTYPE and CTYPE. When mapped to OMG IDL, they become

```
// OMG IDL
typedef sequence<short> BTYPE;
typedef sequence<char> CTYPE;
```

The mapping is to a sequence of appropriate data types as declared in the IDL code. Actual implementation on both sides takes care of the true length at runtime. The sequence definition mapped back to IDL or ODL will not provide nonfixed-length arrays, but will map to a sequence. For this reason, the IDL or ODL unbounded sequence definition is functionally equivalent to the nonfixed-length array definition.

3.1.14.1 *Mapping for SAFEARRAY*

SAFEARRAY is a type of array definition available only in ODL. It is a variable-length, variable-dimension array, whose length and dimension are determined at runtime. The array data type must be defined at compile time. An example of a SAFEARRAY definition in Microsoft ODL is shown here:

```
// Microsoft ODL
SAFEARRAY(element-type) * A_Name;
```

This definition is of a SAFEARRAY of type element-type and name A_Name. It is mapped to OMG IDL to form this sequence:

```
// OMG IDL
typedef sequence <element-type> A_Name;
```

which, as shown, is of type element_type and name A_Name. When the CORBA client receives a multidimensional SAFEARRAY from a COM client, an E_DATA_CONVERSION exception is raised. We will see the use of E_DATA_CONVERSION later on in the chapter.

3.1.15 Mapping for the any Type

The any keyword in OMG IDL can map to any data type. However, because of the complexity of its functionality, an interface definition must be created for it in COM, which is shown below:

```
// Microsoft IDL
typedef [v1_enum] enum CORBAAnyDataTagEnum
{
  anySimpleValTag,
  anyAnyValTag,
  anySeqValTag,
  anyStructValTag,
  anyUnionValTag
} CORBAAnyDataTag;

typedef union CORBAAnyDataUnion switch(
  CORBAAnyDataTag whichOne )
{
  case anyAnyValTag:
    ICORBA_Any *anyVal;
  case anySeqValTag:
  case anyStructValTag:
    struct
    {
      [string, unique] char * repositoryId;
      unsigned long cbMaxSize;
      unsigned long cbLengthUsed;
      [size_is(cbMaxSize), length_is(cbLengthUsed), unique]
      union CORBAAnyDataUnion *pVal;
    } multiVal;
  case anyUnionValTag:
    struct
    {
      [string, unique] char * repositoryId;
      long disc;
      union CORBAAnyDataUnion *value;
    } unionVal;
  case anyObjectValTag:
    struct
    {
      [string, unique] char * repositoryId;
```

```
    VARIANT val;
   } objectVal;
  case anySimpleValTag: // All other types
    VARIANT simpleVal;
} CORBAAnyData;

.... uuid(74105F50-3C68-11cf-9588-AA0004004A09) ]
interface ICORBA_Any: IUnknown
{
  HRESULT _get_value( [out] VARIANT * val );
  HRESULT _put_value( [in] VARIANT val );
  HRESULT _get_CORBAAnyData( [out] CORBAAnyData * val );
  HRESULT _put_CORBAAnyData( [in] CORBAAnyData val );
  HRESULT _get_typeCode( [out] ICORBA_TypeCode ** tc );
}
```

The above interface definition shows the *any* mapping to COM. The interface is properly defined to handle all possible data type conversions. Note that VARIANT represents the data types in the IDL interface. *It* can be considered a subset of any because it cannot represent complex data types such as struct and union. For these the IStream pointer is used. IStream represents a stream of data that does not have any specific interpretation attached to it other than that it is made up of 8-bit characters.

The IStream pointer can be used to move data to and from the stream. However, since IStream is a general representation, the implementation itself must interpret that data. If for some reason the implementation does not represent these types as an IStream, E_DATA_CONVERSION is returned as the value of SCODE.

The interface definition code above shows five methods. The first two—_get_value and _put_value—retrieve and put the data from the OMG any type. They use the VARIANT data type to indicate that the OMG any does not have any complex data types and values associated with it. The next two methods—_get_CORBAAnyData and _put_CORBAAnyData—use the CORBAAny-Data data type and are used for complex data structures. The last method—_get_typeCode—is used to obtain the data type code employed by the client implementation. The OMG IDL any data type is as complex as it is because it has to handle all possible data type formations within the application.

Microsoft does not have the any data type, so there is no need for mappings.

3.1.16 Mapping for VARIANT

The COM VARIANT type is somewhat similar to CORBA's any. It is COM's way of specifying a variable data type, but its allowable set of data types is currently limited to those supported by OLE Automation. VARTYPE is an enumeration type used in the VARIANT structure that defines the members of the structure vt. Its value acts as the discriminator for the embedded union and governs the union's interpretation. Listed in Table 3.5 are the VARTYPE values along with descriptions of their use to represent the OMG IDL any data type.

Table 3.5   Valid OLE VARIANT Data Types

Value	Description
VT_EMPTY	No value was specified. If an argument is left blank, you should not return VT_EMPTY for the argument. Instead, you should return the VT_ERROR value: DISP_E_MEMBERNOTFOUND
VT_EMPTY | VT_BYREF	Illegal.
VT_UI1	An unsigned 1-byte character is stored in bVal.
VT_UI1 | VT_BYREF	A reference to an unsigned 1-byte character was passed; a pointer to the value is in pbVal.
VT_I2	A 2-byte integer value is stored in iVal.
VT_I2 | VT_BYREF	A reference to a 2-byte integer was passed; a pointer to the value is in piVal.
VT_I4	A 4-byte integer was stored in lVal.
VT_I4 | VT_BYREF	A reference to a 4-byte integer was passed; a pointer to the value is in plVal.
VT_R4	An IEEE 4-byte real value is stored in fltVal.
VT_R4 | VT_BYREF	A reference to an IEEE 4-byte real was passed; a pointer to its value is in pfltVal.
VT_R8	An 8-byte IEEE real value is stored in dblVal.
VT_R8 | VT_BYREF	A reference to an 8-byte IEEE real was passed; a pointer to its value is in pdblVal.

Table 3.5   Valid OLE VARIANT Data Types   (Continued)

Value	Description
VT_CY	A currency value was specified. A currency number is stored as an 8-byte, two's complement integer, scaled by 10,000 to give a fixed-point number with 15 digits to the left of the decimal and 4 digits to the right. The value is in cyVal.
VT_CY | VT_BYREF	A reference to the currency value was passed; a pointer to the value is in pcyVal.
VT_BSTR	A string was passed; it is stored in bstrVal. This pointer must be obtained and freed via the BSTR functions.
VT_BSTR | VT_BYREF	A reference to a string was passed. A BSTR*, which points to a BSTR, is in pbstrVal. The referenced pointer must be obtained or freed via the BSTR functions.
VT_NULL	A propagating NULL value was specified. This should not be confused with the NULL pointer. The NULL value is used for tri-state logic as with SQL.
VT_NULL | VT_BYREF	Illegal.
VT_ERROR	An SCODE was specified. The type of error is specified in code. Generally, operations on error values should raise an exception or propagate the error to the return value, as appropriate.
VT_ERROR | VT_BYREF	A reference to the SCODE was passed. A pointer to the value is in pscode.
VT_BOOL	A Boolean (True/False) was specified. A value of 0xFFFF (all bits one) indicates True; a value of 0 (all bits zero) indicates False. No other values are legal.
VT_BOOL | VT_BYREF	A reference to a Boolean value was passed. A pointer to the Boolean value is in pbool.

Table 3.5   Valid OLE VARIANT Data Types   (Continued)

Value	Description
VT_DATE	A value denoting the date and time was specified. Dates are represented as double-precision numbers, where midnight, January 1, 1900 is 2.0, January 2, 1900 is 3.0 and so on. The value is passed is date. This is the same numbering system used by most spreadsheet programs, although some incorrectly believe that February 29, 1900 existed, and thus set January 1, 1900 to 1.0. The date can be converted to and from an MS-DOS representation using VariantTimeToDosDateTime.
VT_DATE | VT_BYREF	A reference to a date was passed. A pointer to the value is in pdate.
VT_DISPATCH	A pointer to an object was specified. The pointer is in pdispVal. This object is only known to implement IDispatch; the object can be queried as to whether it supports any other desired interface by calling QueryInterface on the object. Objects that do not implement IDispatch should be passed using VT_UNKNOWN.
VT_DISPATCH | VT_BYREF	A pointer to a pointer to an object was specified. The pointer to the object is stored in the location referred to by ppdispVal.
VT_VARIANT	Illegal. VARIANTARGs must be passed by reference.
VT_VARIANT | VT_BYREF	A pointer to another VARIANTARG is passed in pvarVal. This referenced VARIANTARG will never have the VT_BYREF bit set in vt, so only one level of indirection can ever be present. This value can be used to support languages that allow functions to change the types of variables passed by reference.
VT_UNKNOWN	A pointer to an object that implements the IUnknown interface is passed in punkVal.
VT_UNKNOWN | VT_BYREF	A pointer to a pointer to the IUnknown interface is passed in ppunkVal. The pointer to the interface is stored in the location referred to by ppunkVal.

Table 3.5   Valid OLE VARIANT Data Types   (Continued)

Value	Description
VT_ARRAY	<anything>	An array of data <anything> was passed. (VT_EMPTY and VT_NULL are illegal types to combine with VT_ARRAY.) The pointer in pByrefVal points to an array descriptor, which describes the dimensions, size and in-memory location of the array. The array descriptor is never accessed directly, but instead is read and modified using functions.

Source: OMG

COM's VARIANT is mapped to CORBA's any with no data loss. If at runtime a CORBA client passes an inconvertible any to a COM server, a DATA_CONVERSION exception is raised.

3.1.17   Mapping for Pointers

Microsoft's IDL supports three types of pointers:

- Reference pointer; a non-null pointer to a single item. The pointer cannot represent a data structure with cycles as aliasing (two pointers to the same address).

- Unique pointer; a (possibly null) pointer to a single item. The pointer cannot represent a data structure with cycles or aliasing.

- Full pointer; a (possibly null) pointer to a single item. Full pointers can be used for data structures, which form cycles or have aliases.

IDL reference pointers are mapped to a CORBA sequence with one element, which because reference pointers are supposed to point to one element, is an appropriate match. The Unique pointer and the Full pointer, if not pointing to data structures forming cycles or aliasing, are mapped to a CORBA bounded sequence having zero or one item. Passing a full pointer with cycles or aliases from a COM client to a CORBA server results in a return of E_DATA_CONVERSION because the CORBA server cannot map the cycled values properly, and expects the COM client to convert the data into a format it understands. Similarly, if the COM server returns a full pointer containing aliases or cycles to a CORBA client, the CORBA client raises a DATA_CONVERSION exception since it cannot handle aliased full pointers either.

3.2   Interface Mapping

Both COM and CORBA provide interfaces, which they use to exhibit services and which other applications use to interact with the system. A system can provide any number of interfaces depending on the tasks it handles. For this reason, all interfaces have unique identifiers.

3.2.1   Mapping for Interface Identifiers

In both COM and CORBA, the client application makes use of interface identifiers to retrieve information about an interface. Both systems allow convenient string representation of the identifiers, but underneath, the identifiers are raw numbers. The system maintains a mapping from that number to a textual representation.

In CORBA the RepositoryId is a unique identifier for an interface, among other things. COM's slightly different approach to maintaining interface identifiers is the Win32 DCE UUID (Universally Unique IDentifier) format, which COM calls IID (Interface IDentifier). The RepositoryId maps bidirectionally to the COM IID; COM interface identifiers, on the other hand, map bidirectionally to the CORBA RepositoryId. COM interface pointers are mapped bidirectionally to CORBA object references with the appropriate mapping of IDL and ODL interfaces to OMG IDL.

3.2.2   Mapping for Exception Types

CORBA supports exceptions, which are a structured way of representing error conditions. Returning error codes is a simple and limited form of error handling, as it does not allow the *callee* to return a significant amount of error information. In contrast, exceptions allow the *callee* to provide enough information about the error for proper processing. This exception-specific information is a specialized form of a record. Thus, it may consist of any basic or complex data type. Exceptions are classified as System (or Standard) and User.

COM provides error information to clients using a return of type HRESULT, in which a zero value implies a successful operation. The return value can be converted into an SCODE, which in Win32 platform an SCODE is equivalent to HRESULT. This SCODE can then be used by the application to determine if the operation succeeded or failed. The error or success code contained within the SCODE consists of a "facility" major code and a 16-bit minor code. In Win32 the "facility" major code is 13 bits; in Win16, 6 bits.

CORBA allows an application to define its own custom exception definition, which can be returned to the client by the CORBA server on the basis of the situations defined. COM does not provide any standard way to determine the completion status of an invocation, so it is not possible within a COM environment to predict the errors an interface might return. This does not mean that the return error codes are unlimited or previously unspecified. In fact, the status code that can be returned from a COM operation must be fixed when the operation is defined, but there is currently no defined, machine-readable way to discover it.

The richness in the CORBA exception model requires that additional protocol be defined on the COM side for mapping. To map CORBA User exceptions to COM, an additional parameter is added to the end of the COM operation signature, which the COM client checks for the presence of User exception data.

As we will now see, System exceptions are slightly simpler than their user-defined counterparts, as their information is returned in a standard OLE Error object. The COM client uses the OLE object to retrieve the details of the error.

3.2.2.1 Mapping for System Exceptions

System, or Standard, exceptions are used by the ORB and Oas to signal system errors. They do not necessarily mean a failed CORBA operation, but can be returned as a result of any operation invocation. To map a System exception to COM, two things need to be done. First, since COM relies on HRESULT as an indication of success or failure, an appropriate HRESULT must be generated. Second, an OLE object must be created for providing the System exception information.

CORBA System exceptions are assigned a 16-bit numerical ID starting at 0x200 to be used as the HRESULT code. It is available in the lower 16-bit of HRESULT. The COM facility code FACILITY_ITF is used as the facility code in HRESULT because the CORBA exceptions are interface specific. Bits 12 and 13 of the HRESULT contain a bit mask indicating the completion status of the CORBA request. A bit value of 00 indicates that the operation did not complete; a bit value of 01 indicates that the operation did complete; and one of 02 indicates that the operation may have completed. Table 3.6 shows the HRESULT constants and their values that are possible in mapping System exceptions from CORBA to COM.

Table 3.6   Mappings of Standard Exceptions to SCODE

HRESULT **Constant**	HRESULT **Value**
ITF_E_UNKNOWN_NO	0x40200
ITF_E_UNKNOWN_YES	0x41200
ITF_E)UNKNOWN_MAYBE	0x42200
ITF_E_BAD_PARAM_NO	0x40201
ITF_E_BAD_PARAM_YES	0x41201
ITF_E_BAD_PARAM_MAYBE	0x42201
ITF_E_NO_MEMORY_NO	0x40202
ITF_E_NO_MEMORY_YES	0x41202
ITF_E_NO_MEMORY_MAYBE	0x42202
ITF_E_IMP_LIMIT_NO	0x40203
ITF_E_IMP_LIMIT_YES	0x41203
ITF_E_IMP_LIMIT_MAYBE	0x42203
ITF_E_COMM_FAILURE_NO	0x40204
ITF_E_COMM_FAILURE_YES	0x41204
ITF_E_COMM_FAILURE_MAYBE	0x42204

Table 3.6   Mappings of Standard Exceptions to SCODE   *(Continued)*

HRESULT **Constant**	HRESULT **Value**
ITF_E_INV_OBJREF_NO	0x40205
ITF_E_INV_OBJREF_YES	0x41205
ITF_E_INV_OBJREF_MAYBE	0x42205
ITF_E_NO_PERMISSION_NO	0x40206
ITF_E_NO_PERMISSION_YES	0x41206
ITF_E_NO_PERMISSION_MAYBE	0x42206
ITF_E_INTERNAL_NO	0x40207
ITF_E_INTERNAL_YES	0x41207
ITF_E_INTERNAL_MAYBE	0x42207
ITF_E_MARSHAL_NO	0x40208
ITF_E_MARSHAL_YES	0x41208
ITF_E_MARSHAL_MAYBE	0x42208
ITF_E_INITIALIZE_NO	0x40209
ITF_E_INITIALIZE_YES	0x41209
ITF_E_INITIALIZE_MAYBE	0x42209
ITF_E_NO_IMPLEMENT_NO	0x4020A
ITF_E_NO_IMPLEMENT_YES	0x4120A
ITF_E_NO_IMPLEMENT_MAYBE	0x4220A
ITF_E_BAD_TYPECODE_NO	0x4020B
ITF_E_BAD_TYPECODE_YES	0x4120B
ITF_E_BAD_TYPECODE_MAYBE	0x4220B
ITF_E_BAD_OPERATION_NO	0x4020C
ITF_E_BAD_OPERATION_YES	0x4120C
ITF_E_BAD_OPERATION_MAYBE	0x4220C
ITF_E_NO_RESOURCES_NO	0x4020D
ITF_E_NO_RESOURCES_YES	0x4120D
ITF_E_NO_RESOURCES_MAYBE	0x4220D
ITF_E_NO_RESPONSE_NO	0x4020E

Table 3.6   Mappings of Standard Exceptions to SCODE   (Continued)

HRESULT **Constant**	HRESULT **Value**
ITF_E_NO_RESPONSE_YES	0x4120E
ITF_E_NO_RESPONSE_MAYBE	0x4220E
ITF_E_PERSIST_STORE_NO	0x4020F
ITF_E_PERSIST_STORE_YES	0x4120F
ITF_E_PERSIST_STORE_MAYBE	0x4220F
ITF_E_BAD_INV_ORDER_NO	0x40210
ITF_E_BAD_INV_ORDER_YES	0x41210
ITF_E_BAD_INV_ORDER_MAYBE	0x42210
ITF_E_TRANSIENT_NO	0x40211
ITF_E_TRANSIENT_YES	0x41211
ITF_E_TRANSIENT_MAYBE	0x42211
ITF_E_FREE_MEM_NO	0x40212
ITF_E_FREE_MEM_YES	0x41212
ITF_E_FREE_MEM_MAYBE	0x42212
ITF_E_INV_IDENT_NO	0x40213
ITF_E_INV_IDENT_YES	0x41213
ITF_E_INV_IDENT_MAYBE	0x42213
ITF_E_INV_FLAG_NO	0x40214
ITF_E_INV_FLAG_YES	0x41214
ITF_E_INV_FLAG_MAYBE	0x42214
ITF_E_INTF_REPOS_NO	0x40215
ITF_E_INTF_REPOS_YES	0x41215
ITF_E_INTF_REPOS_MAYBE	0x42215
ITF_E_BAD_CONTEXT_NO	0x40216
ITF_E_BAD_CONTEXT_YES	0x41216
ITF_E_BAD_CONTEXT_MAYBE	0x42216
ITF_E_OBJ_ADAPTER_NO	0x40217
ITF_E_OBJ_ADAPTER_YES	0x41217

Table 3.6   Mappings of Standard Exceptions to SCODE   *(Continued)*

HRESULT **Constant**	HRESULT **Value**
ITF_E_OBJ_ADAPTER_MAYBE	0x42217
ITF_E_DATA_CONVERSION_NO	0x40218
ITF_E_DATA_CONVERSION_YES	0x41218
ITF_E_DATA_CONVERSION_MAYBE	0x42218

Source: OMG

The OLE error object contains information on the System exception's minor code and RepositoryId. Its use is optional, and it is mapped according to the following rules:

- The COM View must implement the standard COM interface ISupportErrorInfo so that the View can respond affirmatively when the client asks if error objects are supported by the View interface.
- The COM View must call SetErrorInfo with a NULL value for the IErrorInfo pointer parameter when the mapped CORBA operation is completed successfully. This ensures that the error object on that thread is thoroughly destroyed.

The two mapping rules state that if the OLE Error Object is provided then 1) the ISupportErrorInfo interface should be implemented so that the COM client gets a proper answer to the queries about the Error Object, 2) the SetErrorInfo value should be nullified in case of no exception being raised. Table 3.7 lists the OLE error object properties.

The following code snippet implements the OLE error object. It includes some C++ code that must be supported by the COM View.

```
SetErrorInfo(0L, NULL); // Initialize the thread-local error object
try
{
    // Call the CORBA operation
}
catch(…)
{
    …
    CreateErrorInfo(&pICreateErrorInfo);
```

Table 3.7   Error Object Usage for CORBA System Exceptions

Property	Description
BstrSource	`<interface name>.<operation name>` *where the interface and operation names are those of the CORBA interface that this Automation View is representing.*
BstrDescription	CORBA System Exception: [`<exception repository id>`] `minor code` [`<minor code>`][`<completion status>`] *where the* `<exception repository id>` *and* `<minor code>` *are those of the CORBA system exception.* `<completion status>` *is "YES", "NO" or "MAYBE" based upon the value of the system exception's CORBA completion status. Spaces and square brackets are literals and must be included in the string.*
BstrHelpFile	Unspecified
DwHelpContext	Unspecified
GUID	The IID of the COM View Interface

Source: OMG

```
    pICreateErrorInfo->SetSource(…);
    pICreateErrorInfo->SetDescription(…);
    pICreateErrorInfo->SetGUID(…);
    pICreateErrorInfo->QueryInterface(IID_IErrorInfo,&pIErrorInfo);
    pICreateErrorInfo->SetErrorInfo(0L,pIErrorInfo);
    pIErrorInfo->Release();
    pICreateErrorInfo->Release();
    …
}
```

The code block shown above supports the error object. The first line of the code initializes the error information to NULL. It is followed by the `try` and `catch` blocks and finally the `Release` statements, which decrement the reference count.

The code phrases `try` and `catch` are C++ exception-handling keywords. If an exception is generated by the CORBA invocation in the `try` block, the catch block first creates the error information object (which happens to be an OLE object) and then sets the source and description of the error and the error information object's Globally Unique Identifier (GUID). `QueryInter-`

face, a standard COM method of locating interfaces and their pointers, locates the error information interface, which `IID_IErrorInfo` references. If the interface is supported, its pointer is retrieved in `pIErrorInfo`. Actual information about the error is set in the error information object via `Set-ErrorInfo`.

The COM client accessing the OLE error object has to write extra code to access the error information. This code will be something like the snippet that follows.

```
// After obtaining a pointer to an interface on the COM view, the client
// does the following one time.
pIMyMappedInterface->QueryInterface(IID_ISupportErrorInfo,
                                     &pISupportErrorInfo);
hr = pISupportErrorInfo->InterfaceSupportsErrorInfo(
                                     IID_MyMappedInterface);
BOOL bSupportsErrorInfo = (hr == NOERROR ? TRUE : FALSE);
...
// Call to the COM operation...
HRESULT hrOperation = pIMyMappedInterface->...
if( bSupportsErrorInfo )
{
  HRESULT hr = GetErrorInfo(0, &pIErrorInfo);
  // S_FALSE means that error data is not available
  // NO_ERROR means it is
  if( hr == NO_ERROR )
  {
    pIErrorInfo->GetSource(...);
    // Has repository is & minor code. hrOperation (above)
    // has the completion status encoded into it.
    pIErrorInfo->GetDescription(...);
  }
}
```

Simply, the COM client checks to see if the error interface is supported. If so, it uses the interface to locate the mapped interface from CORBA, which will provide the individual methods the client can call to retrieve the data.

3.2.2.2   Mapping for User Exception Types

User exceptions, defined in IDL with the keyword exception, are custom-defined by users and employed by CORBA to return exception-related information to the client. The User exception must be known and recognized by both the client and server for information to pass from one to the other.

Mapping CORBA User exceptions to COM requires the Exceptions structure, because the exceptions provide much information that can be stored using different data types. The Exceptions structure contains the type and identifier of the exception (defined in the CORBA Interface Repository), and its interface pointer. Since the structure content is dynamic, it needs a dynamic naming mechanism, illustrated by the following template:

```
// Microsoft IDL and ODL
typedef enum
{
NO_EXCEPTION, USER_EXCEPTION
} ExceptionType;
typedef struct
{
  ExceptionType   type;
  LPTSTR    repositoryId;
  <ModuleName><InterfaceName>UserException *  piUserException;
} <ModuleName><InterfaceName>Exceptions;
```

Any operation mapped from OMG IDL to IDL that raises a User exception passes the Exceptions structure as its last parameter—this is always an output parameter because the server needs to return the exception data in it, and it is always an indirect reference because of the way COM manages memory. In COM it is the caller's responsibility to release memory when calling remote server operations. When a last, output parameter is passed as an indirect reference, the callee can treat it as optional. If the caller does not expect the server or called procedure to return an exception, it simply passes a NULL as the last, output parameter. If it *does* expect an exception to be returned, it allocates memory for the Exceptions structure and passes that as the last, output parameter. When the last, output parameter is a non-NULL and the callee has to return an exception, the callee is responsible for allocating any memory needed.

```
// Microsoft IDL
interface IAccount
{
HRESULT Withdraw( [in] float fAmount,
                  [out] float pfNewBalance,
                  [out] BankExceptions **ppException);
}
```

Here `BankExceptions` is the Exceptions structure, passed indirectly as the last output parameter to the `Withdraw` method.

If no exception is raised, a value of `S_OK` is passed as the return value in `HRESULT`. If an exception is raised by the CORBA server, the return value depends on whether the `Exceptions` structure was passed and on the exception type. The following snippet shows IDL User exception definition:

```
// OMG IDL
module Bank
{
  ...
  exception InsufFunds{ float balance };
  exception InvalidAmount { float amount };
  ...
  interface Account
  {
    exception NotAuthorized{};
    float Deposit( in float Amount) raises (InvalidAmount, NotAuthorized);
  };
};
```

Here is the exception when mapped to IDL or ODL:

```
// Microsoft IDL and ODL
struct BankInsufFunds
{
float balance;
};
struct BankInvalidAmount
{
  float amount;
};
struct BankAccountNotAuthorized
{
};
interface IBankAccountUserExceptions : IUnknown
{
  HRESULT get_InsufFunds([out] BankInsufFunds * exceptionBody );
  HRESULT get_InvalidAmount([out] BankInvalidAmount * exceptionBody );
  HRESULT get_NotAuthorized([out] BankAccountNotAuthorized *
                                                 exceptionBody );
};
```

```
typedef struct
{
  ExceptionType      type;
  LPTSTR      repositoryId;
  IBankAccountUserExceptions * piUserException;
} BankAccountExceptions;
```

As the code shows, for every CORBA User exception, a COM structure is defined. Thus, a COM interface that raises exceptions is created for the CORBA interface, taking its name from the module name, the interface name, and the word Exception. The code also shows that the IBank-AccountUserExceptions interface has a get method for each User exception defined in CORBA. Each get takes in one output parameter that retrieves the exception data. Finally, COM defines a structure for the OMG IDL definition—BankAccountExceptions—that has three members: type, which stores the type of exception generated; repositoryId, the repository identifier for the exception definition; and IBankAccountUserExceptions, the interface created by COM. This exception is derived from IUnknown.

3.2.3   Mapping for COM Errors

The COM server returns an error to the client in HRESULT format: a zero value for success, a nonzero value for failure. The nonzero HRESULT should be converted into an SCODE so that the actual error can be identified. COM errors map directly into CORBA error codes; COM system errors map into CORBA Standard exceptions; and COM user-defined errors map to CORBA User exceptions. COM system error codes are defined with the FACILITY_NULL and FACILITY_RPC facility codes, which map to CORBA Standard exceptions.

Table 3.8 lists the mapping of COM FACILITY_NULL error codes to CORBA Standard exceptions, and Table 3.9 lists those from COM FACILITY_RPC error codes to CORBA Standard exceptions. COM SCODEs not listed in the tables are mapped to CORBA User exceptions and require the use of the raises expression in the OMG IDL.

Table 3.8   Mapping from COM `FACILITY_NULL` *Error Codes to CORBA Standard Exceptions*

COM	CORBA
E_OUTOFMEMORY	NO_MEMORY
E_INVALIDARG	BAD_PARAM
E_NOTIMPL	NO_IMPLEMENT
E_FAIL	UNKNOWN
E_ACCESSDENIED	NO_PERMISSION
E_UNEXPECTED	UNKNOWN
E_ABORT	UNKNOWN
E_POINTER	BAD_PARAM
E_HANDLE	BAD_PARAM

Source: OMG

`COM_ERROR` is a special User exception defined in the mapping from CORBA to COM. When it is the only exception raised, the mapped COM operation should not have the additional exception parameter. Every CORBA mapping to COM that raises a User exception, including the mapping of operations described in the next section, is found as an extra, last parameter in the COM definition. This parameter passes the exception data from the server process to the calling COM client, enabling a CORBA implementation of a pre-existing COM interface to be mapped back to COM without altering the COM operation's original signature. In short, it prevents any loss of data. This is a special case that in effect means that a `COM_ERROR` `raises` clause can be added to an operation to indicate that the operation was originally defined in COM.

3.3   *Mapping for Operations*

An interface comprises a collection of like operations that are callable by the users of the interface, that is, the client applications of the CORBA

Table 3.9   Mapping from COM `FACILITY_RPC` *Error Codes to CORBA Standard Exceptions*

COM	CORBA
RPC_E_CALL_CANCELLED	TRANSIENT
RPC_E_CANPOST_INSENDCALL	COMM_FAILURE
RPC_E_CANTCALLOUT_INEXTERNALCALL	COMM_FAILURE
RPC_E_CONNECTION_TERMINATED	NV_OBJREF
RPC_E_SERVER_DIED	INV_OBJREF
RPC_E_SERVER_DIED_DNE	INV_OBJREF
RPC_E_INVALID_DATAPACKET	COMM_FAILURE
RPC_E_CANTTRANSMIT_CALL	TRANSIENT
RPC_E_CLIENT_CANTMARSHAL_DATA	MARSHAL
RPC_E_CLIENT_CANTUNMARSHAL_DATA	MARSHAL
RPC_E_SERVER_CANTMARSHAL_DATA	MARSHAL
RPC_E_SERVER_CANTUNMARSHAL_DATA	MARSHAL
RPC_E_INVALID_DATA	COMM_FAILURE
RPC_E_INVALID_PARAMETER	BAD_PARAM
RPC_E_CANTCALLOUT_AGAIN	COMM_FAILURE
RPC_E_SYS_CALL_FAILED	NO_RESOURCES
RPC_E_OUT_OF_RESOURCES	NO_RESOURCES
RPC_E_NOT_REGISTERED	NO_IMPLEMENT
RPC_E_DISCONNECTED	INV_OBJREF
RPC_E_RETRY	TRANSIENT
RPC_E_SERVERCALL_REJECTED	TRANSIENT
RPC_E_NOT_REGISTERED	NO_IMPLEMENT

Source: OMG

server and framework. A CORBA operation is defined in OMG IDL by its signature, consisting of the operation name, the parameter it takes, if any, and its return value. User exceptions cannot be raised by an operation unless they are defined in this signature. System exceptions in contrast, need not be defined and can be generated any time a system failure occurs.

The context of a system at any point in time defines the system state. The client makes use of it to convey data to an invoked operation. If there is a great deal of information in the context, passing it to the server may cause overhead. For this reason, CORBA has specified that the context be passed implicitly, as a hidden parameter. Also, the bulk of the information in the context represents the entire system, and it would not make sense for operations to receive all that data.

The parameters passed from client to the server and vice versa are directional. That means that the signature of the operation defines the direction of travel in the form of a parameter qualified as in, out, or inout. The in parameter passes from caller to callee; the out parameter passes from callee to caller; and the inout parameter travels in both directions. The OMG IDL in, out and inout map directly to the IDL and ODL [in], [out] and [inout].

Here is an OMG IDL definition.

```
// OMG IDL
#pragma ID::BANK::Bank "IDL:BANK/Bank:1.2"
interface Bank
{
  Account OpenAccount(
          in float StartingBalance,
          in AccountTypes AccountType );
  void Transfer(
          in Account Account1,
          in Account Account2,
          in float Amout) raises(InSufFunds);
}
```

The statements above contain two operations: Bank::OpenAccount and Bank::Transfer. Bank::OpenAccount takes two parameters. The first, StartingBalance of type float, is an input parameter, as indicated by its qualifier. The second, also an input parameter, is AccountType of type AccountTypes and has a return value of type Account. Recall that an operation's return value can be any legitimate basic or derived data type.

The second interface, `Bank::Transfer`, has three parameters, all input. The first is `Account1` of type `Account`; the second is `Account2` also of type `Account`; and the third is `Amount` of type `float`. This operation does not return any value, as shown by `void`. It can raise the User exception `InSufFunds`.

The mapping of this operation from OMG IDL to IDL looks like this:

```
// Microsoft IDL
[ object, uuid(682d22fb-78ac-0000-0c03-4d0000000000),
pointer_default(unique) ]
interface IBank : IUnknown
{
  HRESULT OpenAccount(
          [in] float StartingBalance,
          [in] AccountTypes AccountType,
          [out] IAccount **ppiNewAccount);
  HRESULT Transfer(
          [in] IAccount * Account1,
          [in] IAccount * Account2,
          [in] float Amount,
          [out] IBankUserExceptions **ppiUserException);
};
```

Here is the mapping to ODL:

```
// Microsoft ODL
[uuid(682d22fb-78ac-0000-0c03-4d0000000000) ]
interface IBank: IUnknown
{
  HRESULT OpenAccount(
          [in] float StartingBalance,
          [in] AccountTypes AccountType,
          [out, retval] IAccount **ppiNewAccount );
  HRESULT Transfer(
          [in] IAccount * Account1,
          [in] IAccount * Account2,
          [in] float Amount,
          [out] IBankUserExceptions **ppiUserException);
};
```

The most noticeable difference between the OMG IDL operation signatures and the IDL and ODL signatures is in the return value. Another difference is that the COM mapping of CORBA operations must obey the COM memory ownership and allocation rules specified.

In the OMG IDL definition, operation `Bank::OpenAccount` returns an object of type `Account`. In the COM definition—both IDL and ODL—`Bank::OpenAccount` returns `HRESULT`. The return value is also tagged in the COM operation definition as the third parameter, apparently of the output type. It is of type `IAccount` and is returned as a pointer to a pointer.

The second operation `Bank::Transfer` in OMG IDL does not return any data and has the exception defined. The equivalent COM mapping shows `Bank::Transfer` return `HRESULT`. Also notable is the fourth, output, parameter, added only in COM mappings, which returns the exception data. It is of type `IBankUserExceptions` and is actually a pointer to a pointer of type `IBankUserExceptions`. `HRESULT` is the only way the COM client can be notified of any errors via the exceptions within the CORBA server.

We now look at a mapping from IDL or ODL to OMG IDL:

```
// Microsoft ODL
interface IFoo: IUknown
{
  HRESULT stringify(
          [in] VARIANT value,
          [out, retval] LPSTR * pszValue );
  HRESULT permute(
          [inout] short * value );
  HRESULT trypermute(
          [inout] short * value,
          [out] long newValue );
};
```

When mapped to OMG IDL this becomes

```
// OMG IDL
typedef long HRESULT
interface IFoo:CORBA::Composite, CosLifeCycle::LifeCycleObject
{
  string stringify(
          in any value ) raises(COM_ERROR);
  HRESULT permute(
          inout short value);
  HRESULT trypermute(
          inout short value,
          out long newValue);
};
```

The ODL definition of the first operation, `IFoo::stringify`, has two parameters. The first is an input parameter called `value` and is of type `VARIANT`. The `VARIANT` data type in COM maps to `any` in CORBA. This operation returns `HRESULT`, which when mapped to OMG IDL, develops a completely different signature. We also see that it can raise a User-defined exception, `COM_ERROR`. The second parameter, `pszValue`, which is a pointer to `LPSTR` (a string pointer), becomes the `string` return value in OMG IDL. The other two operations are fairly simple, and the mappings are verbatim.

3.3.1 Mapping for Oneway Operations

OMG IDL has a way to intelligently qualify the direction and the delivery mechanism of an operation. It uses the keyword `oneway` to indicate the invocation semantics the communication service must provide. This is the only attribute used for such a definition. As implied by the keyword, the delivery of this operation is one way only. It is a best-effort delivery and does not guarantee any response from to the callee. The best-effort delivery mechanism makes an at-once effort to deliver the request.

The client application invoking a `oneway` operation should not wait for any return value, as none will be delivered. Nor will a User-defined exception be allowed, as none of its related data can be returned. If the operation is a `oneway`, the system does not have to marshal and unmarshal the data back from the server to the client. This saves the time by avoiding the data transformation process.

IDL's `maybe` operation attribute may provide the closest match to the `oneway` keyword for OMG IDL, since with both the caller does not expect any data back. However, the `maybe` attribute does not provide at-most-once semantics as `oneway` does. Therefore, the mapping of a `oneway` operation from OMG IDL is to an equivalent operation with no parameter or return value.

3.4 Mapping for Attributes

Attributes are constituents of an interface. They are confined within an interface. Attributes aid in providing behavior to the interface. Attributes essentially are shorthand for a pair of accessor functions to an object's data: one to retrieve and possibly one to set a value. They must be contained within an interface and can be either read-only (qualified by the `readonly` keyword) or read/write. The accessor methods of attributes can raise only System exceptions; User exceptions are not possible.

Here is the code for an OMG IDL attribute definition:

```
// OMG IDL
struct CustomerData
{
  CustomerId   Id;
  string       Name;
  string       SurName;
};
#pragma ID::BANK::Account "IDL:BANK/Account:3.1"

interface Account
{
  readonly attribute float Balance;
  float Deposit( in float amount ) raises( InvalidAmount );
  float withdrawal( in float amount ) raises( InsufFunds, InvalidAmount );
  float Close();
};
#pragma ID::BANK::Customer "IDL:BANK/Customer:1.2"

interface Customer
{
  attribute CustomerData Profile;
};
```

Two interfaces are defined: `Account` and `Customer`. The `Account` interface has an attribute called `Balance`, which is read-only, as qualified by the `readonly` keyword. The `Balance` attribute is formed of a simple data, `float`.

The `Customer` interface has an attribute called `Profile`, which is read/write (this is the default if an attribute is not specifically defined as read-only). The `Profile` attribute is formed with the help of a complex data structure called `CustomerData`.

Conversion of attributes from OMG IDL to IDL and ODL requires separate mappings of read/write attributes and read-only attributes.

3.4.1 Mapping for Read-Write Attributes

When the OMG IDL definition illustrated in the last code snippet is mapped to IDL or ODL, the following results. Here, only the read/write attribute is mapped.

```
// Microsoft IDL
[ object, uuid(682d22fb-78ac-0000-0c03-4d0000000000),
pointer_default(unique) ]
interface ICustomer : IUnknown
{
  HRESULT _get_Profile( [out] CustomerData * Profile );
  HRESULT _put_Profile( [in] CustomerData * Profile );
};

// Microsoft ODL
[ uuid(682d22fb-78ac-0c03-4d0000000000) ]
interface ICustomer : IUnknown
{
  [propget] HRESULT Profile( [out] CustomerData * Profile );
  [propput] HRESULT Profile( [in] CustomerData * Profile );
};
```

Notice that the IDL and ODL definitions do not have an explicit attribute defined in the interface. However, they both have get and put methods associated with the attribute, which is how they describe the attribute's presence there.

In IDL the get method is created by the attribute name preceded by _get_. Hence, the get method for Profile is _get_Profile. The put method is similarly created as _put_Profile. The get method takes an output parameter, as it retrieves a value; the put method takes an input parameter, as it sets a value.

The ODL definition is different from that of IDL. The get and put methods have the same name, but get is qualified by [propget]; put, by [propput]. Also, get has an output parameter and put has an input parameter.

3.4.2 Mapping for Read-Only Attributes

The mapping of the read-only attribute obviously is different from that of the read/write attribute. Primarily, a read-only attribute does not need a put method. In the OMG IDL definition code on page 131 the interface

`Account` has the read-only attribute `Balance`. Here is the mapping of `Balance` (the other mappings are irrelevant for this discussion and so are not illustrated):

```
// Microsoft IDL
[ object, uuid(682d22fb-78ac-0000-0c03-4d0000000000) ]
interface IAccount : IUnknown
{
  HRESULT _get_Balance( [out] float Balance );
};

// Microsoft ODL
[ uuid(682d22fb-78ac-0000-0c03-4d0000000000) ]
interface IAccount : IUnknown
{
  [propget] HRESULT Balance( [out] float Balance );
};
```

As expected, there are no put methods here. The explanation for the get methods are as stated in the explanation for the mapping of the read / write attributes.

In Microsoft IDL and ODL scripts there are no attributes; instead there are properties, which are supported only by ODL and the OLE Type libraries. Of course, this means that the only mappings of properties are from ODL and the OLE Type libraries to OMG IDL. However, since they are the exact reverse of OMG IDL mappings to ODL, they will not be discussed here.

3.5   Inheritance Mapping

CORBA and COM differ in the interface inheritance. In CORBA an interface can have both single and multiple inheritance. There is no built-in mechanism to access interfaces without an inheritance relationship. The runtime interfaces of an object, as defined in CORBA, use a description of the object's principle type, which is defined in OMG IDL. CORBA allows many ways to implement interfaces, including implementation inheritance.

Even though syntactically COM allows only single inheritance, it provides a standard mechanism by which an object can have multiple interfaces and by which clients can query for them at runtime. COM does not allow a common way to determine whether two interfaces are referring to the same object, nor does it permit enumeration of all the supported interfaces by an entity. Nevertheless, some COM objects have a specific set of relationships that are conceptually equivalent to multiple inheritance, although discovering this relationship is possible only if ODL or OLE Type libraries are available for it. COM supports two main implementation techniques, aggregation and delegation. A C++-style implementation inheritance is not supported.

Because of the multiple inheritance model supported by CORBA, it is difficult to map CORBA to COM, but it is relatively easy to map COM to CORBA. A singly inherited CORBA definition mapping to COM is straightforward—the base interface for all CORBA inheritance trees is IUnknown. Although most derived interfaces can be queried using IUnknown::QueryInterface, each individual interface in the inheritance hierarchy can also be queried separately.

The following rules apply to CORBA-to-COM inheritance mapping.

- Each OMG IDL interface that does not have a parent is mapped to an MIDL interface deriving from IUnknown.
- Each OMG IDL interface that inherits from a single parent interface is mapped to an MIDL interface that derives from the mapping for the parent interface.
- Each OMG IDL interface that inherits from multiple parent interfaces is mapped to an MIDL interface deriving from IUnknown.
- For each CORBA interface, the mapping for operations precedes the mapping for attributes.
- The resulting mapping of operations within an interface is ordered by operation name. The ordering is lexicographic by bytes in machine-collating order.
- The resulting mapping of attributes within an interface is ordered by attribute name. The ordering is lexicographic by bytes in machine-collating order. If the attribute is not read-only, the _get_<attribute name> method immediately precedes the _set_<attribute name> method.

Here is the OMG IDL inheritance definition:

```
// OMG IDL
interface A
{
  void opA();
  attribute long val;
};
interface B : A
{
  void opB();
};
interface C : A
{
  void opC();
};
interface D : B, C
{
  void opD();
};
interface E
{
  void opE();
};
interface F : D, E
{
  void opF();
};
```

When mapped to COM the definition looks like this:

```
// Microsoft IDL
[ object, uuid(b97267fa-7855-e044-71fb-12fa8a4c515f) ]
interface IA : IUnknown
{
  HRESULT opA();
  HRESULT _get_val( [out] long * val );
  HRESULT _set_val( [in] long val );
};
[ object, uuid(fa2452c3-78425-ff44-11fb-1345fc2fa851f) ]
interface IB : IA
{
  HRESULT opB();
};
[ object, uuid(114552c3-78425-ff44-11fb-2289de2fa851f) ]
interface IC : IA
{
```

```
  HRESULT opC();
};
[ object, uuid(112cc552-78425-ff44-11fb-2289de2fa851f) ]
interface ID : IUnknown
{
  HRESULT opD();
};
[ object, uuid(114552c3-78425-00f2-8994-2289de2fa851f) ]
interface IE : IUnknown
{
  HRESULT opE();
};
[ object, uuid(1145eec3-78425-ff44-11fb-2289de2fa851f) ]
interface IF : IUnknown
{
  HRESULT opF();
};
```

Note that interface D in OMG IDL has a multiple inheritance and is derived from B and C. When mapped to IDL, ID derives from IUnknown. Hence, the multiple inheritance becomes a single inheritance.

3.6   *Interface Repository Mapping*

The Interface Repository in CORBA is where interfaces are stored. It is a common namespace that the client can use to locate a particular interface type in response to a query. Although basically similar, the CORBA Interface Repository and the COM Type libraries exhibit subtle differences. For example, the Type libraries are not presented as a common namespace, but occupy separate files. Thus, the client has to know which library to look in for a specific set of interfaces.

The following mapping can be used by implementations to invoke an Object::get_interface on CORBA object references to COM objects to retrieve an InterfaceDef. For accessing CORBA objects from COM, implementations may allow retrieval of the ITypeInfo for a CORBA object interface using the IProvideClassInfo COM interface.

Table 3.10   The Mapping of the CORBA Interface Repository to the OLE Type Library Mappings

TypeCode	TYPEDESC
Repository	
ModuleDef	ITypeLib
InterfaceDef	ITypeInfo
AttributeDef	VARDESC
OperationDef	FUNCDESC
ParameterDef	ELEMDESC
TypeDef	ITypeInfo
ConstantDef	VARDESC
ExceptionDef	

Source: OMG

With this we finish the chapter on mapping from CORBA to COM and vice versa. The chapter was designed around the specifications of the mapping provided by OMG. Mapping between CORBA and COM is necessary because both have been accepted by the computing industry and developers have been busy developing applications on them. Inevitably, users will want to interoperate between COM and CORBA applications. Sometimes the server may be a COM server and the client a CORBA application; at other times the roles will be reversed. In such a scenario, the interoperability offered by these mappings can be of great use and will save many development dollars.

CHAPTER 4

OLE Automation and CORBA: Mappings

OLE (Object Linking and Embedding) Automation[1] technology was introduced by Microsoft and is considered the precursor of that company's COM and DCOM systems. It is a technique by which objects containing and/or generating commonly needed information can be used by different servers. Automation comprises two primary visible components: *Automation objects* and *Automation controllers*. Automation objects are generators or sources of commonly desired information or data; they are reusable and can be used by multiple servers. Automation controllers are applications that act as servers and that desire the information/data supplied by the different Automation objects. *Automation* itself is a dedicated application-level communication protocol that the Automation objects and controllers employ to carry out their interactions.

In this chapter, mappings of the data types and interfaces are bidirectional. We will use Microsoft ODL to describe the Automation objects; however, not all ODL constructs are supported by Automation, so we limit our discussion only to those that are.

---

[1] The terms *Automation* and *Ole Automation* for the Microsoft technology will be used interchangeably in this chapter.

4.1   Architectural Overview

Figure 4.1 depicts the components of a remote method invocation on a CORBA server from an Automation server. The seven components shown are the *OLE Automation controller*, the *COM communication* component, the *COM System Registry*, the *Automation View*, the `TypeInfo` component, the *ORB*, and the *object implementation*. The arrows indicate the call path or the flow of control when an Automation controller invokes a remote CORBA method, which is implemented in a CORBA server. Also shown are two distinct component technologies and the bridging object.

The Automation View component acts as the bridge between the OLE Automation side supported by COM and the CORBA-compliant ORB. It is an OLE Automation server whose dispatch interface, called the Automation View Interface, is isomorphic to the mapped OMG IDL interface. On the Automation side, which is the client side of the application, the Automation

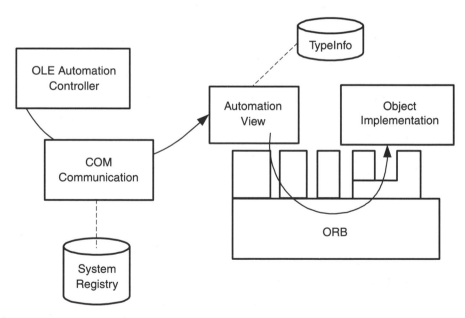

Figure 4.1   CORBA Object Architectural Overview

View encapsulates the CORBA objects and maps every incoming Automation call into a CORBA method invocation based on a one-on-one correspondence. It does not specify the creation and storage of the type information. The parameters of the involved methods are translated bidirectionally the CORBA and the OLE references. The object implementation component is the CORBA object that is communicated with the help of the ORB infrastructure.

The situation is much the same when the OLE Automation object is the server and the CORBA object or implementation is the client. Subtle differences arise because CORBA is distributable and COM is not, as we will see. An OLE Automation object on the server side needs information about the Automation object. This information can be represented with the help of either ODL or the Automation objects type information. For this, an implementation of one or more dispatch interfaces is necessary, and the server side of the component needs to expose a class factory for its COM class. The next step is to have a CORBA View object provide skeletal implementation of the operations of all interfaces supported by the server object. The CORBA View object is an implementation the server, which acts as a stub to the CORBA clients. This is a legal CORBA object not an Automation object, so any CORBA client can communicate with it.

Since CORBA is distributable, a copy of the CORBA View object does not have to reside on each CORBA client, but is put on the server alongside the Automation object. In contrast, the Automation View must be on each and every client that communicates with the CORBA server. The CORBA View acting as the client to the Automation object does the transformation of parameters coming into and going out of the Automation server. From the other side, CORBA clients that want to talk to the Automation object instantiate the CORBA View, which marshals the data and performs the interprocess communication.

Figure 4.2 depicts the OLE Automation object as the client side and the CORBA object as the server side of the communicating applications separated by the network. Note that the client has the Automation View. Also note that a client CORBA stub is needed for the Automation View to coordinate with the CORBA server application. The client application interacts

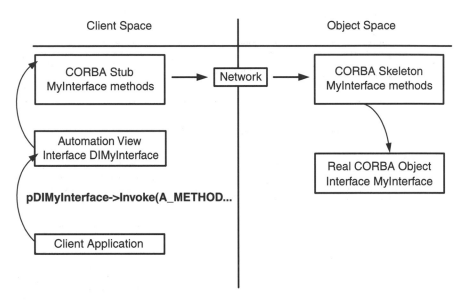

Figure 4.2   Methods of the Automation View Interface Delegated to the CORBA Stub

with the Automation View, which it sees as the server object (this is apparent from the client application's side). On the server side, denoted by the "Object Space," is the CORBA skeleton, which helps link to the actual server object's operations.

Figure 4.3 is a representation of the CORBA object as the client and the OLE Automation object as the server. Note that the terms *client* and *server* are overloaded here, but the meanings are attached to the tasks assigned—the client requests the information and the server provides it. In the figure the CORBA View is on the server domain, confined by the same physical bounds that bind the OLE Automation object. The CORBA stub is within the client application's physical domain, and the skeleton is on the server side. (This is common to the previous discussion of the OLE Automation object being the client and the CORBA object being the server.) The CORBA View is a truly CORBA-compliant representation of the OLE Automation server object.

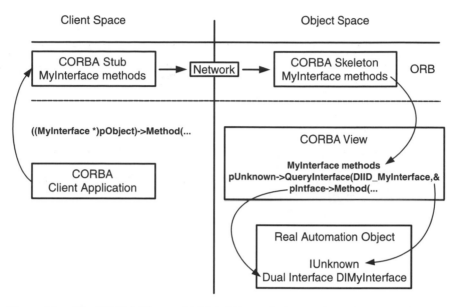

Figure 4.3   The CORBA View: a CORBA Object, which Is a Client of a COM Object

4.2   *Main Features of the Mappings*

The following lists repectively outline the main features of the mappings from OLE Automation to CORBA and vice versa. As these features are self-explanatory, they need no further discussion.

OLE Automation to CORBA

- OMG IDL attributes and operations map to Automation properties and methods, respectively.

- OMG IDL interfaces map to Automation interfaces.

- OMG IDL basic types map to corresponding basic types in Automation where possible. Since Automation supports a limited set of data types, the following OMG IDL types cannot be mapped directly:

   - OMG IDL constructed types, such as `struct` and `union`. These map to Automation interfaces with appropriate attributes and operations. User exceptions are mapped the same way.

143

- OMG IDL unsigned types . These map as closely as possible to Automation types, and overflow conditions are identified.
- OMG IDL sequences and arrays map to Automation SAFEARRAYS.

CORBA to OLE Automation

- ODL or Type library information can be the input for the mapping.
- Automation properties and methods map to OMG IDL attributes and operations, respectively.
- Automation interfaces map to OMG IDL interfaces.
- Automation basic types map to corresponding OMG IDL basic types where possible.
- Automation errors map similarly to COM errors.

4.3   Mapping for Interfaces: CORBA TO OLE Automation

A CORBA interface maps straightforwardly to an Automation View interface. Consider the following code:

```
// OMG IDL
Module MyModule
{
  Interface MyInterface
  {
  // Attributes and operations
  ...
  };
};
```

This maps to the Automation View interface in this way:

```
[odl, dual, uuid(...)]
interface IMyModule_MyInterface: IDispatch
{
// Properties and methods
...
};
```

The OLE Automation mapped interface `IMyModule_MyInterface` is a dual interface, which in COM allows both early and late bindings. It derives from `Idispatch`, so it contains the methods from `IDispatch` as well as the `vtable` for its own property `get`/`set` methods. The late binding is facilitated by `IDispatch::Invoke`; the early binding, by the COM `vtable`.

4.4   Mapping for Attributes and Operations

An OMG IDL operation maps one-to-one to an isomorphic Automation operation, and an OMG IDL attribute maps to an ODL property. Each read/write ODL property has a `get` method that retrieves the value of the property, and a `set` method that changes the value. The OMG IDL read-only property maps to an ODL property that has a `get`, single method. This method retrieves the value of the property.

A code example will help explain the mapping:

```
// OMG IDL
interface account
{
  attribute float balance;
  readonly attribute string owner;
  void makeLodgement( in float amount, out float balance );
  void makeWithdrawal( in float amount, out float balance );
};
```

This maps to the corresponding Automation View interface:

```
// ODL
[odl, dual, uuid(…)]
interface DIaccount: IDispatch
{
  HRESULT makeLodgement ( [in] float amount,
               [out] float * balance,
               [optional, out] VARIANT * excep_OBJ );
  HRESULT makeWithdrawal( [in] float amount,
               [out] float * balance,
               [optional, out] VARIANT * excep_OBJ );
```

```
    [propget] HRESULT balance( [retval, out] float * IT_retval );
    [propput] HRESULT balance( [in] float balance );
    [propget] HRESULT owner( [retval, out] BSTR * IT_retval );
};
```

The mapping shows that the OMG IDL in, out, and inout parameters map to ODL's [in], [out], and [in,out]. The OMG IDL read/write attribute balance maps to the ODL get and set methods. Both methods are called balance but are tagged differently by the [propget] and [propput] prefixes. They also have different parameters: get, an output parameter; set, an input parameter, for obvious reasons.

The read-only attribute owner from OMG IDL maps to a get method in ODL. An operation of a dual interface always returns HRESULT, but the last argument in the operation's signature may be tagged [retval, out], which is considered syntactically a return value. Because Automation controller macro languages map this special argument to a return value in their language syntax, the equivalent CORBA operation's return value is mapped to the last argument of the Automation View interface's operation.

All operations on the Automation View interface have an optional out parameter of type VARIANT, which returns the contents of any exception that occurs during the invocation. The return value must be the last parameter in the Automation operation. If the CORBA operation has no return value, the optional parameter comes last in the corresponding Automation operation, but if the CORBA operation does have a return value, that value directly follows.

4.5 Mapping for Interfaces: OLE Automation to CORBA

Each ODL interface maps directly to an OMG IDL interface. This includes all methods and properties except for IUnknown and IDispatch. The following code illustrates the mapping:

```
// ODL
[odl, dual, uuid(…)]
```

```
interface IMyModule_account: IDispatch
{
  [propget] HRESULT balance( [retval, out] float * ret );
};
```

This, when mapped to OMG IDL, is

```
// OMG IDL
interface MyModule_account
{
  readonly attribute float balance;
};
```

We see that the `balance` method from ODL is mapped to an attribute in OMG IDL. The signature `[propget]` informs the system that it has to map to a `readonly` attribute, and the signature `[retval, out]` preceding `ret`, which is of type `float`, states that if the method does not have a parameter, its return type maps to `long`. This allows `COM SCODE` to be passed to the CORBA client.

4.6   *Mapping of the Inheritance Model*

CORBA supports both single- and multiple-level inheritance in its OMG IDL definition, whereas COM supports only single-level. Both types must be considered in mappings from CORBA to OLE Automation.

4.6.1   OMG IDL Single Inheritance

Singly inherited OMG IDL interfaces map directly to singly inherited Automation View interfaces. The mapping is one-to-one, as no conversion is needed. Here is a code example of a singly inherited hierarchy model:

```
// OMG IDL
module MyModule
{
  interface account
  {
    attribute float balance;
    readonly attribute string owner;
    void makeLodgement( in float amount, out float balance );
```

```
    void makeWithdrawal( in float amount, out float theBalance );
  };

  interface checkingAccount: account
  {
    readonly attribute float overdraftLimit;
    boolean orderChequeBook();
  };
};
```

When mapped to the Automation View interface this OMG IDL becomes

```
// ODL
[odl, dual, uuid(20c31e22-dcb2-aa79-1dc4-34a4d297579)]
interface IMyModule_account: IDispatch
{
  HRESULT makeLodgement( [in] float amount, [out] float * balance,
               [optional, out] VARIANT * excep_OBJ );
  HRESULT makeWithdrawal( [in] float amount, [out] float * balance,
               [optional, out] VARIANT * excep_OBJ );
  [propget] HRESULT balance( [retval, out] float * IT_retval );
  [propput] HRESULT balance( [in] float balance );
  [propget] HRESULT owner( [retval, out] BSTR * IT_retval );
};

[odl, dual, uuid(ffe752b2-af3f-2a28-1de4-21754778ab4b)]
interface IMyModule_checkingAccount: IMyModule_account
{
  HRESULT orderChequeBook( [optional, out] VARIANT * excep_OBJ,
             [retval, out] short * IT_retval );
  [propget] HRESULT overdraftLimit( [retval, out] short * IT_retval );
};
```

In the OMG IDL definition we see that the interface checkingAccount is derived from the interface account. The same single inheritance is shown in the Automation View interface mapping. In the Automation View interface we see that IMyModule_checkingAccount is inherited from IMyModule_account, so the single inheritance level is maintained.

4.6.2 OMG IDL Multiple Inheritance

The mapping from a multiply inherited OMG IDL definition to an Automation View interface is not direct, because Automation does not support multiple inheritance. The mapping needs to split the hierarchy where the multiple inheritance occurs so as to form multiple singly inherited strands. The algorithm that determines the splitting is the left branch traversal of the tree. At the point of multiple inheritance, the interface that comes first in an ordering of the parent interfaces is included in what is called the main strand, and the other interfaces are assigned to secondary strands.

Figure 4.4 shows the classical diamond-shaped multiple inheritance system. The hierarchy can be stated as follows:

- B and C derive from A.
- D derives from B and C.
- E derives from D.

The point of multiple inheritance is D, which inherits from B and C. The mapping of this scheme to the Automation View Interface is as shown in Figure 4.5.

As shown, D is the point where the hierarchy splits, and it inherits from B and C. According to the left branch traversal algorithm, the main strand is A-B-D, and the secondary strand is A-C. To access all of the object's

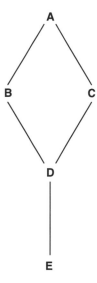

Figure 4.4   A CORBA Interface Hierarchy Using Multiple Inheritance

methods, a controller must navigate among these disjoint strands via `QueryInterface`. Such navigation is expected of COM clients and might be an acceptable requirement of C++ Automation controllers, but many Automation controller environments do not support it. For that reason, a solution that can be applied to all Automation controller environments was devised, called *aggregation*. At the point of multiple inheritance the operations of the secondary strands are aggregated into the interface of the main strand. In simple words, the C operations are added to the D operations; that is, D now contains C's operation as well as its own. (A's operations are not added because A is already present in the main strand through inheritance.) Thus, the continuity is maintained even after splitting and, more important, the Automation controller holding the reference to D can access all the methods without having to call `QueryInterface`.

This is a simple technique for converting the multiple inheritance CORBA to the single inheritance of Automation. Nevertheless, some constraints must be respected. First, a reliable, deterministic, and portable way to ascertain the inheritance chains at the points of multiple inheritance is

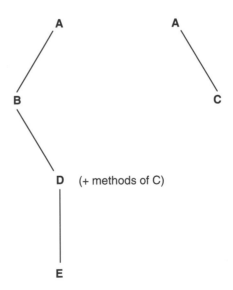

Figure 4.5   The Mapped Automation Hierarchy: Split at the Point of Multiple Inheritance

necessary, and these chains must be explicitly ordered. Also, to obtain interoperability with respect to dual interfaces, a precise model for ordering operations and attributes within an interface must be specified. A good set of guiding principles is outlined in the following paragraphs.

Within an interface, attributes should appear before operations and both should be ordered lexicographically by bytes in machine-collating sequence. For read-only attributes, the [propget] method immediately precedes the [propput] method. This ordering determines the position of the vtable portion of a dual interface. At points of multiple inheritance, the base interface should be ordered from left to right lexicographically by bytes in machine-collating order. (In all cases, the ordering is based on ISO Latin-1.) Thus, the leftmost branch at a point of multiple inheritance is the first among the base classes, not necessarily the one listed first in the inheritance declaration.

Here is the OMG IDL hierarchy code and its mapping to the Automation View interface:

```
// OMG IDL
module MyModule
{
  interface A
  {
    void aOp1();
    void zOp1();
  };
  interface B: A
  {
    void aOp2();
    void zOp2();
  };
  interface C: A
  {
    void aOp3();
    void zOp3();
  };
  interface D: C, B
  {
    void aOp4();
    void zOp4();
  };
};
```

When mapped to the Automation View interface, it looks like this:

```
// ODL
// strand 1:  A-B-D
[odl, dual, uuid(8db15b54-c647-553b-1dc9-6d098ec49328)]
interface DIMyModule_A: IDispatch
{
  HRESULT aOp1( [optional, out] VARIANT * excep_OBJ );
  HRESULT zOp1( [optional, out] VARIANT * excep_OBJ );
};
[odl, dual, uuid(ef8943b0-cef8-21a5-1dc0-37261e082e51)]
interface DIMyModule_B: DIMyModule_A
{
  HRESULT aOp2( [optional, out] VARIANT * excep_OBJ );
  HRESULT zOp2( [optional, out] VARIANT * excep_OBJ );
};
[odl, dual, uuid(67528a67-2cfd-e5e3-1de2-d59a444fe593)]
interface DIMyModule_D: DIMyModule_B
{
  // C's aggregated operations
  HRESULT aOp3( [optional, out] VARIANT * excep_OBJ );
  HRESULT zOp3( [optional, out] VARIANT * excep_OBJ );
  // D's normal operations
  HRESULT aOp4( [optional, out] VARIANT * excep_OBJ );
  HRESULT zOp4( [optional, out] VARIANT * excep_OBJ );
};
// strand 2: A-C
[odl, dual, uuid(327885f8-ae9e-19c0-1dd5-d1ea05bcaae5)]
interface DIMyModule_C: DIMyModule_A
{
  HRESULT aOp3( [optional, out] VARIANT * excep_OBJ );
  HRESULT zOp3( [optional, out] VARIANT * excep_OBJ );
};
```

The mapping from the Automation View interface to CORBA is just the opposite of a single-inheritance mapping from CORBA to the Automation View interface, and need not be illustrated.

4.7 Mapping for Basic Data Types

The basic data types supported by OLE Automation are a subset of the data types supported by ODL, because not all of the data types recognized by ODL can be marshaled by the `IDispatch` interface and by the implementation of `ItypeInfo::Invoke`. Table 4.1 lists and describes the OLE Automation basic data types. Table 4.2 shows the mapping of data types from CORBA to Automation.

4.7.1   Special Cases

The Automation view must map the basic data types when data is passed from OLE Automation to CORBA and vice versa. However, during the mapping some abnormalities may develop, which must be handled appropriately.

If the Automation `long` parameter is a negative number, the View operation returns an `HRESULT` of `DISP_E_OVERFLOW`. If the `CORBA::ULong` parameter

Table 4.1   OLE Automation Basic Data Types

Type	Description
boolean	True = -1, False = 0
double	64-bit IEEE floating-point number
float	32-bit IEEE floating-point number
long	32-bit signed integer
short	16-bit signed integer
void	Allowed only as return type for a function, or in a function pointer parameter list to indicate no parameters.
BSTR	Length-prefixed string. Prefix is an integer
CURRENCY	8-byte fixed-point number.
DATE	64-bit floating-point fractional number of days since December 30, 1899
SCODE	Built-in error type. In Win16, does not include additional data contained in an HRESULT. In win32, identical to HRESULT
IDispatch *	Pointer to IDispatch interface. From the viewpoint of the mapping, an IDispatch pointer parameter is an object reference.
IUnknown *	Pointer to IUnknown interface. (Any OLE interface can be represented by its IUnknown interface.)

Source: OMG

Table 4.2   CORBA-to-OLE Automation: Data Type Mappings

CORBA Type	OLE Automation Type
boolean	boolean
char	short
double	double
float	float
long	long
octet	short
short	short
Unsigned long	long
Unsigned short	long

Source: OMG

is greater than the maximum value of a long, the View operation returns an HRESULT of DISP_E_OVERFLOW. If the long is negative or greater than the maximum value of CORBA::UShort, the View operation returns an HRESULT of DISP_E_OVERFLOW. True and false values for CORBA boolean are, respectively, one and zero, whereas true and false values of Automation boolean are, respectively, negative one and zero. Therefore, true values need to be adjusted accordingly.

4.7.2   Strings

OMG IDL supports bounded and unbounded strings, and both string types map to OLE BSTR. For example, for the OMG IDL definitions

```
// OMG IDL
string sortCode<20>;
string name;
```

the corresponding ODL code is

```
// ODL
BSTR sortCode;
BSTR name;
```

On Win32 platforms, a BSTR maps to a Unicode string. BSTR is the only support for internationalization of strings defined at this time.

4.7.3 A Complete IDL-to-ODL Mapping for the Basic Data Types

Although not the only choices, at this time OMG IDL is the appropriate language to define a CORBA interface and ODL is the appropriate language to define an Automation View interface. The following OMG IDL code describes a CORBA interface that exercises all of the CORBA base data types—attribute, operation `in` parameter, operation `out` parameter, operation `inout` parameter, and return value.

```
// OMG IDL
module MyModule
{
  interface TypesTest
  {
    attribute boolean boolTest;
    attribute char charTest;
    attribute double doubleTest;
    attribute float floatTest;
    attribute long longTest;
    attribute octet octetTest;
    attribute short shortTest;
    attribute string stringTest;
    attribute string<10> stringnTest;
    attribute unsigned long ulongTest;
    attribute unsigned short ushortTest;

    readonly attribute short readonlyShortTest;
    // Sets all the attributes
    boolean setAll(
      in boolean booltest,
      in char charTest,
      in double doubleTest,
      in float floatTest,
      in long longTest,
      in octet octetTest,
      in short shortTest,
      in string stringTest,
      in string<10> stringnTest,
      in unsigned long ulongTest,
      in unsigned short ushortTest);
    // Gets all the attributes
    boolean getAll(
      out boolean booltest,
      out char charTest,
```

```
        out double doubleTest,
        out float floatTest,
        out long longTest,
        out octet octetTest,
        out short shortTest,
        out string stringTest,
        out string<10> stringnTest,
        out unsigned long ulongTest,
        out unsigned short ushortTest);
      boolean setAndIncrement(
        inout boolean booltest,
        inout char charTest,
        inout double doubleTest,
        inout float floatTest,
        inout long longTest,
        inout octet octetTest,
        inout short shortTest,
        inout string stringTest,
        inout string<10> stringnTest,
        inout unsigned long ulongTest,
        inout unsigned short ushortTest);

      boolean boolReturn();
      char charReturn();
      double doubleReturn();
      float floatReturn();
      long longReturn();
      octet octetReturn();
      short shortReturn();
      string stringReturn();
      string<10> stringReturn();
      unsigned long ulongReturn();
      unsigned short ushortReturn();
    }; // End of Interface TypesTest
}; // End of Module MyModule
```

The following ODL code illustrates the mapping of the preceding code to the Automation View interface.

```
[odl, dual, uuid(180d4c5a-17d2-a1a8-1de1-82e7a9a4f93b)]
interface DIMyModule_TypesTest: IDispatch
{
  HRESULT boolReturn( [optional, out] VARIANT * excep_OBJ,
                [retval, out] short * IT_retval );
  HRESULT charReturn( [optional, out] VARIANT * excep_OBJ,
                [retval, out] short * IT_retval );
```

```
HRESULT doubleReturn( [optional, out] VARIANT * excep_OBJ,
                [retval, out] double * IT_retval );
HRESULT floatReturn( [optional, out] VARIANT * excep_OBJ,
                [retval, out] float * IT_retval );
HRESULT getAll( [out] short * boolTest,
                [out] short * charTest,
                [out] double * doubleTest,
                [out] float * floatTest,
                [out] long * longTest,
                [out] short * octetTest,
                [out] short * shortTest,
                [out] BSTR * stringTest,
                [out] BSTR * stringnTest,
                [out] long * ulongTest,
                [out] long * ushortTest,
                [optional, out] VARIANT * excep_OBJ,
                [retval, out] short * IT_retval);
HRESULT longReturn( [optional, out] VARIANT * excep_OBJ,
                [retval, out] long * IT_retval );
HRESULT octetReturn( [optional, out] VARIANT * excep_OBJ,
                [retval, out] short * IT_retval );
HRESULT setAll( [in] short boolTest,
                [in] short charTest,
                [in] double doubleTest,
                [in] float floatTest,
                [in] long longTest,
                [in] short octetTest,
                [in] short shortTest,
                [in] BSTR stringTest,
                [in] BSTR stringnTest,
                [in] long ulongTest,
                [in] long ushortTest,
                [optional, out] VARIANT * excep_OBJ,
                [retval, out] short * IT_retval);
HRESULT setAndIncrement( [in,out] short * boolTest,
                [in,out] short * charTest,
                [in,out] double * doubleTest,
                [in,out] float * floatTest,
                [in,out] long * longTest,
                [in,out] short * octetTest,
                [in,out] short * shortTest,
                [in,out] BSTR * stringTest,
                [in,out] BSTR * stringnTest,
                [in,out] long * ulongTest,
                [in,out] long * ushortTest,
                [optional, out] VARIANT * excep_OBJ,
                [retval, out] short * IT_retval);
```

```
HRESULT shortReturn( [optional, out] VARIANT * excep_OBJ,
                [retval, out] short * IT_retval );
HRESULT stringReturn( [optional, out] VARIANT * excep_OBJ,
                [retval, out] BSTR * IT_retval );
HRESULT stringnReturn( [optional, out] VARIANT * excep_OBJ,
                [retval, out] BSTR * IT_retval );
HRESULT ulongReturn( [optional, out] VARIANT * excep_OBJ,
                [retval, out] long * IT_retval );
HRESULT ushortReturn( [optional, out] VARIANT * excep_OBJ,
                [retval, out] long * IT_retval );
[propget] HRESULT boolTest([retval, out] short * IT_retval);
[propput] HRESULT boolTest([in] short boolTest);
[propget] HRESULT charTest([retval, out] short * IT_retval);
[propput] HRESULT charTest([in] short charTest);
[propget] HRESULT doubleTest([retval, out] double * IT_retval);
[propput] HRESULT doubleTest([in] double doubleTest);
[propget] HRESULT floatTest([retval, out] float * IT_retval);
[propput] HRESULT floatTest([in] float floatTest);
[propget] HRESULT longTest([retval, out] long * IT_retval);
[propput] HRESULT longTest([in] long longTest);
[propget] HRESULT octetTest([retval, out] short * IT_retval);
[propput] HRESULT octetTest([in] short octetTest);
[propget] HRESULT readonlyShortTest([retval, out] short * IT_retval);
[propget] HRESULT shortTest([retval, out] short * IT_retval);
[propput] HRESULT shortTest([in] short shortTest);
[propget] HRESULT stringTest([retval, out] BSTR * IT_retval);
[propput] HRESULT stringTest([in] BSTR stringTest);
[propget] HRESULT stringnTest([retval, out] BSTR * IT_retval);
[propput] HRESULT stringnTest([in] short stringnTest);
[propget] HRESULT ulongTest([retval, out] long * IT_retval);
[propput] HRESULT ulongTest([in] long ulongTest);
[propget] HRESULT ushortTest([retval, out] long * IT_retval);
[propput] HRESULT ushortTest([in] long ushortTest);
};
```

4.7.4   Automation Basic Data Types

In Table 4.3 are the basic data types supported by OLE Automation as parameters and return values, and their OMG IDL counterparts.

The Automation CURRENCY type is a 64-bit integer scaled by 10,000, giving a fixed-point number with 15 digits to the left of the decimal point and 4 digits to the right. The COM::Currency type is defined as follows:

```
module COM
{
  struct Currency
  {
    unsigned long lower;
    long upper;
  };
};
```

This mapping is transitional and should be revised when the extended data type revisions to OMG IDL, slated to include a 64-bit integer, are adopted.

The Automation DATE type is an IEEE 64-bit floating-point number representing the number of days since December 30, 1899.

When the CORBA View, which performs the data type conversions, encounters an error condition, it raises the CORBA DATA_CONVERSION System exception. This will apply if, for example, the supplied COM::Currency value does not translate to a meaningful Automation CURRENCY value. It also applies if the CORBA double value is negative or converts to an impossible date. True and false values for CORBA boolean are, respectively, one and zero, whereas they are, respectively, negative one and zero for Automation boolean. Thus, as before, the true values need to be adjusted.

Table 4.3   Mapping of Automation Data Types to OMG IDL Types

OLE Automation Type	OMG IDL Type
boolean	boolean
short	short
double	double
float	float
long	long
BSTR	string
CURRENCY	COM::Currency
DATE	double
SCODE	long

Source: OMG

4.8   Mapping for Object References

The OMG IDL code below shows two interfaces, the second of which uses the first as an attribute, as *in, out,* and *inout* parameters and as a return value.

```
// OMG IDL
module MyModule
{
// A simple object we can use for testing object references
  interface Simple
  {
    attribute short shortTest;
  }; // End of interface Simple

  interface ObjRefTest
  {
    attribute Simple simpleTest;
    Simple simpleOp( in Simple inTest,
                 out Simple outTest,
                 inout Simple inoutTest );
  }; // End of interface ObjRefTest
}; // End of module MyModule
This code maps to the Automation View interface as follows:
[odl, dual, uuid(c166a426-89d4-f515-1dfe-87b88727b4ea)]
interface DIMyModule_Simple: IDispatch
{
  [propget] HRESULT shortTest( [retval, out] short * IT_retval );
  [propout] HRESULT shortTest( [in] short shortTest );
};
[odl, dual, uuid(04843769-120e-e003-1dfd-6b75107d01dd)]
interface DIMyModule_ObjRefTest: IDispatch
{
  HRESULT simpleOp( [in] DIMyModule_Simple  * inTest,
                 [out] DIMyModule_Simple **outTest,
                 [in,out] DIMyModule_Simple **inoutTest,
                 [optional, out] VARIANT * excep_Obj,
                 [retval, out] DIMyModule_Simple ** IT_retval );
  [propget] HRESULT simpleTest(
                 [retval, out] DIMyModule_Simple ** IT_retval );
  [propout] HRESULT simpleTest(
                 [in] DIMyModule_Simple * simpleTest );
};
```

As shown, `simpleOp` from OMG IDL—which takes `Simple` as the in, out, and `inout` parameters and also returns `Simple`—maps to `simpleOp` in

`DIMyModule_ObjRefTest`. It does the same here. Note that the fourth (last but one) parameter returns any exception data that occurs. The fifth (last) parameter has the return value, type `DIMyModule_Simple`, which is the equivalent of `Simple` on the Automation side).

The mapping of object references from Automation to OMG IDL is the reverse of the mapping just described.

4.8.1 Object Reference Parameters and IForeignObject

One of the requirements of the specifications is that Automation and COM Views expose the `IForeignObject` interface in addition to the interface isomorphic to the mapped CORBA interface. `IForeignObject` extracts a valid CORBA object reference from a View object in the following way:

- The client calls `Automation-View-A::M`, passing an `IDispatch`-derived pointer to `Automation-View-B`.

- `Automation-View-A::M` calls `IDispatch::QueryInterface` for `IForeignObject`.

- `Automation-View-A::M` calls `IForeignObject::GetForeign-Reference` for the reference to the CORBA object `B`.

- `Automation-View-A::M` calls `CORBA-Stub-A::M` with the reference, narrowed to interface type `B`, as the object reference `in` parameter.

Figure 4.6 shows the Automation View object with the required interfaces. Automation View object `A` has an operation `M`, which takes Automation View object `B` as its `in` parameter.

4.9 Mapping for Enumerated Types

CORBA `enums` maps directly Automation `enums`, as this code illustrates:

```
// OMG IDL
module MyModule
{
  enum color {red, green, blue};
  interface foo
```

```
  {
    void op1( in color col );
  };
};

// ODL
typedef enum {red, green, blue} MyModule_color;
[odl, dual, uuid(7d1951f2-b5d3-8b7c-1dc3-aa0d5b3d6a2b)]
interface DIMyModule_foo: IDispatch
{
  HRESULT op1( [in] MyModule_color col,
                [optional, out] VARIANT * excep_OBJ );
};
```

From OMG IDL the OLE Automation maps the value of enum to the actual
platform-supported range; this data type is the integer. On a Win32 platform an integer is 4 bytes and equivalent to long. Thus, if the passed-in
value for a CORBA enum is more than the maximum value that can be
stored in an Automation long an overflow occurs. The Automation view
then returns an HRESULT of DISP_E_OVERFLOW.

Integer is the default, and in most cases is a very satisfactory assumption,
but it is not the only possible data type. The choice of data type for enum is
up to the implementing vendor.

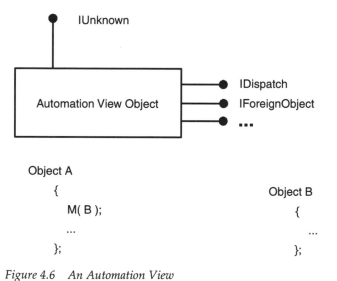

Figure 4.6   An Automation View

Here is a mapping of an enumerated type from ODL to OMG IDL:

```
// ODL
typedef enum MyModule_color {red, green, blue};
[odl, dual, uuid(…)]
interface DIMyModule_foo: IDispatch
{
  HRESULT op1( [in] MyModule_color col );
};
```

The above ODL, when mapped to OMG IDL, is

```
// OMG IDL
module COM
{
  enum MyModule_color {red, green, blue};
  interface foo: COM::CORBA_View
  {
    long op1( in MyModule_color col );
  };
};
```

The only thing to point out here is that the ODL interface definition DIMyModule_foo is derived from Idispatch, and that the equivalent OMG IDL interface definition foo is derived from COM::CORBA_View.

4.10   Mapping for Arrays and Sequences

OMG IDL arrays and sequences, bounded and unbounded, are mapped to ODL SafeArrays. A SafeArray has a header describing certain characteristics of an array, including its bounding, and thus is relatively safe for marshaling. ODL declarations of SafeArrays do not have bound specifiers, so OLE provides an API for allocating and manipulating SafeArrays that includes a resizing procedure.

In IDL, bounded sequences have a maximum bound specified during their creation or initialization, and they can grow up to that maximum. Unbounded sequences do not have any upper bounds and grow as new elements are added to them. Both types require certain changes when mapped to ODL SafeArrays: Bounded sequences do not grow dynamically up to the specified maximum but are statically initialized at creation; unbonded sequences have a default maximum bound, which can be extended by Automation APIs when necessary.

The Automation View retains bounding and resizing information because, as mentioned, the ODL `SafeArray` declaration does not contain any boundary specifiers. When a `SafeArray` is submitted as an `in` parameter, the Automation API dynamically repackages it as a CORBA array or bounded or unbounded sequence. When it is mapped as an `out` parameter, the API dynamically repackages the CORBA array or sequence as a `SafeArray`. When an unbounded sequence outgrows the corresponding `SafeArray`, the API increases the `SafeArray` size by one allocation unit (the size of which is set by the system vendor). If a `SafeArray` is mapped from a bounded sequence and a View client attempts to write more to it than the maximum, the View considers this a runtime error and returns an `HRESULT` of `DISP_E_OVERFLOW`.

Multidimensional OMG IDL arrays and multidimensional `SafeArrays` map to each other. The left-to-right order in the OMG IDL array corresponds to the ascending order in the SafeArray. Bounding information for each dimension, as well as the number of dimensions, is not available in the static Type library information or ODL definition, but is available only at runtime. For this reason, `SafeArrays`, which have more than one dimension, are mapped first to an identical linear format and then to a sequence in the normal way. The linearization of the multidimensional `SafeArray` is as follows:

- The number of elements in the sequence is the product of the dimensions.

- For a `SafeArray` with dimensions do, d1, and d2, the location of an element [p0][p1][p2] is

$$\text{pos}[p0][p1][p2] = p0*d1*d2 + p1*d2 + p2$$

Calculating the linear offset of a multidimensional array is quite simple. The rightmost element is the least significant dimension and the leftmost element is the most. The least significant element starts at zero and runs up to the value specified. At that point the dimension to the right, starting at zero, increments by one. This process repeats through the most significant dimension. Every one-element increment becomes a position in the linear structure. (Analogously to multiple nested `for` loops in C or C++, the number of nestings depends on the number of dimensions.)

For a dimension of 5,6,7, say, the total length of the linear structure is 5 * 6 * 7 = 360, which gives 0 to 359 possible elements in the linear structure. The linear position of the element at location [4][5][1] is 4 * 8 * 9 + 5 * 9 + 1 = 334.

4.11 Mapping for CORBA Complex Types

CORBA complex data types do not map directly to OLE Automation, because they are not supported by it. This calls for an indirect approach, in which CORBA types such as `struct`, `union`, and `Exception` are mapped to pseudo-Automation interfaces. The objects that implement these interfaces, called pseudo-objects, do not expose the `IForeign-Object` interface. Pseudo-Automation interfaces are dual interfaces, but they do not derive directly from `IDispatch`, as Automation View interfaces do. Instead, they derive from `DIForeignComplexType`, defined here:

```
// ODL
[odl, dual, uuid(…)]
interface DIForeignComplexType: IDispatch
{
  [propget] HRESULT INSTANCE_repositoryId(
              [retval, out] BSTR * IT_retval);
  HRESULT INSTANCE_clone([in] IDispatch * pDispatch,
              [retval, out] IDispatch ** IT_retval);
};
```

The UUID for `DIForeignComplexType` is `{A8B553C0-3B72-11cf-BBFC-444553540000}`. This interface can also be implemented as a generic (nondual) Automation interface, in which case it is named `DforeignComplexType` and its UUID is `{E977F900-3B75-11cf-BBFC-444553540000}`.

`DIForeignComplexType::INSTANCE_clone` provides the client with a way to duplicate a complex type, not just a reference to it, by creating a new instance of the type with values identical to the input instance. `INSTANCE_repositoryId` supports `DICORBAAny` when, at the request of `DICORBAAny`'s read-only typeCode property, it wraps an instance of a complex type to produce a type code for the instance. (We will discuss mapping for `any` shortly.)

4.11.1   Mapping for Structure Types

A CORBA structure is a user-defined complex data type. It maps only indirectly to OLE Automation, through an intermediate pseudo-`struct`—that is, a pseudo-Automation interface containing properties that correspond to the members of the structure and have identical names. A Pseudo-`struct` derives from `DICORBAStruct`, which in turn derives from `DIForeign-ComplexType`. The ODL definition of `DICORBAStruct` is

```
// ODL
[odl, dual, uuid(…)]
interface DICORBAStruct: DIForeignComplexType
{

};
```

The UUID for `DICORBAStruct` is `{A8B553C1-3B72-11CF-BBFC-444553540000}`. This is a dual interface, but it can also be implemented as generic (nondual), in which case it is named `DCORBAStruct` and its UUID is `{E977F901-3B75-11CF-BBFC-444553540000}`.

The methodless `DICORBAStruct` marks the interface as originating in the mapping of a CORBA `struct`. This information, which can be stored in a type library, is essential for mapping the type back to CORBA. `DICORBA-Struct` acts as a placeholder, directing the mapping and at the same time retaining the capability for inverse mappings. The mapping of a CORBA `struct` to a pseudo-`struct` follows:

```
// IDL
struct S
{
  long l;
  double d;
  float f;
};
```

Here is how the CORBA `struct` definition maps to an Automation interface:

```
// IDL
interface S
{
  attribute long l;
  attribute double d;
  attribute float f;
};
```

The mapped Automation dual interface derives from `DICORBAStruct`.

4.11.2   Mapping for Union Types

Just as a CORBA structure maps to a pseudo-`struct`, a CORBA `union` maps to a pseudo-`union`. A pseudo-`union` contains properties that correspond to the members of the union, and it also has a discriminator property (OMG IDL unions can discriminate), named `UNION_D`,   that corresponds to the OMG IDL union discriminant. The Automation discriminant functions like a CORBA union. If a union element is accessed from the pseudo-`union` and the current value of the discriminant does not match the property requested, the pseudo-`union` returns `DISP_E_TYPEMISMATCH`. When an element is set, the discriminant's value is set to the value that corresponds to that element—the element type—on the discriminant list.

A pseudo-union derives from the methodless interface `DICORBAUnion`, which, in turn derives from `DIForeignCompleType`, as shown here:

```
// ODL
[odl, dual, uuid(…)]
interface DICORBAUnion: DIForeignComplexType
{

};
```

The UUID for `DICORBAUnion` is `{A8B553C2-3B72-11CF-BBFC-444553540000}`. It can also be implemented as generic (nondual), in which case it is called `DCORBAUnion` and its UUID is `{E977F902-3B75-11CF-BBFC-444553540000}`.

A mapping of a CORBA union to a Pseudo-Union follows:

```
// IDL
interface A;
union U switch(long)
{
  case 1: long l;
  case 2: float f;
  default: A obj;
};
```

The above union when mapped to a Pseudo-Union is

```
// IDL
interface A;
interface U
{
  // switch discriminant
  readonly attribute long UNION_d;
  attribute long l;
  attribute float f;
  attribute A obj;
};
```

The mapped Automation dual interface derives from DICORBAUnion.

4.12 Mapping for TypeCodes

The OMG IDL TypeCode data type maps to the DICORBATypeCode interface, which is defined as follows:

```
// ODL
typedef enum
{
   tk_null = 0, tk_void, tk_short, tk_long, tk_ushort,
   tk_ulong, tk_float, tk_double, tk_octet,
   tk_any, tk_typeCode, tk_principle, tk_objref,
   tk_struct, tk_union, tk_enum, tk_string,
   tk_sequence, tk_array, tk_alias, tk_except
} CORBATCKind;

[odl, dual, uuid(…)]
interface DICORBATypeCode: DIForeignComplexType
```

```
{
  [propget] HRESULT kind( [retval, out] TCKind * IT_retval );

  // for tk_objref, tk_struct, tk_union, tk_alias, tk_except
  [propget] HRESULT id( [retval, out] BSTR * IT_retval );
  [propget] HRESULT name( [retval, out] BSTR * IT_retval );

  // tk_struct, tk_union, tk_enum, tk_except
  [propget] HRESULT member_count( [retval, out] long * IT_retval );
  HRESULT member_name( [in] long index,
              [retval, out] BSTR * IT_retval );
  HRESULT member_type( [in] long index,
              [retval, out] IDispatch * IT_retval );

  // tk_union
  HRESULT member_label( [in] long index,
              [retval, out] VARIANT * IT_retval );
  [propget] HRESULT discriminator_type(
              [retval, out] IDispatch ** IT_retval );
  [propget] HRESULT default_index(
              [retval, out] long * IT_retval );

  // tk_string, tk_array, tk_sequence
  [propget] HRESULT length(
              [retval, out] long * IT_retval );

  // tk_sequence, tk_array, tk_alias
  [propget] HRESULT content_type(
              [retval, out] IDispatch ** IT_retval );
};
```

The UUID for `DICORBATypeCode` is `{A8B553C3-3B72-11CF-444553540000}`, and, like the other interfaces, this one can be implemented as generic with the name `DCORBATypeCode` and the UUID `{E977F903-3B75-11CF-BBFC-4445535440000}`.

Visual Basic constants corresponding to the values of `CORBATCKind` should be declared as follows:

```
Global const CORBATCKind_tk_null = 0
Global const CORBATCKind_tk_void = 1
...
```

Since `DICORBATypeCode` derives from `DIForeignComplexType`, the objects that implement it are, in effect, pseudo-objects.

4.13   *Mapping for any*

The OMG IDL any data type maps to the DICORBAAny interface. DICORBA-Any is declared as follows:

```
// ODL
[odl, dual, uuid(…)]
interface DICORBAAny: DIForiegnComplexType
{
  [propget] HRESULT value(
                [retval, out] VARIANT * IT_retval );
  [propput] HRESULT value(
                [in] VARIANT val );
  [propget] HRESULT typeCode(
                [retval, out] DICORBATypeCode ** IT_retval );
};
```

The UUID for DICORBAAny is {A8B553C4-3B72-11CF-BBFC-444553540000}. When implemented as generic (nondual), this interface becomes DCORBAAny, and its UUID is {E977F904-3B75-BBFC-444553540000}.

DICORBAAny derives from DIForeignComplexType, so objects that implement it are, in effect, pseudo-objects. Since the VARIANT property of DICORBAAny represents a Safearray or a pointer to a DICORBAStruct or DICORBAUnion interface, this mapping of any is valid for a CORBA array, sequence, structure, or union.

4.14   *Mapping for Typedefs*

Mapping an OMG IDL typedef definition to OLE depends on the actual typedef'd type. In itself typedef does not provide any information, but becomes sensible only when it has a data type. No mapping is provided for typedef for the standard data types, float, double, long, short, unsigned long, unsigned short, char, boolean, and octet. For complex data types, the mapping creates intermediate aliases called pseudo-objects. For interfaces, the mapping creates an alias for the Automation View object. A conforming implementation may register `typedef` aliases in the Windows System Registry.

4.15   Mapping for Constants

Of the two models, only OMG IDL supports constants, so, obviously, no mapping for CORBA constants is provided. Mappings for `enums` are a different story. The vendor can create a separate header file containing an appropriate constant declaration for the client language, and this can be used to build the system. For example:

```
// OMD IDL
const long Max = 100;
```

can map to Visual Basic as

```
' Visual Basic
Global Const Max = 100
```

Hence, it turns out to be vendor and implementation specific and no standardization can be applied to it.

4.16   Mapping CORBA Exceptions to Automation Exceptions

CORBA supports Systems, or Standard, and User exceptions, which were discussed in an earlier chapter. Before we study the mappings for both types to OLE Automation, we will spend a few minutes on OLE Automation exception handling. Since the exception paradigms of the two models are different, a clear view from both sides will promote understanding of the mapping.

4.16.1   Exception Handling in OLE Automation

Automation does not follow the classical exception handling as seen in CORBA or C++. By now we know that Automation methods can be invoked in two ways (hence, *dual* interfaces): the `IDispatch::Invoke` method and, if the dual interface is supported, the `vtable` method. These methods return a 32-bit value of type `HRESULT` (as in all COM methods). `HRESULT` values, which have the severity bit (31 being the high bit) set, indicate an error during the call and thus are considered error codes. (On the Win16 platform, an `SCODE` was defined as the lower 31 bits of an `HRESULT`; on Win32 platform they are identical for all intents and purposes.) `HRESULT` also has a twobit field called the facility, one of the predefined values for which is `FACILITY_DISPATCH`. A vendor-specific implementation can check on these two fields to determine the error conditions and act appropriately.

`IDispatch::Invoke` returns error information to the caller if requested. It does so with the help of a parameter called `EXCEPINFO*`. The caller can pass either a null pointer in this parameter placeholder or the address of the `EXCEPINFO` structure. A null pointer means that no error information is required; a non-null pointer means that the caller wants to know what went wrong. If the callee returns the error information in the `EXCEPINFO` structure pointer, the `HRESULT` value will be `DISP_E_EXCEPTION`.

Dual interfaces that use `vtable` retrieve error information another way. They create and pass OLE error objects to the caller which contain information similar to that in the `EXCEPINFO` structure.

4.16.2 CORBA Exceptions

The Automation error-handling model does not directly support CORBA exceptions. Instead, all Automation View interface methods have an additional, optional `out` parameter of type *VARIANT*, which is filled in by the View in response to a CORBA exception. Both CORBA System and User exceptions map to pseudo-Automation interfaces called pseudo-exceptions. These derive from `IForeignException`, which derives from `IForiegnComplexType`:

```
// ODL
[odl, dual, uuid(…)]
interface DIForeignException: DIForeignComplexType
{
```

```
[propget] HRESULT EX_majorCode(
                [retval, out] long * IT_retval );
[propget] HRESULT EX_repositoryID(
                [retval, out] BSTR * IT_retval );
};
```

The UUID for `DIForeignException` is `{A8B553C7-3B72-11CF-444553540000}` implemented as generic (nondual), `DIForeignException` becomes `DForeignException` with the UUID `{E977F907-3B75-11CF-444553540000}`.

The attribute `EX_majorCode` defines the broad category of exceptions raised and has one of the following numeric values:

```
NO_EXCEPTION = 0
SYSTEM_EXCEPTION = 1
USER_EXCEPTION = 2
```

These values may be specified as an `enum` in the `typelibrary` information, as follows:

```
typedef enum {NO_EXCEPTION,
SYSTEM_EXCEPTION,
USER_EXCEPTION}
CORBA_ExceptionType;
```

The attribute `EX_repositoryID` is the exception type's unique repository ID from the CORBA Interface Repository.

4.16.3   CORBA User Exceptions

CORBA exceptions, in general, are mapped to pseudo-exception objects. For example, CORBA User exception is mapped to a properties-only pseudo-exception. Pseudo-exception object properties have a one-to-one correspondence with those of the CORBA User exceptions and derive from the methodless interface `DICORBAUserException`. Here we have the ODL definition of `DICORBAUserException`:

```
// ODL
[odl, dual, uuid(…)]
interface DICORBAUserException: DIForeignException
{

};
```

DICORBAUserException's   UUID   is   {A8B553C8-3B72-11CF-444553540000}. As a generic (nondual) interface, named DCORBAUser-Exception, its UUID is {E977F908-3B75-11CF-BBFC-444553540000}.

Here is an OMG IDL exception mapped to ODL:

```
// OMG IDL
exception reject
{
  string reason;
};
// ODL
[odl, dual, uuid(6bfaf02d-9f3b-1658-1dfb-7f056665a6bd)]
interface Direject: DICORBAUserException
{
  [propget] HRESULT reason(
                  [retval, out] BSTR reason );
};
```

4.16.3.1   *Operations That Raise User Exceptions*

If the optional parameter supplied by the caller causes a User exception, the parameter is filled in with the IDispatch pointer to an exception pseudo-Automation interface, which returns an HRESULT of S_FALSE. The Automation View fills in the VARIANT by setting its vt field to VT_DISPATCH and its pdispval field to point to the pseudo-exception. If no exception occurs, the optional parameter is filled with an IForeign-Exception pointer on a pseudo-exception object whose EX_majorCode property is set to NO_EXCEPTION.

If the optional parameter is not supplied and an exception occurs, then

- If the operation was invoked via IDispatch::Invoke,
    - The operation returns DISP_E_EXCEPTION.
    - If the caller provided an EXCEPINFO, it is filled by the View.
- If the method was called via the vtable of a dual interface, the OLE Error Object is filled by the view.

Note that in order to support error objects, Automation Views must implement the standard OLE interface ISUPPORTERRORINFO.

Table 4.4 shows the EXCEPINFO structure fields and their descriptions. EXCEPINFO reports errors when a call is invoked via IDispatch::Invoke. Table 4.5 shows the properties and descriptions of the error object, which reports exception details when dual interfaces are used to invoke remote calls.

Table 4.4   EXCEPINFO Usage for CORBA User Exceptions

Field	Description
wCode	Must be Zero
bstrSource	`<interface name>.<operation name>` *where the interface and operation names are those of the CORBA interface, which this Automation View is representing.*
bstrDescription	CORBA User Exception [`<exception repository id>`] *where the repository id is that of the CORBA user exception.*
bstrHelpFile	Unspecified
dwHelpContext	Unspecified
pfnDeferredFillIn	NULL
scode	DISP_E_EXCEPTION

Source: OMG

Table 4.5   Error Object Usage for CORBA User Exceptions

Property	Description
bstrSource	`<interface name>.<operation name>` *where the interface and operation names are those of the CORBA interface, which this Automation View is representing.*
bstrDescription	CORBA User Exception [`<exception repository id>`] *where the* `repository id` *is that of the CORBA user exception.*
bstrHelpFile	Unspecified
dwHelpContext	Unspecified
GUID	The IID of the Automation View Interface

Source: OMG

4.16.4   CORBA System Exceptions

CORBA System Exceptions map to `DICORBASystemException`, which derives from `DIForeignException`. This code defines ODL `DICORBASystemException`:

```
// ODL
[odl, dual, uuid(…)]
interface DICORBASystemException: DIForeignException
{
  [propget] HRESULT EX_minorCode(
            [retval, out] long * IT_retval );
  [propget] HRESULT EX_completionStatus(
            [retval, out] long * IT_retval );
};
```

`DICORBASystemException`'s UUID is `{1E5FFCA0-563B-11CF-B8FD-444553540000}`, but if it is implemented as generic (nondual) it becomes `DCORBASystemException`, its UUID `{1E5FFCA1-563B-11CF-B8FD-444553540000}`.

The attribute `EX_minorCode` defines the type of System exception raised, while `EX_completionStatus` has one of the following numeric values:

```
COMPLETION_YES = 0
COMPLETION_NO = 1
COMPLETION_MAYBE = 2
```

These values may be specified as an `enum` in the `typelibrary` information as

```
typedef enum { COMPLETION_YES,
               COMPLETION_NO,
               COMPLETION_MAYBE } CORBA_ExceptionType;
```

The operation may complete while an exception or erroneous condition is occurring. If so, `EX_minorCode` provides the error code and `EX_completionStatus` provides the completion status. These two attributes also apply when the error is so critical that the method does not complete at all.

4.16.4.1   *Operations That Raise System Exceptions*

Like the User exception, the System exception can be returned to the caller in the optional last parameter, if provided. (All the methods have this last optional parameter.) If a system exception occurs, the optional parameter is filled with an `IForeignException` pointer to the pseudo-exception and the Automation return value is `S_FALSE`. If no exception occurs, the optional parameter is filled with an `IForeignException` pointer whose `EX_majorCode` property is set to `NO_EXCEPTION`.

If no optional parameter is supplied and a System exception occurs, it will be one of a subset of CORBA System exceptions mapped to semantically equivalent `FACILITY_DISPATCH   HRESULT` values (listed in Table 4.6), and the equivalent `HRESULT` value will be returned. For all other exceptions, the Standard-exception-to-`SCODE` mapping and its corresponding `HRESULT` are used, according to the following scheme:

- If the operation was invoked via `IDispatch::Invoke`:
  - The operation returns `DISP_E_EXCEPTION`.
  - If the caller provided an `EXCEPINFO`, then it is filled with the `SCODE` field set to the new `HRESULT` value.
- If the method was called via the `vtable` of a dual interface,
  - The OLE error object is filled.
  - The method returns the new `HRESULT`.

Table 4.6   Mappings of CORBA Exceptions to COM Error Codes

CORBA Exception	COM Error Codes
BAD_OPERATION	DISP_E_MEMBERNOTFOUND
NO_RESPONSE	DISP_E_PARAMNOTFOUND
BAD_INV_ORDER	DISP_E_BADINDEX
INV_IDENT	DISP_E_UNKNOWNNAME
IND_FLAG	DISP_E_PARAMNOTFOUND
DATA_CONVERSION	DISP_E_OVERFLOW

Source: OMG

Table 4.7 EXCEPINFO Usage for CORBA System Exceptions

Field	Description
wCode	Must be zero
bstrSource	`<interface name>.<operation name>` *where the interface and operation names are those of the CORBA interface, which this Automation View is representing.*

bstrDescription	`CORBA System Exception:[<exception repository id>]`
	`minor code [<minor code>][<completion status>]`
	where the `<exception repository id>` *and* `<minor code>` *are those of the CORBA system exception.* `<completion status>` *is "YES", "NO" or "MAYBE" based upon the value of the system exception's CORBA completion status. Spaces and square brackets are literals and must be included in the strings.*

bstrHelpFile	Unspecified
dwHelpContext	Unspecified
pfnDeferredFillIn	NULL
scode	Mapped COM error code the `scode` to COM error mapping table

Source: OMG

Table 4.8 Error Object Usage for CORBA System Exceptions

Property	Description
bstrSource	`<interface name>.<operation name>` *where the interface and operation names are those of the CORBA interface, which this Automation View is representing.*
bstrDescription	*CORBA System Exception:* `[<exception repository id>]` `minor code [<minor code>][<completion status>]` *where the* `<exception repository id>` *and* `<minor code>` *are those of the CORBA system exception.* `<completion status>` *is "YES", "NO" or "MAYBE" based upon the value of the system exception's CORBA completion status. Spaces and square brackets are literals and must be included in the strings.*
bstrHelpFile	Unspecified
dwHelpContext	Unspecified
GUID	The IID of the Automation View Interface

Source: OMG

Table 4.7 shows the fields and descriptions of the EXCEPINFO structure used in the CORBA system exception. EXCEPINFO is used when the IDispatch::Invoke method makes remote system calls. It is passed as the last optional parameter, which is present in every operation. Table 4.8 lists the properties of system exception error objects and their descriptions, which apply to dual interfaces. The error object is filled with the exception data, which it passes to the caller.

4.17   Summary

In this chapter we have covered the mapping from OMG IDL to ODL or from CORBA to OLE Automation. At every place where it was deemed necessary the reverse mapping was also covered (i.e., mapping from OLE Automation to OMG IDL). The discussion presented was based on the mapping specifications issued by the OMG consortium. The intense discussion presented in the chapter was complemented with figures and tables to make the presentation easier to consume. A thorough and detailed explanation was dedicated to each and every sub-topic. We conclude with the thought that the hard work put toward preparing the chapter will be found beneficial by the readers.

CHAPTER 5   *IDL to C Mapping*

CORBA is independent of the programming that uses it. On its part the language must have the following capabilities in order to map CORBA's functionality, particularly the ORB.

- All OMG IDL basic data types
- All OMG IDL constructed data types
- References to constants defined in OMG IDL
- References to objects defined in OMG IDL
- Operation invocation
- Exception handling
- Access to attributes
- Signatures of the operations defined by the ORB

The mapping allowed by a language determines how convenient the facilities provided by the ORB will be for the particular programmer to use. CORBA must support source portability, so all ORB implementations must support the same mapping for a given language.

5.1   *Mapping for Basic Data Types*

The implementation provides `typedefs` for `CORBA_short`, `CORBA_long`, and so forth, consistent with OMG IDL requirements for the corresponding data. Mappings for the basic data types are shown in Table 5.1.

The OMG IDL `boolean` types map to C as `unsigned char` with only the values one (true) and zero (false) defined; other values produce undefined behavior. `CORBA_boolean` is provided for symmetry with the other basic-data-type mappings. The C mapping of OMG IDL `enum` types is an unsigned integer type capable of representing 2^{32} enumerations. Each enumerator in an `enum` is `#defined` with an appropriate unsigned integer value conforming to the ordering constraints described in the section "Enumerations" to come.

Table 5.1   Data Type Mapping

OMG IDL	C
short	CORBA_short
long	CORBA_long
long long	CORBA_long_long
unsigned short	CORBA_unsigned_short
unsigned long	CORBA_unsigned_long
unsigned long long	CORBA_unsigned_long_long
float	CORBA_float
double	CORBA_double
long double	CORBA_long_double
char	CORBA_char
wchar	CORBA_wchar
boolean	CORBA_boolean
any	Typedef struct CORBA_any {CORBA_TypeCode _type; void * _value;} CORBA_any

The _value member for an any is a pointer to the actual value of the data. In turn the any type supports ownership of its _value member. The programmer can control ownership by setting the release flag in the any when a _value is installed. As the flag's location is implementation-dependent, the ORB provides two functions to set and check its values.

```
void CORBA_any_set_release(CORBA_any*, CORBA_boolean);
CORBA_boolean CORBA_any_get_release(CORBA_any*);
```

CORBA_any_set_release sets the state of the release flag. TRUE means that any effectively "owns" the storage pointed to by _value; FALSE means that the programmer is responsible for the storage. Thus, if we try to deallocate the memory pointed to by _value returned from *any by calling CORBA_free(), and the release flag is set to FALSE, nothing happens. In such cases the release flag value should first be checked via the CORBA_any_get_release function. If FALSE, we should not invoke the CORBA_free() on the _value member because the result will be an undefined behavior. Passing a null pointer to either of the above two functions also produces an undefined behavior.

If CORBA_any_set_release is never called for a given instance of any, the default value of the release flag for that instance is FALSE.

5.2   Scoped Names

A C programmer must use the global names for a type, constant, exception, or operation. We derive the C global name that corresponds to an OMG IDL global name by converting :: to _ and eliminating the leading underscore. Consider the following interface and its equivalent in C:

```
// IDL
typedef string<256> filename_t;
interface example0 {
  enum color {red, green, blue};
  union bar switch (enum foo {room, bell}) { ... };
  ...
};
```

The code to use this interface looks as follows:

```
#include "example0.h"

filename_t FN;

example0_color C = example0_red;

example0_bar myUnion;

switch (myUnion._d) {
  case example0_bar_room: …
  case example0_bar_bell: …
};
```

The use of underscores to replace : : can lead to confusion if there are too many of them. Caution must be exercised in such cases.

5.3   Mapping for Interfaces

All interfaces in C have to be defined globally. Nested interfaces are not allowed. The mapping of an interface declaration is as follows:

```
// IDL
interface example {
  long function1(in long arg1);
};
```

The preceding example generates the following C declarations:

```
typedef CORBA_Object example;

extern CORBA_long example_function1(
  example o,
  CORBA_long arg1,
  CORBA_Environment *ev
);
```

All object references are of opaque type CORBA_Object, which is represented as a pointer. The programmer defines a type with the name of the interface as a CORBA_Object in order to decorate a program with typed references.

CORBA_OBJECT_NIL is legal wherever a CORBA_Object can be used. It passes the is_nil operation. Consider the following example:

```
// IDL
#include "example1.idl"
interface example2 {
example1 op2();
};
```

This is equivalent to the following C declaration:

```
#include "example1.h"
typedef CORBA_Object example2;
extern example1 example2_op2(example2 o, CORBA_Environment *ev);
```

A C fragment for invoking such an operation is as follows:

```
#include "example2.h"
example1 ex1;
example2 ex2;
CORBA_Environment ev;
/* code for binding ex2 */
ex1 = example2_op2(ex2, &ev);
```

5.4   Inheritance and Operation Names

As we know, OMG IDL supports inheritance, which means that interfaces can inherit operations from other interfaces. Consider the following example:

```
// IDL
interface examplederived : examplebase {
  void func( in long arg1, out long arg2 );
}
```

The equivalent code in C is

```
typedef CORBA_Object examplederived ;
extern CORBA_long examplederived_func1(
  examplederived o,
  CORBA_long arg1,
  CORBA_Environment *ev;
);
```

```
extern void examplederived_func(
  examplederived o,
  CORBA_long arg1,
  CORBA_long *arg2,
  CORBA_Environment *ev;
};
```

After this remapping, a C object can access func1 as if it were directly declared in examplederived. Of course, a programmer can invoke examplebase_func1 on an object of type examplederived. The virtual nature of operations in interface definitions causes either function to invoke the same method.

5.5   Mapping for Attributes

The mapping for attributes is best explained through example. Consider the following specification:

```
// IDL
interface foo {
  struct position_t {
    float x, y;
  };
  attribute float radius;
  readonly attribute position_t position;
};
```

This is exactly equivalent to the following illegal OMG IDL specification:

```
// IDL (illegal)
interface foo {
  struct position_t {
    float x, y;
  };
  float _get_radius();
  void _set_radius(in float r);
  position_t _get_position();
};
```

The second specification is illegal because OMG IDL identifiers are not permitted to start with the underscore (_) character.

The language mapping for attributes thus becomes the language mapping for these equivalent operations. The function signatures generated for the above operations are as follows:

```
/* C */
typedef struct foo_position_t {
    CORBA_float x, y;
} foo_position_t;

extern CORBA_float foo__get_radius(foo o, CORBA_Environment *ev);

extern void foo__set_radius(
    foo o,
    CORBA_float r,
    CORBA_Environment *ev
);

extern foo_position_t foo__get_position(foo o, CORBA_Environment *ev);
```

Note that two underscore characters (__) separate the interface name from the `get` or `set` in the function names.

If the `set` accessor function fails to set the attribute value, the method should return one of the Standard exceptions.

5.6   *Mapping for Constants*

The identifiers for constants can be referenced at any point in the user's code where a literal of the type is illegal. In C, these constants are `#defined`. To resolve the ambiguities that result from `#defined` constants, all names mandated by the mappings for any of the structured types start with an underscore.

The mappings for wide-character and wide-string constants are identical to those for character and string constants, except that IDL literals are preceded by `L` in C. For example, the IDL constant

```
const wstring ws = "Hello World";
```

in C maps to

```
#define ws L"Hello World"
```

5.7   Mapping for Constructed Data Types

The mappings for the constructed data types—structures, unions, arrays, and sequences—vary depending on whether the data structure is of fixed or variable length. A variable-length type is one of the following:

- The type any
- A bounded or unbounded string or wide string
- A bounded or unbounded sequence
- An object reference or reference to a transmissible pseudo-object
- A structure or union that contains a member of a variable-length type
- An array with a variable-length element type
- A typedef to a variable-length type

Treating fixed- and variable-length data structures differently allows more flexibility in the allocation of out parameters and return values from an operation. This permits more flexibility in the client-side stub, such as when an operation returns a sequence of strings of strings. Here the operation can allocate the string storage in one area that is later deallocated in a single call.

When the parameter-passing modes require heap allocation, an ORB function provides it. The allocation functions types include variable-length struct, variable-length union, sequence, any, string, wstring, and an array of a variable-length type. The return value of all these must be freed using CORBA_free(). For one of these listed types, T, the ORB implementation provides the following type-specific allocation function:

```c
/* C */
T *T__alloc();
```

The functions are defined globally, using the fully scoped name of T converted to a C language name followed by the suffix __alloc (note the double underscore). For any, string, and wstring, the allocation functions are, respectively,

```c
/* C */
CORBA_any *CORBA_any_alloc();
```

```
char *CORBA_string_alloc();
CORBA_wchar* CORBA_wstring_alloc(CORBA_unsigned_long len);
```

5.8 Mapping for Structure Types

OMG IDL structures map directly onto C `structs`. Remember that all such types potentially include padding.

5.9 Mapping for Union Types

OMG IDL discriminated unions are mapped onto C `structs`. Consider the following OMG IDL declaration:

```
// IDL
union Foo switch (long) {
  case 1: long x;
  case 2: float y;
  default: char z;
};
```

In C this is equivalent to the following `struct`:

```
/* C */
typedef struct {
  CORBA_long _d;
  union {
    CORBA_long x;
    CORBA_float y;
    CORBA_char z;
  } _u;
} Foo;
```

The discriminator in the `struct` is always referred to as _d; the union in the `struct`, as _u.

Reference to union elements is as in normal C:

```
/* C */
Foo *v;
/* make a call that returns a pointer to a Foo in v */
```

```
switch(v->_d) {
  case 1: printf("x = %ld\n", v->_u.x); break;
  case 2: printf("y = %f\n", v->_u.y); break;
  default: printf("z = %c\n", v->_u.z); break;
}
```

An ORB implementation need not use a C union to hold the OMG IDL union elements, but may use a C struct instead. In either case, the programmer accesses the union elements via the _u member.

5.10   Mapping for Sequence Types

The OMG IDL data type sequence permits the passing of unbounded arrays between objects. Here is the OMG IDL declaration:

```
// IDL
typedef sequence<long,10> vec10;
```

In C, this is converted to

```
typedef struct {
  CORBA_unsigned_long _maximum;
  CORBA_unsigned_long _length;
  CORBA_long *_buffer;
} vec10;
```

An instance of this type is declared as follows:

```
vec10 x = {10L, 0L, (CORBA_long *)NULL};
```

Prior to passing &x as an in parameter, the programmer must set the _buffer member to point to a CORBA_long array of 10 elements; and the _length member, to the actual number of elements to transmit. No action is necessary prior to the passing of the address of a vec10* as an out parameter (or the receipt of a vec10* as the function return). For the returned sequence the client stub allocates storage; for bounded sequences, it also allocates a buffer of the specified size; and for unbounded sequences, it also allocates a buffer big enough to hold what was returned by the object. Upon successful return from the invocation, the _maximum member contains the size of the allocated array, the _buffer member points to allocated storage, and the _length member contains the number of values returned in the _buffer member. The client is responsible for freeing the allocated sequence using CORBA_free().

As with passing &x as an in parameter, prior to passing &x as an inout parameter, the programmer sets the _buffer member to point to a CORBA_long array of 10 elements and the _length member to the actual number of elements to transmit. If the invocation is successful, the _length member contains the number of values copied into the buffer pointed to by the _buffer member. However, if more data must be returned than the original buffer can hold, the callee can deallocate the original _buffer member using CORBA_free() (honoring the release flag) and assign _buffer to point to new storage.

For bounded sequences, it is an error to set the _length or _maximum member to a value larger than the specified bound.

Sequence types support ownership of their _buffer members. By setting a release flag in the sequence when a buffer is installed, programmers can control ownership of the memory pointed to by _buffer. The location of this release flag is implementation dependent, so the following two ORB-supplied functions allow for it to be set and checked:

```
void CORBA_sequence_set_release(void*, CORBA_boolean);
CORBA_boolean CORBA_sequence_get_release(void*);
```

CORBA_sequence_set_release sets the state of the release flag. If TRUE, the sequence effectively "owns" the storage pointed to by _buffer; if FALSE, the programmer is responsible for it. For example, if a sequence is returned from an operation with its release flag set to FALSE, calling CORBA_free() on the returned sequence pointer will not deallocate the memory pointed to by _buffer. Before calling CORBA_free() on the _buffer member of a sequence directly, the programmer should check the release flag using CORBA_sequence_get_release. If it returns FALSE, invoking CORBA_free() on the _buffer member produces undefined behavior; so does passing a null pointer, or a pointer to something other than a sequence type, to either CORBA_sequence_set_release or CORBA_sequence_get_release.

The creator of a sequence should use only `CORBA_sequence_set_release`. If it is not called for a given sequence instance, then the default value of the release flag for that instance is `FALSE`.

Two sequence types are the same type if their sequence element type and size arguments are identical. For example, this code declares `s1`, `s2`, `s3`, and `s4` to be of the same type:

```
// IDL
const long SIZE = 25;
typedef long seqtype;
typedef sequence<long, SIZE> s1;
typedef sequence<long, 25> s2;
typedef sequence<seqtype, SIZE> s3;
typedef sequence<seqtype, 25> s4;
```

The OMG IDL type

```
// IDL
sequence<type,size>
```

maps to

```
#ifndef _CORBA_sequence_type_defined
#define _CORBA_sequence_type_defined
typedef struct {
    CORBA_unsigned_long _maximum;
    CORBA_unsigned_long _length;
    type *_buffer;
} CORBA_sequence_type;
#endif /* _CORBA_sequence_type_defined */
```

The `ifdef`s are needed to prevent duplicate definition where the same type is used more than once. The type name used in the C mapping is the type name of the effective type, for example, in

```
typedef CORBA_long FRED;
typedef sequence<FRED,10> FredSeq;
```

the sequence is mapped to

```
struct { ... } CORBA_sequence_long;
```

If the `type` in

```
// IDL
sequence<type,size>
```

consists of more than one identifier (e.g, unsigned long), the generated type name consists of the string `CORBA_sequence_` concatenated to the string consisting of the concatenation of each identifier separated by underscores (e.g, `unsigned_long`). If the `type` is `string`, the string `string` generates the type name. If the `type` is `sequence`, the string `sequence` generates the type name, recursively. For example,

```
sequence<sequence<long> >
```

generates a type of

```
CORBA_sequence_sequence_long
```

These generated type names may be used to declare instances of a sequence type. In addition to providing a type-specific allocation function for each sequence, an ORB implementation must provide a buffer allocation function for each sequence type. These functions allocate vectors of type `T` for `sequence<T>`. They are defined at global scope and are named similarly to sequences:

```
T *CORBA_sequence_T_allocbuf(CORBA_unsigned_long len);
```

Here, `T` refers to the type name. Thus, for the type

```
// IDL
sequence<sequence<long> >
```

the sequence buffer allocation function is named

```
/* C */
T *CORBA_sequence_sequence_long_allocbuf
(CORBA_unsigned_long len);
```

Buffers allocated via these allocation functions are freed by `CORBA_free()`.

5.11 Mapping for Strings

OMG IDL strings are mapped to 0-byte-terminated character arrays—that is, the length of the string is encoded in the character array itself through the placement of the 0 byte. Note that the storage for C strings is one byte longer than the stated OMG IDL bound, as shown in the following OMG IDL declarations:

```
// IDL
typedef string<10> sten;
typedef string sinf;

/* C */
typedef CORBA_char *sten;
typedef CORBA_char *sinf;
```

Instances of these types are declared as

```
/* C */
sten s1 = NULL;
sinf s2 = NULL;
```

Two string types are the same if their size arguments are identical. For example, this code declares `sx` and `sy` to be of the same type:

```
/* C */
const long SIZE = 25;
typedef string<SIZE> sx;
typedef string<25> sy;
```

Before passing s1 or s2 as an in parameter, the programmer must assign the address of a character buffer containing a 0-byte-terminated string to the variable. The caller cannot pass a null pointer as the string argument.

The programmer does nothing before passing &s1 or &s2 as an out parameter (or receiving an sten or sinf as the return result). The client stub allocates storage for the returned buffer: a buffer of the specified size for bounded strings and one big enough to hold unbounded strings. Upon successful return from the invocation, the character pointer contains the address of the allocated buffer. The client must free the allocated storage using CORBA_free().

Prior to passing &s1 or &s2 as an inout parameter, the programmer must assign to the variable the address of a character buffer containing a 0-byte terminated array. If the returned string is larger than the original buffer, the client stub calls CORBA_free() on the original string and allocates a new buffer for the new string.

For this reason the client should never pass an `inout` string parameter that was not allocated via `CORBA_string_alloc`. It must use `CORBA_free()` to free the allocated storage regardless of whether a reallocation was necessary.

Strings are dynamically allocated using the following ORB-supplied function, which allocates `len+1` bytes—enough to hold the string and its terminating null character:

```
/* C */
CORBA_char *CORBA_string_alloc(CORBA_unsigned_long len);
```

Strings allocated in this manner are freed via `CORBA_free()`.

5.12   Mapping for Wide Strings

The mapping for wide strings is similar to that for strings, except: (1) wide strings are mapped to null-terminated (note: wide null) wide-character arrays instead of 0-byte-terminated character arrays; and (2) wide strings are dynamically allocated with the ORB-supplied function `CORBA_wchar* CORBA_wstring_alloc(CORBA_unsigned_long len);` instead of `CORBA_string_alloc`. The length argument, `len`, is the number of `CORBA::WChar` units to be allocated, including one additional unit for the null terminator.

5.13   Mapping for Fixed Types

If an implementation has a native fixed-point decimal type that matches the CORBA specifications of the `fixed` type, the OMG IDL `fixed` type may be mapped to the native type. Otherwise, the mapping is as shown in the following OMG IDL declarations:

```
fixed<15,5> dec1; // IDL
typedef fixed<9,2> money;
```

In C, these become

```
typedef struct {/* C */
    CORBA_unsigned_short _digits;
    CORBA_short _scale;
    CORBA_char _value[(15+2)/2];
} CORBA_fixed_15_5;

CORBA_fixed_15_5 dec1 = {15u, 5};

typedef struct {
    CORBA_unsigned_short _digits;
    CORBA_short _scale;
    CORBA_char _value[(9+2)/2];
} CORBA_fixed_9_2;

typedef CORBA_fixed_9_2 money;
```

An instance of `money` is declared:

```
money bags = {9u, 2};
```

For application portability, the mapping must provide the following minimal set of functions and operations on the `fixed` type. Since C does not support parameterized types, the `fixed` arguments are represented as `void*` pointers. The type information is instead conveyed within the representation itself, so the `_digits` and `_scale` of every `fixed` operand must be set prior to invocation. Only the `_value` field of the result, denoted by `*rp`, may be left unset. Otherwise, the behavior of the functions is undefined.

```
/* Conversions: all signs are the same. */
CORBA_long CORBA_fixed_integer_part(const void *fp);

CORBA_long CORBA_fixed_fraction_part(const void *fp);

void CORBA_fixed_set(void *rp, const CORBA_long i,
const CORBA_long f);

/* Operations, of the form: r = f1 op f2 */
void CORBA_fixed_add(void *rp, const void *f1p,
const void *f2p);

void CORBA_fixed_sub(void *rp, const void *f1p,
const void *f2p);

void CORBA_fixed_mul(void *rp, const void *f1p,
const void *f2p);
```

```
void CORBA_fixed_div(void *rp, const void *f1p,
const void *f2p);
```

These operations must maintain proper fixed-point decimal semantics for the precision and scale of the intermediate results prior to assignment to the result variable. Truncation without rounding may occur if the result type cannot express the intermediate result exactly.

Instances of the `fixed` type are dynamically allocated via the ORB-supplied function `CORBA_fixed_d_s* CORBA_fixed_alloc(CORBA_unsigned_short d);`

5.14 Mapping for Arrays

OMG IDL arrays map directly to C arrays. All array indices run from 0 to `<size - 1>`. For each named array type in OMG IDL, the mapping provides a C `typedef` for a pointer to the array's *slice*—that is, another array with all the dimensions of the original except the first. For example, given the following OMG IDL definition,

```
// IDL
typedef long LongArray[4][5];
```

the C mapping provides the following definitions:

```
/* C */
typedef CORBA_long LongArray[4][5];
typedef CORBA_long LongArray_slice[5];
```

Appending `_slice` to the original array name creates the generated name of the slice `typedef`.

If the operation's return result, or an `out` parameter for an array holding a variable-length type, is an array, the array storage is dynamically allocated by the stub; a pointer to the array slice of the dynamically allocated array is returned as the value of the client stub function. When the data is no longer needed, the programmer must return the dynamically allocated storage by calling `CORBA_free()`.

An array, `T`, of a variable-length type is dynamically allocated using the following ORB-supplied function:

```
/* C */
T_slice *T__alloc();
```

This function is identical to the allocation functions described in the section "Mapping for Constructed Types," except that the return type is a pointer to the array slice, not to the array.

5.15   Mapping for Exception Types

Each exception type is defined as a `struct` tag and a `typedef` with the C global name for the exception. An identifier for the exception, in string literal form, is also `#defined`, as is a type-specific allocation function. For example,

```
// IDL
exception foo {
    long dummy;
};
```

yields the following C declarations:

```
/* C */
typedef struct foo {
    CORBA_long dummy;
    /* ...may contain additional
     * implementation-specific members...
     */
} foo;

#define ex_foo <unique identifier for exception>

foo *foo__alloc();
```

The identifier for the exception uniquely identifies the exception type. For example, it could be the exception's Interface Repository identifier.

The allocation function for each exception type dynamically allocates an instance of the exception and returns a pointer to it. Exceptions allocated by these functions are freed via `CORBA_free()`.

Since IDL exceptions cannot have members, but C `structs` must have at least one, IDL exceptions with no members map to C `structs` with one which is opaque to applications. Both the type and the name of the single member are implementation specific.

5.16   *Implicit Arguments to Operations*

In C additional leading parameters precede the operation-specific parameters of all operations declared in an interface:

- The first parameter, a `CORBA_Object` input parameter, designates the object to process the request.

- The last parameter, a `CORBA_Environment*` output parameter, permits the return of exception information.

- If an operation in OMG IDL has a context specification, a `CORBA_Context` input parameter precedes `CORBA_Environment*` and follows any operation-specific arguments.

As described above, the `CORBA_Object` type is opaque; the `CORBA_Environment` type, partially opaque. The section "Handling Exceptions," to come, describes the nonopaque portion of the exception structure and illustrates how to handle exceptions in client code. The `CORBA_Context` type also is opaque; see OMG Dynamic Invocation Interface specification (www.omg.org) for more information on how to create and manipulate context objects.

5.17   *Interpretation of Functions with Empty Argument Lists*

A function declared with an empty argument list takes no operation-specific arguments.

5.18   Argument-Passing Considerations

For all OMG IDL types (except arrays), if the signature specifies an argument as an `out` or `inout` parameter, the caller must always pass the address of a variable of that type (or the value of a pointer to that type); the callee must dereference the parameter to get to the type. For arrays, the caller must pass the address of the array's first element.

For `in` parameters, the parameter value must be passed for all of the basic types, enumeration types, and object references. For all arrays, the address of the array's first element must be passed, but for all other structured types, whether fixed- or variable-length, the address of a variable of that type must be passed. For strings, a `char*` and `wchar*` must be passed.

For `inout` parameters, the address of a variable of the correct type must be passed for all basic types, enumeration types, object references, and structured types. For strings, the address of a `char*` and `*` of a `wchar` must be passed. For all arrays, the address of the first element must be passed.

Consider the following OMG IDL specification:

```
// IDL
interface foo {
    typedef long Vector[25];
    void bar(out Vector x, out long y);
};
```

The client code for invoking the `bar` operation looks like

```
/* C */
foo object;
foo_Vector_slice x;
CORBA_long y;
CORBA_Environment ev;
/* code to bind object to instance of foo */
foo_bar(object, &x, &y, &ev);
```

For `out` parameters of type variable-length `struct`, variable-length `union`, `string`, `sequence`, an array holding a variable-length type, or `any`, the ORB allocates storage for the output value using the appropriate type-specific allocation function. The client may use and retain that storage indefinitely, and must indicate when the value is no longer needed by calling the procedure CORBA_free, whose signature is

```
/* C */
extern void CORBA_free(void *storage);
```

The parameter to `CORBA_free()` is the pointer that returns the `out` parameter. `CORBA_free()` releases the ORB-allocated storage occupied by the `out` parameter, including storage indirectly referenced, such as for a sequence of strings or an array of object references. If a client does not call `CORBA_free()` before reusing the pointers to the `out` parameters, that storage might be wasted. Passing a null pointer to `CORBA_free()` is allowed; `CORBA_free()` simply ignores it and returns without error.

5.19   *Return-Result Passing*

When an operation is defined to return a nonvoid return result, the following rules hold:

- If the return result is of the type `float`, `double`, `long`, `short`, `unsigned long`, `unsigned short`, `char`, `wchar`, `fixed`, `boolean`, `octet`, or `Object`, or an `enum`, the value is returned as the operation result.
- If the return result is of the fixed-length type `struct` or `union`, the value of the C `struct` representing that type is returned as the operation result. If the return result is of the variable-length type `struct`, `union`, `sequence`, or `any`, then a pointer to a C `struct` representing that type is returned.
- If the return result is of type `string` or `wstring`, a pointer to the first character of the string is returned.
- If the return result is of type `array`, a pointer to the slice of the array is returned.

Consider the following interface:

```
// IDL
interface X {
    struct y {
    long a;
    float b;
};
```

```
long op1();
    y op2();
};
```

Here are the C declarations that ensue from processing the specification:

```
/* C */
typedef CORBA_Object X;

typedef struct X_y {
    CORBA_long a;
    CORBA_float b;
} X_y;
extern CORBA_long X_op1(X object, CORBA_Environment *ev);

extern X_y X_op2(X object, CORBA_Environment *ev);
```

For operation results of type variable-length `struct`, variable-length `union`, `wstring`, **string**, `sequence`, `array`, or `any`, the ORB allocates storage for the return value using the appropriate type-specific allocation function. The client may use and retain that storage indefinitely, and must indicate when it no longer needs the value by calling the procedure `CORBA_free()`.

5.19.1   Argument/Result Passing: Summary

Table 5.2 describes what the client passes as an argument and receives as a result. For brevity, the `CORBA_` prefix is omitted from the type names.

The client is responsible for providing storage for all arguments as `in` parameters. These are listed in Table 5.3.

Argument-Passing Cases

- The caller allocates all necessary storage, except what may be encapsulated and managed within the parameter itself. For `inout` parameters, the caller provides the initial value, which the callee may change. For `out` parameters, the caller allocates the storage but need not initialize it, and the callee sets the value. Function returns are by value.

- The caller allocates storage for the object reference. For `inout` parameters, the caller provides an initial value; if the callee wants to reassign the parameter, it first calls `CORBA_Object_release` on the initial value. To continue using an object reference passed in as an `inout`, the

Table 5.2   Basic Argument and Result Passing

Data Type	In	Inout	Out	Return
short	short	short*	short*	short
long	long	long*	long*	long
long long	long_long	long_long*	long_long*	long_long
unsigned short	unsigned_short	unsigned_short*	unsigned_short*	unsigned_short
unsigned long	unsigned_long	unsigned_long*	unsigned_long*	unsigned_long
unsigned long long	unsigned_long_long	unsigned_long_long*	unsigned_long_long*	unsigned_long_long
float	float	float*	float*	float
double	double	double*	double*	double
long double	long_double	long_double*	long_double*	long_double
fixed<d,s>	fixed_d_s*	fixed_d_s*	fixed_d_s*	fixed_d_s
boolean	boolean	boolean*	boolean*	boolean
char	char	char*	char*	char
wchar	wchar	wchar*	wchar*	wchar
octet	octet	octet*	octet*	octet

Table 5.2   Basic Argument and Result Passing   (Continued)

Data Type	In	Inout	Out	Return
enum	enum	enum*	enum*	enum
object reference ptr	object_ptr	object_ptr*	object_ptr*	object_ptr
struct, fixed	struct*	struct*	struct*	struct
struct, variable	struct*	struct*	struct**	struct*
union, fixed	union*	union*	union*	union
union, variable	union*	union*	union**	union*
string	char*	char**	char**	char*
wstring	wchar*	wchar**	wchar**	wchar*
sequence	sequence*	sequence*	sequence**	sequence*
array, fixed	array	array	array	array slice
array, variable	array	array	array	array slice
any	any*	any*	any**	any*

Table 5.3   Client Argument Storage Responsibilities

Type	Inout Param	Out Param	Return Result
short	1	1	1
long	1	1	1
unsigned short	1	1	1
unsigned long	1	1	1
float	1	1	1
double	1	1	1
boolean	1	1	1
char	1	1	1
octet	1	1	1
enum	1	1	1
object reference ptr	2	2	2
struct, fixed	1	1	1
struct, variable	1	3	3
union, fixed	1	1	1
union, variable	1	3	3
string	4	3	3
sequence	5	3	3
array, fixed	1	1	6
array, variable	1	6	6
any	5	3	3

caller must first duplicate the reference. The client is responsible for releasing all out and return object references. All object references embedded in other out and return structures are released automatically by CORBA_free.

- For out parameters, the caller allocates a pointer and passes it by reference to the callee. The callee sets the pointer to point to a valid instance of the parameter's type. For returns, the callee returns a similar pointer, but cannot return a null pointer in either case. In both cases, the caller releases the returned storage. Following the completion of a request, the caller cannot modify any values in the returned storage. To do so, it must first copy the returned instance into a new instance and then modify the new instance.

- For `inout` strings, the caller provides storage for both the input string and the `char*` pointing to it. The callee may deallocate the input string and reassign the `char*` new storage for the output value. The size of the `out` string is therefore not limited by the size of the `in` string. The caller is responsible for freeing the storage for the `out`. The callee cannot return a null pointer for an `inout`, `out`, or return value.

- For `inout` sequences and `any`s assignment or modification may cause deallocation of owned storage before any reallocation occurs, depending upon the state of the `boolean` release in the sequence or `any`.

- For `out` parameters, the caller allocates a pointer to an array slice and passes the pointer by reference to the callee. The callee sets the pointer to a valid instance of the array. For returns, the callee returns a similar pointer. The callee is not allowed to return a null pointer in either case. In both cases, the caller must release the returned storage. Once the request is completed, the caller cannot modify any values in the returned storage until it copies the returned array instance into a new array instance and then modifies the new instance.

5.20   Exception Handling

C language does not have exception handling, so applications pass and receive exceptions via the special `CORBA_Environment` parameter passed to each IDL operation. The `CORBA_Environment` type is partially opaque; the C declaration contains at least the following:

```
/* C */
typedef struct CORBA_Environment {
    CORBA_exception_type _major;
    ...
} CORBA_Environment;
```

The `_major` field indicates whether the invocation terminated successfully. Its possible values are `CORBA_NO_EXCEPTION`, `CORBA_USER_EXCEPTION`, and

CORBA_SYSTEM_EXCEPTION. If the value is one of the latter two, any exception parameters signaled by the object can be accessed.

Five functions are available in the CORBA_Environment structure for accessing the exception information. Their signatures are

```C
/* C */
extern void CORBA_exception_set(
    CORBA_Environment *ev,
    CORBA_exception_type major,
    CORBA_char *except_repos_id,
    void *param
);

extern CORBA_char *CORBA_exception_id(
    CORBA_Environment *ev
);

extern void *CORBA_exception_value(CORBA_Environment *ev);

extern void CORBA_exception_free(CORBA_Environment *ev);

extern CORBA_any* CORBA_exception_as_any(
    CORBA_Environment *ev
);
```

CORBA_exception_set() allows a method implementation to raise an exception. The ev (environment) parameter is passed into the method. The caller must supply a value for the major parameter, whose value constrains the other parameters in the call as follows:

- The value CORBA_NO_EXCEPTION of the major parameter indicates a normal outcome. In this case, both except_repos_id and param must be null. It is *not* necessary to invoke CORBA_exception_set() to indicate a normal outcome, since that is the default behavior if the method simply returns.

- For any other value of major the operation specifies either a User or System exception. The except_repos_id parameter is the repository ID for the exception type. If the exception is declared to have members, the param parameter must be the address of an instance of the exception struct containing the parameters according to the C language mapping, coerced to a void*. In this case, the struct must be allocated with the appropriate T__alloc() function. The CORBA_exception_set() function adopts the allocated memory and frees it when it is no longer needed. Once the allocated exception `struct` is passed to `CORBA_exception_set()`, the application cannot access it because it no longer owns it. If the exception takes no parameters, `param` must be NULL.

If the `CORBA_Environment` argument to `CORBA_exception_set()` already has an exception set, that exception is properly freed before the new exception information is set.

`CORBA_exception_id()` returns a pointer to the character string identifying the exception. The string contains the exception's repository ID. If the function is invoked on a `CORBA_Environment`, which identifies a nonexception, a null pointer is returned. Note that ownership of the returned pointer does not transfer to the caller; instead, the pointer remains valid until `CORBA_exception_free()` is called.

`CORBA_exception_value()` returns a pointer to the structure corresponding to this exception. If invoked on a `CORBA_Environment`, which identifies a nonexception or an exception with no associated information, a null pointer is returned. The returned pointer does not become the callers, but remains valid until `CORBA_exception_free()` is called.

`CORBA_exception_free()` frees any storage allocated in the construction of `CORBA_Environment` or adopted by the `CORBA_Environment` when `CORBA_exception_set()` is called on it. `CORBA_exception_free()` sets the `_major` field to `CORBA_NO_EXCEPTION`. It can be invoked regardless of the value of the `_major` field.

`CORBA_exception_as_any()` returns a pointer to a `CORBA_any` containing the exception. This allows a C application to deal with exceptions for which it has no static (compile-time) information. If it is invoked on a `CORBA_Environment`, which identifies a nonexception, a null pointer is returned. Again, ownership of the returned pointer does not transfer to the caller; instead, the pointer remains valid until `CORBA_exception_free()` is called.

Consider the following example:

```
// IDL
interface exampleX {
    exception BadCall {
        string<80> reason;
```

```
    };
    void op() raises(BadCall);
};
```

This interface defines a single operation, which returns no results and can raise a `BadCall` exception. The following user code shows how to invoke the operation and how to recover from an exception:

```c
/* C */
#include "exampleX.h"

CORBA_Environment ev;
exampleX obj;
exampleX_BadCall *bc;

/*
 * some code to initialize obj to a reference to an object
 * supporting the exampleX interface
 */

exampleX_op(obj, &ev);

switch(ev._major) {
    case CORBA_NO_EXCEPTION:/* successful outcome*/
    /* process out and inout arguments */
    break;
    case CORBA_USER_EXCEPTION:/* a user-defined exception */
        if (strcmp(ex_exampleX_BadCall,
            CORBA_exception_id(&ev)) == 0)
        {
            bc=(exampleX_BadCall*)CORBA_exception_value(&ev);
            fprintf(stderr, "exampleX_op() failed - reason:
                    %s\n", bc->reason);
        }
        else
        { /* should never get here ... */
            fprintf( stderr, "unknown user-defined exception
                    -%s\n",CORBA_exception_id(&ev));
        }
    break;
    default:/* standard exception */
    /*
     * CORBA_exception_id() can be used to determine
     * which particular standard exception was
     * raised; the minor member of the struct
     * associated with the exception (as yielded by
```

```
    * CORBA_exception_value()) may provide additional
    * system-specific information about the exception */
   break;
}
/* free any storage associated with exception */
CORBA_exception_free(&ev);
```

5.21 Method Routine Signatures

The signatures of the methods that implement an object depend not only on the language binding but also on the choice of object adapter. Different object adapters may provide additional parameters to access adapter-specific features.

Most object adapters provide method signatures similar in most respects to those of the client stubs. In particular, the mapping for OMG IDL operation parameters should be the same as that for the client side.

5.22 Include Files

Multiple interfaces may be defined in a single source file. By convention, each source file holds a separate interface. All OMG IDL compilers, by default, generate a header file, named `Foo.h`, from `Foo.idl`. This file should be `#included` by clients and implementations of the interfaces defined in `Foo.idl`. `Foo.h` is sufficient to define all global names associated with the interfaces in `Foo.idl` and any interfaces from which they derive.

5.23 Pseudo-Objects

In the C language mapping, several interfaces are defined as pseudo-objects, on which a client makes calls in the same way it does on ordinary ORB objects. However, the ORB may implement a pseudo-object directly whereas there are restrictions on what a client may do with one. The ORB itself is a pseudo-object with the following partial definition:

```
// IDL
interface ORB {
    string object_to_string (in Object obj);
    Object string_to_object (in string str);
};
```

This means that a C programmer may convert an object reference into its string form by calling

```
/* C */
CORBA_Environment ev;
CORBA_char *str = CORBA_ORB_object_to_string(
    orbobj, obj, &ev
);
```

just as if the ORB were an ordinary object. The C library contains the routine `CORBA_ORB_object_to_string`, and does not do a real invocation. The `orbobj` object reference specifies the ORB of interest, since it is possible to choose the one to convert an object reference to a string.

Although operations on pseudo-objects are invoked in the usual way defined by the C language mapping, there are restrictions on them. In general, pseudo-objects cannot be specified as parameters to an operation on an ordinary object. Also, they are not accessible via the dynamic invocation interface and do not have definitions in the Interface Repository.

The programmer uses pseudo-objects in the same way he or she uses ordinary objects, and some ORB implementations may implement some pseudo-objects that way as well. For example, a context object might be implemented as an ordinary object, assuming it could be efficient enough.

5.23.2 ORB Operations

The operations on the ORB defined in Chapter 2 are used as if the OMG IDL definitions were described in the document and then mapped in the usual way with the C language mapping. For example, the `string_to_object` ORB operation has the following signature:

```
/* C */
CORBA_Object CORBA_ORB_string_to_object(
```

```
    CORBA_Object orb,
    CORBA_char *objectstring,
    CORBA_Environment *ev
);
```

Although here we are using an "object" that is special (an ORB), the method name is generated as `interface_operation` in the same way ordinary object names are. Also, the signature contains an `CORBA_Environment` parameter for error indications.

The same procedure determines the C language binding for the remainder of the ORB and object reference operations.

5.24   *Mapping for Object Implementations*

This section describes the OMG–IDL-to-C–language mapping of the Portable Object Adapter—specifically, how the implementation methods connect to the skeleton.

5.24.1   Operation-Specific Details

Generally, for operation-specific parameters, the method implementing the operation appears to receive the same values that are passed to the stubs.

5.24.2   PortableServer Functions

Objects registered with POAs use sequences of `octet`, specifically `PortableServer::POA::ObjectId`, as object identifiers. However, because C programmers often use strings as object identifiers, the C mapping provides the following functions that convert strings to `ObjectId` and vice versa:

```
/* C */
extern CORBA_char* PortableServer_ObjectId_to_string(
    PortableServer_ObjectId* id,
    CORBA_Environment* env
);
```

```
extern CORBA_wchar_t* PortableServer_ObjectId_to_wstring(
    PortableServer_ObjectId* id
    CORBA_Environment* env
);

extern PortableServer_ObjectId*
PortableServer_string_to_ObjectId(
    CORBA_char* str,
    CORBA_Environment* env
);

extern PortableServer_ObjectId*
PortableServer_wstring_to_ObjectId(
    CORBA_wchar_t* str,
    CORBA_Environment* env
);
```

These functions follow the normal C mapping rules for parameter passing and memory management.

If conversion of an `ObjectId` to a string results in illegal string characters (such as a `NUL`), the first two functions raise the `CORBA_BAD_PARAM` exception.

5.24.3   PortableServer::ServantLocator::Cookie

Since `PortableServer::ServantLocator::Cookie` is an IDL `native` type, its type must be specified by each language mapping. In C, `Cookie` maps to `void*`:

```
/* C */
typedef void* PortableServer_ServantLocator_Cookie;
```

For the C mapping of the `PortableServer::ServantLocator::prein-voke()` operation, the `Cookie` parameter maps to `Cookie*`; for the `postinvoke()` operation, it is passed as `Cookie`:

```
/* C */
extern PortableServer_ServantLocator_preinvoke(
    PortableServer_ObjectId* oid,
    PortableServer_POA adapter,
    CORBA_Identifier op_name,
    PortableServer_ServantLocator_Cookie* cookie
);
```

```
extern PortableServer_ServantLocator_postinvoke(
    PortableServer_ObjectId* oid,
    PortableServer_POA adapter,
    CORBA_Identifier op_name,
    PortableServer_ServantLocator_Cookie cookie,
    PortableServer_Servant servant
);
```

5.24.4 Servant Mapping

A *servant* is a language-specific entity that can incarnate a CORBA object. In C, a servant comprises a data structure that holds the state of the object, along with a collection of *method functions* that manipulate that state in order to implement the CORBA object.

The `PortableServer::Servant` type maps into C as follows:

```
/* C */
typedef void* PortableServer_Servant;
```

`Servant` maps to a `void*`, rather than to a pointer to `ServantBase`, so that all servant types for derived interfaces can be passed to all operations that take a `Servant` parameter without casting. However, it is expected that an instance of `PortableServer_Servant` will point to an instance of a `PortableServer_ServantBase` or its equivalent for derived interfaces, as described below.

Associated with a servant is a table of pointers to method functions. This table is called an *entry point vector*, or EPV, and has the same name as that of the servant type with __epv appended (note the double underscore). The EPV for `PortableServer_Servant` is defined as follows:

```
/* C */
typedef struct PortableServer_ServantBase__epv {
    void* _private;
    void (*finalize)(PortableServer_Servant,
    CORBA_Environment*);
    PortableServer_POA (*default_POA)(
            PortableServer_Servant,
            CORBA_Environment*);
} PortableServer_ServantBase__epv;

extern PortableServer_POA
```

```
PortableServer_ServantBase__default_POA(
    PortableServer_Servant,
    CORBA_Environment*
);
```

The `PortableServer_ServantBase__epv _private` member, which is opaque to applications, allows ORB implementations to associate data with each `ServantBase` EPV. It is expected that EPVs will be shared among multiple servants, so they are suitable for per-servant data. The second member is a pointer to the finalization function for the servant, which is invoked when the servant is etherealized.

The other function pointers correspond to the usual `Servant` operations.

The actual `PortableServer_ServantBase` structure combines an EPV with per-servant data, as shown below:

```
/* C */
typedef PortableServer_ServantBase__epv*
PortableServer_ServantBase__vepv;

typedef struct PortableServer_ServantBase {
    void* _private;
    PortableServer_ServantBase__vepv* vepv;
} PortableServer_ServantBase;
```

The first member is a `void*` that points to data specific to the ORB implementation. This member, which allows ORB implementations to keep per-servant data, is opaque to applications. The second member is a pointer to a pointer to a `PortableServer_ServantBase__epv`. The reason for the double level of indirection is that servants for derived classes contain multiple EPV pointers, one for each base interface as well as one for the interface itself. (This is explained further in the next section.) The name of the second member, `vepv`, is standardized to allow portable access through it.

5.24.5   Interface Skeletons

All C skeletons for IDL interfaces have essentially the same structure as that of `ServantBase`, except that the second member has a type that allows access to all EPVs for the servant, including those for base and most derived interfaces.

For example, consider the following IDL interface:

```
// IDL
interface Counter {
long add(in long val);
};
```

The servant skeleton generated by the IDL compiler for this interface appears as follows (the type of the second member is further defined below):

```
/* C */
typedef struct POA_Counter {
    void* _private;
    POA_Counter__vepv* vepv;
} POA_Counter;
```

As with `PortableServer_ServantBase`, the name of the second member is standardized to `vepv` for portability. The EPV generated for the skeleton is a bit more interesting. For the `Counter` interface defined above, it appears as follows:

```
/* C */
typedef struct POA_Counter__epv {
    void* _private;
    CORBA_Long (*add)(PortableServer_Servant servant,
    CORBA_Long val,
    CORBA_Environment* env);
} POA_Counter__epv;
```

Since all servants are effectively derived from `PortableServer _ServantBase`, the complete set of entry points has to include EPVs for both `PortableServer_ServantBase` and `Counter`:

```
/* C */
typedef struct POA_Counter__vepv {
    PortableServer_ServantBase__epv* _base_epv;
    POA_Counter__epv* Counter_epv;
} POA_Counter__vepv;
```

The first member of the `POA_Counter__vepv` structure is a pointer to the `PortableServer_ServantBase` EPV. To ensure portability of initialization and access code, this member is always named `_base_epv`. Also, it must

always be the first member. The second member is a pointer to a
POA_Counter__epv.

The pointers to EPVs in the VEPV structure are in the order in which the IDL
interfaces appear in a top-to-bottom left-to-right traversal of the inheritance
hierarchy of the most-derived interface. The base of this hierarchy, as far as
servants are concerned, is always PortableServer_ServantBase. An
example is the following complicated interface hierarchy:

```
// IDL
interface A {};
interface B : A {};
interface C : B {};
interface D : B {};
interface E : C, D {};
interface F {};
interface G : E, F {
    void foo();
};
```

The VEPV structure for interface G is generated as follows:

```
/* C */
typedef struct POA_G__epv {
    void* _private;
    void (*foo)(PortableServer_Servant, CORBA_Environment*);
};

typedef struct POA_G__vepv {
    PortableServer_ServantBase__epv* _base_epv;
    POA_A__epv* A_epv;
    POA_B__epv* B_epv;
    POA_C__epv* C_epv;
    POA_D__epv* D_epv;
    POA_E__epv* E_epv;
    POA_F__epv* F_epv;
    POA_G__epv* G_epv;
};
```

Note that each member other than _base_epv is named by appending
_epv to the interface name whose EPV the member points to. These names
are standardized to allow for portable access to these struct fields.

5.24.6 Servant Structure Initialization

Each servant requires initialization and etherealization, or finalization, functions. For `PortableServer_ServantBase`, the ORB implementation provides the following:

```
/* C */
void PortableServer_ServantBase__init(
    PortableServer_Servant, CORBA_Environment*);

void PortableServer_ServantBase__fini(
    PortableServer_Servant, CORBA_Environment*);
```

These functions are named by appending `__init` or `__fini` (note the double underscores) to the name of the servant.

The first argument to the `init` function is a valid `Portable-Server_Servant` whose `vepv` member has been initialized to point to a VEPV structure. The init function performs ORB-specific initialization of the `PortableServer_ServantBase`, and initializes the `fini` struct member of the pointed-to `PortableServer_ServantBase__epv` to point to the `PortableServer_ServantBase_fini()` function, if the `fini` member is null. If it is not null, presumably it has already been correctly initialized by the application. If the `default_POA` member of the `PortableServer_ServantBase__epv` structure is null when the `init` function is called, its value is set to point to the `PortableServer_ServantBase__default_POA()` function, which returns an object reference to the root POA.

If a servant pointed to by the `PortableServer_Servant` passed to an `init` function has a null `vepv` member, or if the `Portable-Server_Servant` argument itself is null, no initialization of the servant is performed, and the `CORBA::BAD_PARAM` Standard exception is raised via the `CORBA_Environment` parameter. This also applies to interface-specific `init` functions, which are described below.

As the default finalization function for servants, `fini` cleans up only ORB-specific private data. It does not make any assumptions about where the servant is allocated, such as that the servant is heap-allocated and trying to call `CORBA_free()` on it. Applications can "override" `fini` for a given servant by initializing the `PortableServer_ServantBase__epv` "finalize" pointer with a pointer to a finalization function specifically for that servant; however, any such overriding function must always ensure that `PortableServer_ServantBase_fini()` is invoked for that servant as part of its implementation. The results of a failure to invoke `PortableServer_ServantBase_fini()` are implementation specific, but may include memory leaks or faults that could crash the application. If a servant passed to a `fini` function has a null `epv` member, or if the `PortableServer_Servant` argument itself is null, no finalization of the servant is performed, and the `CORBA::BAD_PARAM` Standard exception is raised via the `CORBA_Environment` parameter. This also applies to interface-specific `fini` functions, which are described below.

Normally, `PortableServer_ServantBase__init` and `Portable-Server_ServantBase__fini` are not invoked directly by applications, but rather by interface-specific initialization and finalization functions generated by an IDL compiler. For example, the `init` and `fini` functions generated for the `Counter` skeleton are defined as follows:

```c
/* C */
void POA_Counter__init(POA_Counter* servant,
    CORBA_Environment* env)
{
  /*
  * first call immediate base interface init functions
  * in the left-to-right order of inheritance
  */
  PortableServer_ServantBase__init(
      (PortableServer_ServantBase*)servant,env );
  /* now perform POA_Counter initialization */
  ...
}

void POA_Counter__fini(POA_Counter* servant,
   CORBA_Environment* env)
{
  /* first perform POA_Counter cleanup */
  ...
  /*
  * then call immediate base interface fini functions
  * in the right-to-left order of inheritance
  */
```

```
PortableServer_ServantBase__fini(
        (PortableServer_ServantBase*)servant, env);
}
```

The address of a servant must be passed to the `init` function before the servant can be activated or registered with the POA. The results of failing to do so are implementation specific, but can include memory access violations that could crash the application.

5.24.7 Application Servants

It is expected that applications will create their own servant structures so they can add their own servant-specific data members to store Object State. For the `Counter` example shown above, an application servant would probably have a data member to store the counter value:

```
/* C */
typedef struct AppServant {
    POA_Counter base;
    CORBA_Long value;
} AppServant;
```

The application might contain the following implementation of the `Counter::add` operation:

```
/* C */
CORBA_Long
app_servant_add(PortableServer_Servant _servant,
    CORBA_Long val,
    CORBA_Environment* _env)
{
  AppServant* self = (AppServant*)_servant;
  self->value += val;
  return self->value;
}
```

It might initialize the servant statically as follows:

```
/* C */
PortableServer_ServantBase__epv base_epv = {
    NULL, /* ignore ORB private data */
    NULL, /* no servant-specific finalize
            Function needed */
    NULL, /* use base default_POA function */
```

```
};

POA_Counter__epv counter_epv = {
    NULL, /* ignore ORB private data */
    app_servant_add /* point to our add function */
};

/* Vector of EPVs */
POA_Counter__vepv counter_vepv = {
    &base_epv,
    &counter_epv };
};

AppServant my_servant = {
/* initialize POA_Counter */
{
    NULL, /* ignore ORB private data */
    &counter_vepv /* Counter vector of EPVs */
    },
    0 /* initialize counter value */
};
```

Before registering or activating this servant, the application calls:

```
/* C */
CORBA_Environment env;
POA_Counter__init(&my_servant, &env);
```

If it requires a special destruction function for `my_servant`, the application sets the value of the `PortableServer_ServantBase__epv` `finalize` member either before or after calling `POA_Counter__init()`:

```
/* C */
my_servant.epv._base_epv.finalize = my_finalizer_func;
```

Note that if the application statically initialized the `finalize` member before calling the servant initialization function, the explicit assignment to the `finalize` member shown here is not necessary, since the `PortableServer_ServantBase __init()` function will not modify it if it is non-null.

The preceding example illustrates static initialization of the EPV and VEPV structures. Though portable, this initialization method depends on the ordering of the VEPV `struct` members for base interfaces: If the top-to-bottom, left-to-right ordering of the interface inheritance hierarchy changes, the order of these fields also changes. A less fragile way of initializing these fields is to do the initialization at runtime, relying on assignment to the named `struct` fields. Since the names of the fields are used, this approach does not break if the order of base interfaces changes.

Field initialization within a servant initialization function also provides a convenient place to invoke the servant initialization functions. In any case, both approaches are portable, and it is up to the developer to choose the best one for each application.

5.24.8   Method Signatures

With the POA, implementation method signatures are identical to the stubs except for the first argument. If the following interface is defined in OMG IDL,

```
// IDL
interface example4 {
    long op5(in long arg6);
};
```

a method function for the `op5` operation must have the following function signature:

```
/* C */
CORBA_long example4_op5(
    PortableServer_Servant _servant,
    CORBA_long arg6,
    CORBA_Environment* _env
);
```

The `_servant` parameter points to the servant incarnating the CORBA object on which the request was invoked. The method can obtain the object reference for the target CORBA object via the `POA_Current` object. The `_env` parameter is used for raising exceptions. Note that the names of the `_servant` and `_env` parameters are standardized to allow the bodies of method functions to refer to them portably.

The method terminates successfully via a `return` statement returning the declared operation value. Prior to that, the method code must assign legal values to all `out` and `inout` parameters. The method terminates with an error by executing the `CORBA_exception_set` operation before the `return` statement. In this case, the method code is *not* required to assign legal values to any `out` or `inout` parameters, but, because of restrictions in C, it must return a legal function value.

5.25 *Mapping of the Dynamic Skeleton Interface to C*

Here we discuss the C mapping of the Dynamic Skeleton Interface's `ServerRequest` and the Portable Object Adapter's Dynamic Implementation Routine.

5.25.1 Mapping of ServerRequest to C

In the C mapping, a `ServerRequest` is a pseudo-object in the CORBA module that supports the following operations:

```
/* C */
CORBA_Identifier CORBA_ServerRequest_operation(
    CORBA_ServerRequest req,
    CORBA_Environment *env
);
```

This function returns the name of the operation being performed, as shown in the operation's OMG IDL specification.

```
/* C */
CORBA_Context CORBA_ServerRequest_ctx (
    CORBA_ServerRequest req,
    CORBA_Environment *env
);
```

`ServerRequest` can determine any context values passed as part of the operation.

Context is available only to the extent defined in the operation's OMG IDL definition. For example, OMG IDL defines no context for attribute operations.

```
/* C */
void CORBA_ServerRequest_arguments(
    CORBA_ServerRequest req,
    CORBA_NVList* parameters,
```

```
    CORBA_Environment *env
);
```

This function retrieves parameters from `ServerRequest` and finds the addresses for passing pointers to result values to the ORB. It must always be called by each DIR, even when there are no parameters.

The caller passes ownership of the `parameters` NVList to the ORB, but first that NVList must be initialized with the `TypeCodes` and direction flags for each `in`, `out`, and `inout` parameter to the operation being implemented. When the call returns, the NVList is still usable by the DIR, and all `in` and `inout` parameters will have been unmarshaled. At that point pointers to those values also are accessible through the `parameters` NVList.

The implementation routine then processes the call, producing any result values. If the DIR does not report an exception, it replaces pointers to the `inout` values in parameters with the values to be returned, and assigns pointers to `out` values in that NVList. When the DIR returns, all the parameter memory is freed as appropriate, and the ORB frees the NVList itself.

```
/* C */
void CORBA_ServerRequest_set_result(
    CORBA_ServerRequest req,
    CORBA_any* value,
    CORBA_Environment *env
);
```

This function reports any result `value` for an operation. If the operation has no result, it is not called or is called with a `tk_void` TypeCode stored in `value`.

```
/* C */
void CORBA_ServerRequest_set_exception(
    CORBA_ServerRequest req,
    CORBA_exception_type major,
    CORBA_any* value,
    CORBA_Environment *env
);
```

This function reports exceptions, both User and System, to the client that made the original invocation. The parameters are `major`, indicating whether the exception is user- or system-defined, and `value`, the value of the exception, including an exception `TypeCode`.

5.25.2   Mapping of Dynamic Implementation Routine to C

In C, a DIR is a function with this signature:

```
/* C */
typedef void (*PortableServer_DynamicImplRoutine) (
    PortableServer_Servant servant,
    CORBA_ServerRequest request
);
```

A DIR function is invoked by the POA when an invocation is received on an object reference whose implementation has registered a dynamic skeleton. `servant` is the C implementation object incarnating the CORBA object to which the invocation is directed; `request`, the `ServerRequest` used to access explicit parameters and report results (and exceptions).

Unlike other C object implementations, the DIR does not receive a `CORBA_Environment*` parameter, and so the `CORBA_exception_set` API is not used. Instead, `CORBA_ServerRequest_set_exception` provides the `TypeCode` for the exception to the ORB and so does not need to consult the Interface Repository (or rely on compiled stubs) to marshal the exception value.

For a Dynamic Implementation Routine to be registered with a POA, the proper EPV structure and servant must be created first. DSI servants are expected to supply EPVs for both `PortableServer_ServantBase` and for `PortableServer_DynamicImpl`, which is conceptually derived from `PortableServer_ServantBase`, as shown here:

```
/* C */
typedef struct PortableServer_DynamicImpl__epv {
    void* _private;
    PortableServer_DynamicImplRoutine invoke;
    CORBA_RepositoryId (*primary_interface) (
        PortableServer_Servant svt,
        PortableServer_ObjectId id,
```

```
        PortableServer_POA poa,
        CORBA_Environment* env);
} PortableServer_DynamicImpl__epv;

typedef struct PortableServer_DynamicImpl__vepv {
    PortableServer_ServantBase__epv* _base_epv;
    PortableServer_DynamicImpl__epv*
    PortableServer_DynamicImpl_epv;
} PortableServer_DynamicImpl__vepv;

typedef struct PortableServer_DynamicImpl {
    void* _private;
    PortableServer_DynamicImpl__vepv* vepv;
} PortableServer_DynamicImpl;
```

For other servants, initialization and finalization functions for `Portable-Server_DynamicImpl` are also provided and must be invoked.

To properly initialize the EPVs, the application must have implementations of the `invoke` and `primary_interface` functions required by the `PortableServer_DynamicImpl` EPV. The `invoke` method, which is the DIR, receives requests issued to any CORBA object it represents and performs the processing necessary to execute the request.

The `primary_interface` method receives an `ObjectId` value and a POA as input parameters, and returns a valid Interface Repository ID representing the most-derived interface for that `oid`. These methods should be invoked only by the POA as part of serving a CORBA request. Invocation in other circumstances may lead to unpredictable results.

Here is a DSI-based servant:

```
/* C */
/* This function serves as the DIR */

void my_invoke(PortableServer_Servant servant,
        CORBA_ServerRequest req)
{
    /* details omitted */
}

CORBA_RepositoryId my_primary_intf(
    PortableServer_Servant svt,
    PortableServer_ObjectId id,
    PortableServer_POA poa,
```

```
    CORBA_Environment* env)
{
    /* details omitted */
}

/* Application-specific DSI servant type */
typedef struct MyDSIServant {
    POA_DynamicImpl base;
    /* other application-specific data members */
} MyDSIServant;

PortableServer_ServantBase__epv base_epv = {
    NULL, /* ignore ORB private data */
    NULL, /* no servant-specific finalize */
    NULL, /* use base default_POA function */
};

PortableServer_DynamicImpl__epv dynimpl_epv = {
    NULL, /* ignore ORB private data */
    my_invoke, /* invoke() function */
    my_primary_intf, /* primary_interface() function */
};

PortableServer_DynamicImpl__vepv dynimpl_vepv = {
    &base_epv, /* ServantBase EPV */
    &dynimpl_epv, /* DynamicImpl EPV */
};

MyDSIServant my_servant = {
    /* initialize PortableServer_DynamicImpl */
    {
    NULL, /* ignore ORB private data */
    &dynimpl_vepv /* DynamicImpl vector of EPVs */
    };
    /* initialize application-specific data members */
};
```

Registration of the `my_servant` data structure via `Portable-Server_POA_set_servant()` on a suitably initialized POA makes the `my_invoke` DIR function available to handle DSI requests.

5.26   ORB Initialization Operations

The following PIDL is part of the CORBA module, not the ORB interface, which specifies initialization operations for an ORB.

```
// PIDL
module CORBA {
    typedef string ORBid;
    typedef sequence <string> arg_list;
    ORB ORB_init (inout arg_list argv,
            in ORBid orb_identifier);
};
```

The mapping of these operations to C is as follows:

```
/* C */
typedef char* CORBA_ORBid;
extern CORBA_ORB CORBA_ORB_init(int *argc,
    char **argv,
    CORBA_ORBid orb_identifier,
    CORBA_Environment *env);
```

The C mapping for `ORB_init` deviates from the OMG IDL PIDL in its handling of the `arg_list` parameter. To provide a meaningful PIDL definition of the initialization interface, which has a natural C binding, C replaces the `arg_list` structure with `argv` and `argc` parameters. The `argv` parameter is defined as an unbound array of strings (`char **`), the number of strings in which is passed in the `argc` (`int*`) parameter.

If an empty `ORBid` string is used, an `argc` argument can determine which ORB should be returned. It does so by searching the `argv` parameters for one tagged `ORBid`, say, `-ORBid "ORBid_example."` If an empty `ORBid` string is used, and no ORB is indicated by the `argv` parameters, the default ORB is returned.

Whether or not an empty or nonempty `ORBid` string is passed to `ORB_init`, the `argv` arguments are examined to determine if any ORB parameters are given. If a nonempty `ORBid` string is passed to `ORB_init`, all `-ORBid` parameters in the `argv` are ignored. All other `-ORB<suffix>` parameters may be significant during the ORB initialization process.

For C, the order of consumption of `argv` parameters may be significant to an application. To ensure that applications are not required to handle `argv` parameters they do not recognize, the ORB initialization function must be called before the rest of the parameters are consumed. Therefore, after the `ORB_init` call, the `argv` and `argc` parameters will have been modified to remove the ORB-understood arguments. Note that the `ORB_init` call can only reorder or remove references to parameters from the `argv` list; this restriction avoids potential memory management problems caused by an attempt to free parts of the `argv` list or to extend it. This is why `argv` is passed as a `char**` and not a `char***`.

CHAPTER 6

IDL to C++ Mapping

In this chapter, we will walk through the CORBA specification, piece by piece, and describe how IDL[1] is represented in terms of C++. Most of the examples and code fragments will be brief and much like the examples laid out by the OMG in the actual specification.

6.1 Scoped Names

The first part of the specification treats scoped names in the context of C++—basically, the IDL keyword `module` and the corresponding C++ `namespace`. For example: the OMG IDL

```
// IDL
module X
{
  struct S{
    long N;
  };
};
```

---

[1] In this chapter, the terms *OMG IDL* and *IDL* will be used interchangeably.

---

in C++ is

```
// C++
namespace X
{
  struct S{
    Long N;
  };
};
```

Note the similarities between the two. Unlike the other language mappings, here the IDL `module` is replaced with the C++ `namespace` keyword, and the rest is the same.

C++ allows S to be instantiated outside of X, as `X::S`. Furthermore, C++ provides the keyword `using` so that the developer can specify a use of S without X as, say,

```
// C++
using namespace X;
N n;
```

The OMG points out that namespaces are fairly new to C++ (via the ANSI standardization effort), and that there are other ways to specify scope in C++ terms. (See the appendix of OMG documentation.)

6.2   Mappings for Interfaces

As we have seen, `interface` is one of the most important keywords in IDL. C++–CORBA compliance does not permit instances of references (&) or pointers (*) to an IDL `interface` class to be created. This is to allow a multitude of implementations. Thus, IDL such as the following:

```
// IDL
interface foo
{
  struct small{ long L; }
}
```

does not permit an instance of `foo` in C++, such as

```
foo myFoo;
```

or a pointer

```
foo *myFoo;
```

or a reference

```
void aFunction( foo &fooRef );
```

6.3   *Mappings for Object References and Types*

The OMG specifies that the interface itself is a reference and is mapped to two C++ constructs. For any given interface `I`, the two C++ constructs are `I_var`, and `I_ptr`, respectively. Furthermore, the `Ref` construct—for example, `Iref`—has been deprecated. The variable type (`var`) carries an implicit deallocation with its use of a reference. We can think of it as tacit garbage collection.

Inheritance in OMG IDL does not need to be specified as such in C++, although it is certainly possible to do so, and might make a good implementation. Rather, C++ requires only that an object that can "widen" or include all of the functionality of a derived class call a `duplicate()` operation.

The OMG CORBA specification defines three operations using object references:

* `duplicate`—responsible for replicating an object in a different part of memory. This is the only function that can throw CORBA System exceptions.
* `release`—used by the requestor (client) to let the system know that this particular object is no longer necessary. The system can then deallocate the memory associated with that reference.
* `is_nil`—allows a process to check the validity of a reference. If an object is allocated and reacting to calls on a particular reference, this operation returns `TRUE`; otherwise, `FALSE`.

It is also possible to narrow on object references, through _narrow(), which is the opposite of the "widen" functionality. Instead of widening on a derived class, this operation narrows the inheritance hierarchy to a parent class. That is to say, if *B* derives from *A*, it can be narrowed to produce a reference of *A*. This does not work when the derived interface does not support the narrowed reference type.

The OMG does not allow the C++ operator== to check the validity of an object. The is_nil() function instead satisfies this purpose, but it is not allowed to throw any CORBA exceptions.

To bring all of this together, the OMG provides an illustrative case of a valid IDL code fragment and a possible C++ implementation. Here, the example interface is "my interface," or myInt, and the method defined is "my function," or myFcn. First, the IDL:

```
// IDL
interface myInt
{
  myInt myFcn(in myInt arg1, out myInt arg2);
};
```

Now the corresponding C++:

```
// C++
class myInt;
typedef myInt *myInt_ptr;

class myInt : public virtual Object
{
public:
  static myInt_ptr _duplicate( myInt_ptr obj );
  static myInt_ptr _narrow( Object_ptr obj );
  static myInt_ptr _nil();
  virtual myInt_ptr myFcn( myInt_ptr arg1, myInt_out arg2 ) = 0;
protected:
  myInt();
  virtual ~myInt();
private:
  myInt( const myInt& );
  void operator=( const myInt& );
};
```

```
class myInt_var : public _var
{
public:
  myInt_var() : ptr_( myInt::_nil() ) {}
  myInt_var( myInt_ptr p ) : ptr_( p ) {}
  myInt_var( const myInt_var &a ) : ptr_(
                             myInt::_duplicate( myInt_ptr( a ))) {}
  ~myInt_var() { free(); }
  myInt_var &operator=( myInt_ptr p ) {
    reset( p ); return *this;
  }
  myInt_var &operator=(const myInt_var& a ) {
    if (this != &a) {
      free();
      ptr_ = A::_duplicate(A_ptr(a));
    }
    return *this;
  }
  myInt_ptr in() const { return ptr_; }
  myInt_ptr& inout() { return ptr_; }
  myInt_ptr& out() {
    reset( myInt::_nil() );
    return ptr_;
  }
  myInt_ptr _retn() {
    // yield ownership of managed object reference
    myInt_ptr val = ptr_;
    ptr_ = myInt::_nil();
    return val;
  }
  operator const myInt_ptr&() const { return ptr_; }
  operator myInt_ptr&() { return ptr_; }
  myInt_ptr operator->() const { return ptr_; }
protected:
  myInt_ptr ptr_;
  void free() { release(ptr_); }
  void reset( myInt_ptr p ) { free(); ptr_ = p; }
private:
// hidden assignment operators for var types to
// fulfill the rules specified in
// Section 19.3.2
  void operator=(const _var &);
};
```

6.4   *Mappings for Constants*

The OMG IDL constant is a simple mapping, corresponding directly to the C++ `const` keyword. Whether memory is actually allocated depends solely on the scope of the actual declaration. Here is the OMG IDL:

```
// IDL
const string aName = "orielly";

interface anInt
{
  const float pi = 3.1415926;
};
```

and the corresponding C++ code:

```
// C++
static const char +const aName = "orielly";

class anInt
{
public:
  static const Float pi;
};
```

According to the OMG, it is possible, though not always, for a constant to map to an actual value instead of to the constant's name.

6.5   *Mappings for Enums*

The IDL `enum` also maps directly to C++. For example, the following IDL:

```
// IDL
enum WeekDays{ Monday, Tuesday, Wednesday, Thursday, Friday };
```

maps to the following C++:

```
// C++
enum WeekDays{ Monday, Tuesday, Wednesday, Thursday, Friday };
```

6.6   Mappings for Basic Data Types

Table 6.1 lists IDL basic data types and their C++ counterparts. Implicit here is the assumption that the `long` data types map to valid C++ primitives.

Table 6.1   IDL-to-C++ Mapping: Basic Data Types

OMG IDL	C++
short	CORBA::Short
long	CORBA::Long
long long	CORBA::LongLong
unsigned short	CORBA::UShort
unsigned long	CORBA::Ulong
unsigned long long	CORBA::ULongLong
float	CORBA::Float
double	CORBA::Double
long double	CORBA::LongDouble
char	CORBA::Char
wchar	CORBA::Wchar
boolean	CORBA::String
octet	CORBA::Octet

6.7   Mappings for Strings

IDL `string` maps to `char*` in C++, as it does in C. Strings are always considered null-terminated. This is the only nonbasic type that has size requirements. The OMG specifies that for any dynamic allocations to occur, the following C++, within the CORBA namespace, must be used:

```
// C++
namespace CORBA{
  char *string_alloc( ULong len );
  char *string_dup( const char* );
```

```
void string_free( char* );
// and so forth
...
}
```

Note that the `string_alloc` function will either succeed in dynamically allocating a string or fail and return a null value. These three functions cannot throw CORBA System exceptions.

For wide strings, `WString_var` is used in place of `String_var`, making the two declarations look almost identical. The C++ that defines a wide string variable is as follows:

```
// C++
class WString_var
{
public:
  WString_var();
  WString_var( WChar *p );
  WString_var( const WString_var &w );
  ~WString_var();

  WString_var &operator=( WChar *p );
  WString_var &operator=( const WString_var &w );
  operator WChar*();
  operator const WChar*() const;
  WChar &operator[]( ULong index );
  WChar operator[]( ULong index ) const;
};
```

The dynamic allocation of the `WString` functions is identical to the `String` operations.

6.8 Mappings for Structured Types

The structured types in IDL are `struct`, `union`, and `sequence`, but not `array`. These are C++ structures or classes providing a default constructor, a copy constructor, an assignment operator, and lastly, a destructor, and each has a specification for its behavior and return values, if any. Their mappings vary depending on whether the vendor implementing them uses fixed- or variable-length data structures.

Each OMG IDL `struct` type maps to a corresponding C++ type, and all subparts are mapped to C++ data types. To enforce this, no user-defined default constructors, assignment operators, or destructors can be implemented.

6.9   Mapping for Fixed

`Fixed` is considered an abstract data type. The following are the OMG-specified fixed C++ class and function templates (with overloaded operators):

```
// C++ class template
template<CORBA::UShort d, Short s>
class Fixed
{
public:
// Constructors...
  Fixed(int val = 0);
  Fixed(CORBA::LongDouble val);
  Fixed(const Fixed<d,s>& val);
  ~Fixed();
// Conversions...
  operator LongDouble() const;
// Operators...
  Fixed<d,s>& operator=(const Fixed<d,s>& val);
  Fixed<d,s>& operator++();
  Fixed<d,s>& operator++(int);
  Fixed<d,s>& operator--();
  Fixed<d,s>& operator--(int);
  Fixed<d,s>& operator+() const;
  Fixed<d,s>& operator-() const;
  int operator!() const;
// Other member functions
  CORBA::UShort fixed_digits() const;
  CORBA::Short fixed_scale() const;
};
  template<CORBA::UShort d, CORBA::Short s>
  istream& operator>>(istream& is, Fixed<d,s> &val);
  template<CORBA::UShort d, CORBA::Short s>
  ostream& operator<<(ostream& os, const Fixed<d,s> &val);
// C++ function templates for operators...
  template<unsigned short d1, short s1, unsigned short d2,
    short s2)
```

```
Fixed<d r ,s r > operator + (const Fixed<d1,s1> &val1,
    const Fixed<d2,s2> &val2);
Fixed<d r ,s r > operator - (const Fixed<d1,s1> &val1,
    const Fixed<d2,s2> &val2);
Fixed<d r ,s r > operator * (const Fixed<d1,s1> &val1,
    const Fixed<d2,s2> &val2);
Fixed<d r ,s r > operator / (const Fixed<d1,s1> &val1,
    const Fixed<d2,s2> &val2);
Fixed<d1,s1> operator += (const Fixed<d1,s1> &val1,
    const Fixed<d2,s2> &val2);
Fixed<d1,s1> operator -= (const Fixed<d1,s1> &val1,
    const Fixed<d2,s2> &val2);
Fixed<d1,s1> operator *= (const Fixed<d1,s1> &val1,
    const Fixed<d2,s2> &val2);
Fixed<d1,s1> operator /= (const Fixed<d1,s1> &val1,
    const Fixed<d2,s2> &val2);
int operator > (const Fixed<d1,s1> &val1,
    const Fixed<d2,s2> &val2);
int operator < (const Fixed<d1,s1> &val1,
    const Fixed<d2,s2> &val2);
int operator >= (const Fixed<d1,s1> &val1,
    const Fixed<d2,s2> &val2);
int operator <= (const Fixed<d1,s1> &val1,
    const Fixed<d2,s2> &val2);
int operator == (const Fixed<d1,s1> &val1,
    const Fixed<d2,s2> &val2);
int operator != (const Fixed<d1,s1> &val1,
    const Fixed<d2,s2> &val2);
};
```

The digit variables d and s are the results of binary arithmetic functions. According to the OMG, one way to evaluate these functions is through a macro definition.

6.10   Mappings for Unions

IDL's union functionality is mapped to C++ classes with access functions. Much of how the union is built in C++ is implementation dependent. To activate its discriminant functions, the operator _d is defined, which serves as a discriminator modifier. The _default() function sets this value.

6.11   Mappings for Sequences

The IDL `sequence` maps to a C++ class that acts like an array. The OMG specifies that this array-type class must maintain a current and a maximum length, and that bounded sequences' maximum values cannot be controlled by developers. Developers can modify the maximum length of unbounded sequences through the constructors, and they are allowed to modify the current values at any time.

IDL sequences have a one-to-one relationship with corresponding C++ implementations. For instance, for the following IDL:

```
// IDL
typedef sequence<int> IntSeq;
typedef sequence<IntSeq, 5> IntSquaredSeq;
```

the corresponding C++ has two interface classes:

```
// C++
class IntSeq{ … };
class IntSquaredSeq{ … };
```

These classes provide their own constructors, destructors, and so forth.

6.12   Mappings for Array Types

Arrays are mapped in IDL to the same types in the same method as in C++. Note that the assignment to an array element releases the memory associated with the old value. For instance, the following IDL:

```
// IDL
typedef int I[20];
typedef string S[5];
typedef float F[5][10][15];
```

allows the following C++ to be valid:

```
// C++
I i1;
I_var i2;
S s1;
```

```
S_var s2;
F f1;
F_var f2;
i1[0] = i2[1];
s1[1] = s2[1];
f1[0][1][2] = f2[1][0][2];
```

6.13   Mappings for Typedef

For every mapping within the `typedef`, the corresponding alias and mapping for a given type are created. Again, a strong similarity exists between the actual IDL and C++. Consider the following IDL:

```
// IDL
typedef long T;
interface A1;
typedef A1 A2;
typedef sequence<long> S1;
typedef S1 S2;
```

and the C++:

```
// C++
typedef Long T;
// ...definitions for A1...
typedef A1 A2;
typedef A1_ptr A2_ptr;
typedef A1_var A2_var;
// ...definitions for S1...
typedef S1 S2;
typedef S1_var S2_var;
```

6.14   The OMG IDL Any Type

The `any` type is quite possibly the most important functionality in the CORBA specification. Since it can be set to an arbitrary value when necessary, `any` allows a developer to write code once for a particular system or subsystem and use it in many CORBA applications.

The OMG requires two things for the use of any within C++:

- C++ types must be handled in a type-safe manner.
- Values must be handled that are not known until compile time.

The any type is handled safely through C++ overloading with all possible types declared. In this way, any is, in effect, type-safe. For an insertion operation to be possible on any, the following must be defined in C++ for any type foo that can, and must be passed-by-value: Short, UShort, Long, ULong, LongLong, ULongLong, Float, Double, LongDouble, enums, unbounded Strings, and object references (foo_ptr):

```
// C++
void operator <<=( Any&, foo );
```

Other foo values might be too large to pass-by-value. These can be declared as the following in C++:

```
// C++
void operator <<=( Any&, const foo& );
void operator <<=( Any&, foo* );
```

Extracting from any is very much the opposite. For the preceding primitive types that are pass-by-value, the following C++ suffices:

```
// C++
Boolean operator >>=( const Any&, foo& );
```

For the values that expand beyond those bounds:

```
// C++
Boolean operator >>=( const Any&, foo*& );
```

Nonprimitive types are extracted through pointers. To eliminate ambiguity between the boolean, octet, char, wchar, and bounded string types, helper functions are specified within the any class, such as from_boolean() and from_octet(). An any reference can be widened to an object through a similar to_object() functionality.

To handle untyped values within any, the following can be used:

```
// C++
Any( TypeCode_ptr tc, void *value, Boolean release=FALSE );
```

Notice the `TypeCode` sent in as the first parameter. The class uses this code to determine the type of the value—that is, to scope the amount of memory it will need, among other things. Three unsafe operations are defined:

```
// C++
void replace(
   TypeCode_ptr, void *value, Boolean release = FALSE );
TypeCode_ptr type() const;
Const void *value() const;
```

The `replace` function is used for types that cannot be used with the type-safe insertion means. The `type` function returns a pseudo-object type reference for an untyped `any`. Lastly, the `value` function returns a pointer to the memory of the any-typed object.

The entire `any` class is provided in IDL as an appendix to the OMG specification.

6.15   Mappings for Exceptions

The IDL exception class extends the `UserException` class defined in the ORB portion of the specification. It is treated much like a variable-length `struct`, and all members must manage themselves with respect to memory. The main parts of the class such as the copy constructor, destructor, and so on, take care of allocating or deallocating memory. They include a `const char*` as an initial parameter so that arbitrary strings can be generated and maintained as part of the class.

The Standard (System) exceptions are extended from `SystemException`, and both `SystemException` and `UserException` extend on the base `Exception` class. They too are defined in the ORB portion of the specification. Following is the OMG definition of a `SystemException` in C++:

```
// C++
enum CompletionStatus {
   COMPLETED_YES,
   COMPLETED_NO,
   COMPLETED_MAYBE
};
```

```
class SystemException : public Exception
{
public:
  SystemException();
  SystemException( const SystemException & );
  SystemException( ULong minor, CompletionStatus status );
  ~SystemException();
  SystemException &operator=( const SystemException & );
  ULong minor() const;
  void minor( ULong );
  void _raise();
  CompletionStatus completed() const;
  void completed( CompletionStatus );
};
```

Like the Java programming environment, which relies heavily on exception classes, the C++ specification, on which Java is founded, allows this type of exception handling. For most cases, the developer can utilize the base exception at the top of the inheritance hierarchy. For example:

```
// C++
try{
  ...
} catch( const Exception &e ){}
```

Note how similar this looks to Java. Specific types of exceptions can also be caught, such as the two extensions of the base `Exception` class mentioned earlier:

```
// C++
try{
  ...
} catch( const UserException &e ){}
catch( const SystemException &e ){}
catch( const myUserException &e ){}
```

where `myUserException` is an exception that extends `UserException`.

6.16   Argument Passing

CORBA is very detailed regarding how memory is handled in parameter-types passing—specifically `in`, `out`, and `inout` parameters, `readonly`, and so forth. Differences between the C and C++ mappings are covered in brief, and particular attention is paid to the passing of _var types. Table 6.2, from the OMG specification, shows the primitive data types, the parameter-passing method, and the resulting mapping in C++:

Table 6.2 Mapping of OMG IDL Data Types to C++

Data Type	In	Inout	Out	Return
short	Short	Short&	Short&	Short
long	Long	Long&	Long&	Long
long long	LongLong	LongLong&	LongLong&	LongLong
unsigned short	Ushort	Ushort&	Ushort&	Ushort
unsigned long	Ulong	Ulong&	Ulong&	ULong
unsigned long long	ULongLong	ULongLong&	ULongLong&	ULongLong
float	Float	Float&	Float&	Float
double	Double	Double&	Double&	Double
long double	LongDouble	LongDouble&	LongDouble&	LongDouble
boolean	Boolean	Boolean&	Boolean&	Boolean
char	Char	Char&	Char&	Char
wchar	Wchar	Wchar&	Wchar&	WChar
octet	Octet	Octet&	Octet&	Octet
enum	enum	enum&	enum&	enum
object ref. ptr	objref_ptr	objref_ptr&	objref_ptr&	objref_ptr
fixed struct	const struct&	struct&	struct&	struct
variable struct	const struct&	struct&	struct*&	struct*
fixed union	const union&	union&	union&	union
variable union	const union&	union&	union*&	union*
string	const char*	char*&	char*&	char*

Table 6.2   Mapping of OMG IDL Data Types to C++   (Continued)

Data Type	In	Inout	Out	Return
wstring	const wchar*	wchar*&	wchar*&	wchar*
sequence	const sequence&	sequence&	sequence*&	sequence*
fixed array	const array	array	array	array slice*[1]
variable array	const array	array	array slice*&	array slice*
any	const any&	any&	any*&	any*
fixed	const Fixed&	Fixed&	Fixed&	Fixed&

[1] An "array slice" is defined as an array with all dimensions equal to the original except the first one.

Table 6.3 illustrates the _var argument and result passing.

Table 6.3   OMG _var Data Types Mapping to C++

Data Type	In	Inout	Out	Return
object ref. var	const objref_var&	objref_var&	objref_var&	objref_var
struct_var	const struct_var&	struct_var&	struct_var&	struct_var
union_var	const union_var&	union_var&	union_var&	union_var
string_var	const string_var&	string_var&	string_var&	string_var
sequence_var	const sequence_var&	sequence_var&	sequence_var&	sequence_var
array_var	const array_var&	array_var&	array_var&	array_var
any_var	const any_var&	any_var&	any_var&	any_var

The OMG also presents a table of in and out parameter cases and how each should be implemented in terms of assignments, modifications, and the like, to the memory locations that reflect the actual values.

6.17   Miscellaneous Mapping Information

A developer can implement "pseudo-objects" for invoking serverless operations, which do not have to use the exact memory models mentioned above for IDL types. However, with this flexibility come risks, one being that references to pseudo-objects do not necessarily function across different systems. Pseudo-objects do not subclass CORBA::Object as normal IDL classes do. There are, moreover, many similarities, as well as a few key differences, between them and C-PIDL, the C pseudo-object specification. These and other details about pseudo-objects are discussed in the OMG specification.

Server-side mappings differ from client-side mappings primarily in their use of throw operations. A server-side object must implement a throw operation, whereas a client can, and usually does, implement try/catch routines.

Dynamic skeleton mapping is straightforward and is treated in the DSI part of the CORBA specification. Two areas in which it is lacking are its mappings of the DSI ServerRequest and BOA Dynamic Implementation Routine to C++.

6.18   C++ Mapping Definitions

This section presents the actual OMG-specified C++ mapping declarations. Note that alternative mappings exist; these are described in the CORBA C++ specification, Appendix 2. Following are the proposed C++ mapping definitions:

Primitive Types

```
typedef unsigned charBoolean;
typedef unsigned charChar;
typedef wchar_tWChar;
typedef unsigned charOctet;
typedef shortShort;
typedef unsigned shortUShort;
typedef longLong;
typedef …LongLong;
typedef unsigned longULong;
typedef …ULongLong;
typedef floatFloat;
typedef doubleDouble;
typedef long doubleLongDouble;
typedef Boolean&Boolean_out;
typedef Char&Char_out;
typedef WChar&WChar_out;
typedef Octet&Octet_out;
typedef Short&Short_out;
typedef UShort&UShort_out;
typedef Long&Long_out;
typedef LongLong&LongLong_out;
typedef ULong&ULong_out;
typedef ULongLong&ULongLong_out;
typedef Float&Float_out;
typedef Double&Double_out;
typedef LongDouble&LongDouble_out;
```

The `String_var` and `String_out` Classes

```
class String_var
{
public:
  String_var();
  String_var(char *p);
  String_var(const char *p);
  String_var(const String_var &s);
  ~String_var();
  String_var &operator=(char *p);
  String_var &operator=(const char *p);
  String_var &operator=(const String_var &s);
  operator char*();
  operator const char*() const;
  const char* in() const;
  char*& inout();
  char*& out();
  char* _retn();
```

```
  char &operator[](ULong index);
  char operator[](ULong index) const;
};
class String_out
{
public:
  String_out(char*& p);
  String_out(String_var& p);
  String_out(String_out& s);
  String_out& operator=(String_out& s);
  String_out& operator=(char* p);
  String_out& operator=(const char* p)
  operator char*&();
  char*& ptr();
private:
  // assignment from String_var disallowed
  void operator=(const String_var&);
};
```

Any Class

```
class Any
{
public:
  Any();
  Any(const Any&);
  Any(TypeCode_ptr tc, void *value,
  Boolean release = FALSE);
  ~Any();
  Any &operator=(const Any&);
  void operator<<=(Short);
  void operator<<=(UShort);
  void operator<<=(Long);
  void operator<<=(ULong);
  void operator<<=(Float);
  void operator<<=(Double);
  void operator<<=(const Any&);// copying
  void operator<<=(Any*);// non-copying
  void operator<<=(const char*);
  Boolean operator>>=(Short&) const;
  Boolean operator>>=(UShort&) const;
  Boolean operator>>=(Long&) const;
  Boolean operator>>=(ULong&) const;
  Boolean operator>>=(Float&) const;
  Boolean operator>>=(Double&) const;
  Boolean operator>>=(Any*&) const;
  Boolean operator>>=(char*&) const;
```

```
// special types needed for boolean, octet, char,
// and bounded string insertion
// these are suggested implementations only
struct from_boolean {
  from_boolean(Boolean b) : val(b) {}
  Boolean val;
};
struct from_octet {
  from_octet(Octet o) : val(o) {}
  Octet val;
};
struct from_char {
  from_char(Char c) : val(c) {}
  Char val;
};
struct from_wchar {
  from_char(WChar c) : val(c) {}
  WChar val;
};
struct from_string {
  from_string(char* s, ULong b,
  Boolean nocopy = FALSE) :
  val(s), bound(b) {}
  char *val;
  ULong bound;
};
struct from_wstring {
  from_wstring(WChar* s, ULong b,
  Boolean nocopy = FALSE) :
  val(s), bound(b) {}
  WChar *val;
  ULong bound;
};
void operator<<=(from_boolean);
void operator<<=(from_char);
void operator<<=(from_wchar);
void operator<<=(from_octet);
void operator<<=(from_string);
void operator<<=(from_wstring);
// special types needed for boolean, octet,
// char extraction
// these are suggested implementations only
struct to_boolean {
  to_boolean(Boolean &b) : ref(b) {}
  Boolean &ref;
};
```

```
struct to_char {
  to_char(Char &c) : ref(c) {}
  Char &ref;
};
struct to_wchar {
  to_wchar(WChar &c) : ref(c) {}
  WChar &ref;
};
struct to_octet {
  to_octet(Octet &o) : ref(o) {}
  Octet &ref;
};
struct to_object {
  to_object(Object_ptr &obj) : ref(obj) {}
  Object_ptr &ref;
};
struct to_string {
  to_string(char *&s, ULong b) : val(s), bound(b) {}
  char *&val;
  ULong bound;
};
struct to_wstring {
  to_wstring(WChar *&s, ULong b)
    : val(s), bound(b) {}
  WChar *&val;
  ULong bound;
};
Boolean operator>>=(to_boolean) const;
Boolean operator>>=(to_char) const;
Boolean operator>>=(to_wchar) const;
Boolean operator>>=(to_octet) const;
Boolean operator>>=(to_object) const;
Boolean operator>>=(to_string) const;
Boolean operator>>=(to_wstring) const;
void replace(TypeCode_ptr, void *value,
Boolean release = FALSE);
TypeCode_ptr type() const;
const void *value() const;
private:
  // these are hidden and should not be implemented
  // so as to catch erroneous attempts to insert
  // or extract multiple IDL types mapped to unsigned char
  void operator<<=(unsigned char);
  Boolean operator>>=(unsigned char&) const;
};
```

The `Any_var` Class

```
class Any_var
{
public:
  Any_var();
  Any_var(Any *a);
  Any_var(const Any_var &a);
  ~Any_var();
  Any_var &operator=(Any *a);
  Any_var &operator=(const Any_var &a);
  Any *operator->();
  const Any& in() const;
  Any& inout();
  Any*& out();
  Any* _retn();
  // other conversion operators for parameter passing
};
```

The `Exception` Class

```
// C++
class Exception
{
public:
  Exception(const Exception &);
  virtual ~Exception();
  Exception &operator=(const Exception &);
  virtual void _raise() = 0;
protected:
  Exception();
};
```

The `SystemException` Class

```
// C++
enum CompletionStatus { COMPLETED_YES, COMPLETED_NO,
COMPLETED_MAYBE };
class SystemException : public Exception
{
public:
  SystemException();
  SystemException(const SystemException &);
  SystemException(ULong minor, CompletionStatus status);
  ~SystemException();
  SystemException &operator=(const SystemException &);
  ULong minor() const;
  void minor(ULong);
```

```
  CompletionStatus completed() const;
  void completed(CompletionStatus);
  static SystemException* _narrow(Exception*);
};
```

The UserException Class

```
// C++
class UserException : public Exception
{
public:
  UserException();
  UserException(const UserException &);
  ~UserException();
  UserException &operator=(const UserException &);
  static UserException* _narrow(Exception*);
};
```

The UnknownUserException Class

```
// C++
class UnknownUserException : public UserException
{
public:
  Any &exception();
  static UnknownUserException* _narrow(Exception*);
  virtual void raise();
};
```

The Release and is_nil Classes

```
// C++
namespace CORBA {
void release(Object_ptr);
void release(Environment_ptr);
void release(NamedValue_ptr);
void release(NVList_ptr);
void release(Request_ptr);
void release(Context_ptr);
void release(TypeCode_ptr);
void release(POA_ptr);
void release(ORB_ptr);
Boolean is_nil(Object_ptr);
Boolean is_nil(Environment_ptr);
Boolean is_nil(NamedValue_ptr);
Boolean is_nil(NVList_ptr);
Boolean is_nil(Request_ptr);
Boolean is_nil(Context_ptr);
```

```
Boolean is_nil(TypeCode_ptr);
Boolean is_nil(POA_ptr);
Boolean is_nil(ORB_ptr);
...
}
```

The Object Class

```
// C++
class Object
{
public:
  static Object_ptr _duplicate(Object_ptr obj);
  static Object_ptr _nil();
  InterfaceDef_ptr _get_interface();
  Boolean _is_a(const char* logical_type_id);
  Boolean _non_existent();
  Boolean _is_equivalent(Object_ptr other_object);
  ULong _hash(ULong maximum);
  Status _create_request(
    Context_ptr ctx,
    const char *operation,
    NVList_ptr arg_list,
    NamedValue_ptr result,
    Request_out request,
    Flags req_flags
  );
  Status _create_request(
    Context_ptr ctx,
    const char *operation,
    NVList_ptr arg_list,
    NamedValue_ptr result,
    ExceptionList_ptr,
    ContextList_ptr,
    Request_out request,
    Flags req_flags
  );
  Request_ptr _request(const char* operation);
  Policy_ptr _get_policy(PolicyType policy_type);
  DomainManagerList* _get_domain_managers();
  Object_ptr _set_policy_override(
    const PolicyList& policies,
    SetOverrideType set_or_add
  );
};
```

The `Environment` Class

```
// C++
class Environment
{
public:
  void exception(Exception*);
  Exception *exception() const;
  void clear();
  static Environment_ptr _duplicate(Environment_ptr ev);
  static Environment_ptr _nil();
};
```

The `NamedValue` Class

```
// C++
class NamedValue
{
public:
  const char *name() const;
  Any *value() const;
  Flags flags() const;
  static NamedValue_ptr _duplicate(NamedValue_ptr nv);
  static NamedValue_ptr _nil();
};
```

The `NVList` Class

```
// C++
class NVList
{
public:
  ULong count() const;
  NamedValue_ptr add(Flags);
  NamedValue_ptr add_item(const char*, Flags);
  NamedValue_ptr add_value(const char*, const Any&,
    Flags);
  NamedValue_ptr add_item_consume(
    char*,
    Flags
  );
  NamedValue_ptr add_value_consume(
    char*,
    Any *,
    Flags
  );
  NamedValue_ptr item(ULong);
  Status remove(ULong);
```

```
  static NVList_ptr _duplicate(NVList_ptr nv);
  static NVList_ptr _nil();
};
```

The ExceptionList Class

```
// C++
class ExceptionList
{
public:
  ULong count();
  void add(TypeCode_ptr tc);
  void add_consume(TypeCode_ptr tc);
  TypeCode_ptr item(ULong index);
  Status remove(ULong index);
};
```

The ContextList Class

```
class ContextList
{
public:
  ULong count();
  void add(const char* ctxt);
  void add_consume(char* ctxt);
  const char* item(ULong index);
  Status remove(ULong index);
};
```

The Request Class

```
// C++
class Request
{
public:
  Object_ptr target() const;
  const char *operation() const;
  NVList_ptr arguments();
  NamedValue_ptr result();
  Environment_ptr env();
  ExceptionList_ptr exceptions();
  ContextList_ptr contexts();
  void ctx(Context_ptr);
  Context_ptr ctx() const;
  Any& add_in_arg();
  Any& add_in_arg(const char* name);
  Any& add_inout_arg();
  Any& add_inout_arg(const char* name);
  Any& add_out_arg();
```

```
    Any& add_out_arg(const char* name);
    void set_return_type(TypeCode_ptr tc);
    Any& return_value();
    Status invoke();
    Status send_oneway();
    Status send_deferred();
    Status get_response();
    Boolean poll_response();
    static Request_ptr _duplicate(Request_ptr req);
    static Request_ptr _nil();
};
```

The Context Class

```
// C++
class Context
{
public:
    const char *context_name() const;
    Context_ptr parent() const;
    Status create_child(const char*, Context_out);
    Status set_one_value(const char*, const Any&);
    Status set_values(NVList_ptr);
    Status delete_values(const char*);
    Status get_values(const char*, Flags, const char*,
        NVList_out);
    static Context_ptr _duplicate(Context_ptr ctx);
    static Context_ptr _nil();
};
```

The TypeCode Class

```
// C++
class TypeCode
{
public:
    class Bounds { … };
    class BadKind { … };
    TCKind kind() const;
    Boolean equal(TypeCode_ptr) const;
    const char* id() const;
    const char* name() const;
    ULong member_count() const;
    const char* member_name(ULong index) const;
    TypeCode_ptr member_type(ULong index) const;
    Any *member_label(ULong index) const;
    TypeCode_ptr discriminator_type() const;
    Long default_index() const;
```

```cpp
  ULong length() const;
  TypeCode_ptr content_type() const;
  UShort fixed_digits() const;
  Short fixed_scale() const;
  Long param_count() const;
  Any *parameter(Long) const;
  static TypeCode_ptr _duplicate(TypeCode_ptr tc);
  static TypeCode_ptr _nil();
};
```

The ORB Class

```cpp
// C++
class ORB
{
public:
  typedef sequence<Request_ptr> RequestSeq;
  char *object_to_string(Object_ptr);
  Object_ptr string_to_object(const char*);
  Status create_list(Long, NVList_out);
  Status create_operation_list(OperationDef_ptr,
    NVList_out);
  Status create_named_value(NamedValue_out);
  Status create_exception_list(ExceptionList_out);
  Status create_context_list(ContextList_out);
  Status get_default_context(Context_out);
  Status create_environment(Environment_out);
  Status send_multiple_requests_oneway(
    const RequestSeq&
  );
  Status send_multiple_requests_deferred(
    const RequestSeq&
  );
  Boolean poll_next_response();
  Status get_next_response(Request_out);
  // Obtaining initial object references
  typedef char* ObjectId;
  class ObjectIdList {…};
  class InvalidName {…};
  ObjectIdList *list_initial_services();
  Object_ptr resolve_initial_references(
    const char *identifier
  );
  Boolean work_pending();
  void perform_work();
  void shutdown(Boolean wait_for_completion);
  void run();
```

```
    Boolean get_service_information(
      ServiceType svc_type,
      ServiceInformation_out svc_info
    );
    static ORB_ptr _duplicate(ORB_ptr orb);
    static ORB_ptr _nil();
};
```

ORB Initialization

```
// C++
typedef char* ORBid;
static ORB_ptr ORB_init(
  int& argc,
  char** argv,
  const char* orb_identifier = ""
);
```

6.19   Summary

The C++ mapping for CORBA is well-suited to its task because of C++'s many similarities to IDL, and because both are preprocessed for macro definitions. Like the rest of the mappings in this book, however, it is still a "work in progress." Thus, since it will change, although not a great deal, it is important for builders of ORB systems to stay current.

The OMG Web site http://www.omg.org keeps the updated specifications and notices of events. Sitting in on some of the ORBOS task force meetings concerning the language mappings and other aspects of CORBA "plumbing" at the site can be very fruitful.

CHAPTER 7

IDL to Java Language Specification Mapping

This chapter covers the following topics: keywords; mapping syntax; special considerations; the main goals of CORBA; and two important CORBA classes.

7.1 Mapping Syntax

7.1.1 Any Type

The class `org.omg.CORBA.Any` is the mapping for IDL's `Any` type, which has the ability to extract and insert instances of existing types. If an extract operation has a mismatched type, the exception `CORBA::BAD_OPERATION` is thrown. See, for example, the class definition that follows:

```
package org.omg.CORBA;

public abstract class Any {
        public abstract org.omg.CORBA.TypeCode type();
        public abstract void type( org.omg.CORBA.TypeCode t );
        public abstract short extract_short() throws
                org.omg.CORBA.BAD_OPERATION;
```

```
        public abstract void insert_short( short s );
        public abstract int extract_long() throws
                org.omg.CORBA.BAD_OPERATION;
        public abstract void insert_long( int i );
        public abstract long extract_longlong() throws
                org.omg.CORBA.BAD_OPERATION;
        public abstract void insert_longlong ( long l );
        public abstract short extract_ushort() throws
                org.omg.CORBA.BAD_OPERATION;
        public abstract void insert_ushort( short s );
        public abstract int extract_ulong() throws
                org.omg.CORBA.BAD_OPERATION;
        public abstract void insert_ulong( int i );
        public abstract long extract_ulonglong() throws
                org.omg.CORBA.BAD_OPERATION;
        public abstract void insert_ulonglong ( long l );
        public abstract float extract_float() throws
                org.omg.CORBA.BAD_OPERATION;
        public abstract void insert_float( float f );
        public abstract double extract_double() throws
                org.omg.CORBA.BAD_OPERATION;
        public abstract void insert_double( double d );
        public abstract boolean extract_boolean() throws
                org.omg.CORBA.BAD_OPERATION;
        public abstract void insert_boolean( boolean b );
        public abstract char extract_wchar() throws
                org.omg.CORBA.BAD_OPERATION;
        public abstract void insert_wchar( char c );
        public abstract byte extract_octet() throws
                org.omg.CORBA.BAD_OPERATION;
        public abstract void insert_octet( byte b );
        public abstract char extract_char() throws
                org.omg.CORBA.BAD_OPERATION;
        public abstract void insert_char( char c )
                throws org.omg.CORBA.DATA_CONVERSION;

        public abstract String extract_string() throws
                org.omg.CORBA.BAD_OPERATION;
        public abstract void insert_string( String s )
                throws org.omg.CORBA.DATA_CONVERSION,
                org.omg.CORBA.MARSHAL;
        public abstract String extract_wstring() throws
                org.omg.CORBA.BAD_OPERATION;
        public abstract void insert_wstring( String s ) throws
                org.omg.CORBA.MARSHAL;

        public abstract void insert_any( org.omg.CORBA.Any a );
```

```
        public abstract org.omg.CORBA.Any extract_any()
                throws org.omg.CORBA.BAD_OPERATION;

        public abstract void insert_Object( org.omg.CORBA.Object o );
        public abstract void insert_Object(
                org.omg.CORBA.Object o,
                org.omg.CORBA.TypeCode t ) throws org.omg.CORBA.MARSHAL;
        public abstract org.omg.CORBA.Object extract_Object()
                throws org.omg.CORBA.BAD_OPERATION;
}
```

The above `org.omg.CORBA.Any` class has methods to check equality and stream data, although they are not listed.

Certain predefined types in IDL do not directly or simply map to existing Java classes, which is the main reason behind the creation for the `Any` class. Generally, the streaming methods are not to be used by programmers using CORBA in Java, but are there to assist portable interfaces for ORB stubs and skeletons.

7.1.2 Array

An array is mapped from IDL to Java the same way IDL bounded sequence is mapped, with `Holder` appended to the name of the generated Java class. The bounds of the array access are checked when marshaling occurs, and an element accessed out of bounds results in the exception CORBA::MARSHAL being thrown. The length of the array can be obtained via an IDL constant, which is mapped to Java according to the regular constant generation rules. For example, if the IDL code is

```
// An array of longs with 10 elements.
const long arrayBounds = 10;
typedef long AnArray[ arrayBounds ];
```

the resulting Java code is

```
public final class AnArrayHolder implements
                org.omg.CORBA.portable.Streamable {
        public int[] value;

        public AnArrayHolder() { … }
        public AnArrayHolder( int[] initial ) { … }
```

```
        public void _read( org.omg.CORBA.portable.InputStream i ) { ... }
        public void _write( org.omg.CORBA.portable.OutputStream o ) { ... }
        public void org.omg.CORBA.TypeCode _type() { ... }
}
```

7.1.3   Basic Types

Java's basic types are mapped to corresponding types in IDL, as dictated by the CORBA specification. The mapping is shown in Table 7.1.

Although it is straightforward, two items—strings and IDL characters—should be given special attention.

Strings are not a basic type but rather true objects. Thus, they must be marshaled as regular objects, which is an inherently slower process than is

Table 7.1   Basic Type Mapping for IDL to Java

IDL Type	Java Type	Exceptions
boolean	boolean	
char	char	CORBA:DATA_CONVERSION
double	double	
float	float	
long	int	
long long	long	
octet	byte	
short	short	
string	java.lang.String	CORBA::DATA_CONVERSION CORBA::MARSHAL
unsigned long	int	
unsigned long long	long	
unsigned short	short	
wchar	char	
wstring	java.lang.String	CORBA::MARSHAL

sending over a basic type, such as an integer or character. Also, strings are prone to marshaling errors, which may cause a `CORBA::MARSHAL` exception to be thrown.

IDL characters (`chars`) are only 16 bits in length, whereas Java supports 32-bit characters. If a character being sent from one object to another is out of range for a given character set, the exception `CORBA::DATA_CONVERSION` is thrown. A further complication is that a `string` in Java is made up entirely of characters, so the exception `CORBA::DATA_CONVERSION` may also be thrown when a `string` is marshaled.

7.1.4 Boolean

Java's `true` and `false` keywords map directly to the IDL keywords `TRUE` and `FALSE`.

7.1.5 Character

Range checking takes place when a 32-bit Java character is converted to a 16-bit IDL character. As previously mentioned, the `CORBA::DATA_CONVERSION` exception may be thrown to signal that the conversion failed. To avoid range checking, IDL provides the `wchar` type. Java's 32-bit character maps directly to IDL's `wchar`.

7.1.6 Constant

Constant declarations fall into two categories, which differ in scope. Variables declared `public final static` in Java are mapped from constants declared in the interface definition in IDL. An IDL constant not declared within an IDL interface maps to a new public interface in Java, within which a `public final static` variable, `value`, holds the value of the constant declared in IDL.

For example, this IDL code:

```
module Example {
      const long LongConstant = -123;
};
```

is generated into the following Java code:

```
package Example;

public interface LongConstant {
        public final static int value = (int)(-123L);
}
```

7.1.7   Context

A context specifies how strings are resolved before they are transmitted with a request invocation. The IDL code for Context is shown here:

```
pseudo interface Context {
        readonly attribute Identifier context_name;
        readonly attribute Context parent;

        Context create_child( in Identifier child_ctx_name );
        void set_one_value( in Identifier propname, in any propvalue );
        void set_values( in NVList values );
        void delete_values( in Identifier propname );
        NVList get_values( in Identifier scope_type, in Flags op_flags, in
                Identifier pattern );
};
```

The resulting Java code is

```
package org.omg.CORBA;

public abstract class Context {
        String context_name;
        Context parent;
        public abstract String context_name();
        public abstract Context parent();

        public abstract Context create_child( String child_ctx_name );
        public abstract void set_one_value(
                String propname, org.omg.CORBA.Any propvalue );
        public abstract void set_values( NVList values );
        public abstract void delete_values( String propname );
        public abstract NVList get_values( String scope_type,
                int op_flags, String pattern );
}
```

7.1.8   Context List

A context list is similar to a named value list in that it has a variable number of `contexts`. The IDL code for `ContextList` is shown here:

```
pseudo interface ContextList {
        readonly attribute unsigned long count;

        void add( in string context );
        string item( in unsigned long index ) raises( CORBA::Bounds );
        void remove( in unsigned long index ) raises( CORBA::Bounds );
};
```

The resulting Java code is

```
package org.omg.CORBA;

public abstract class ContextList {
        int count;
        public abstract int count();

        public abstract void add( String context );
        public abstract String item( int index ) throws
                org.omg.CORBA.Bounds;
        public abstract void remove( int index ) throws
                org.omg.CORBA.Bounds;
}
```

7.1.9   Enumeration

The IDL `enum` type maps to a Java `final` class Java that is the IDL enum's name. That class is then given `public final static` integer variables that start at zero and end at one less than the number of enumeration values listed. Furthermore, the Java class has `public final static` integer variables of the class itself. New instances of the class are created with a parameter of the `final static` integer variables to achieve strong type checking while allowing enumerations to be used in the Java `switch` statement.

For example, if the IDL code is

```
enum AnEnumeration { zero, one, two };
```

the resulting Java code is

```
public final class AnEnumeration {
        public final static int _zero = 0;
        public final static AnEnumeration  = new AnEnumeration( _zero );

        public final static int _one = 1;
        public final static AnEnumeration  = new AnEnumeration( _one );

        public final static int _two = 2;
        public final static AnEnumeration  = new AnEnumeration( _two );

        public int value() { … }
        public static AnEnumeration from_int( int value ) { … }

        private AnEnumeration ( int value ) { … }
}
```

7.1.10   Environment

Exception information can be obtained by invoking the exception operations on the Environment class, the definition of which follows:

```
package org.omg.CORBA;

public abstract class Environment {
        void exception( java.lang.Exception except );
        java.lang.Exception exception();
        void clear();
}
```

7.1.11   Exception

An IDL exception maps to Java in the same way an IDL structure does, creating a class with instance variables and constructors that stem from Java's exception classes. The CORBA System exceptions, such as CORBA::MARSHAL, inherit from the Java exception java.lang.RuntimeException. User-defined exceptions inherit indirectly from the main Java exception java.lang.Exception.

7.1.12 Exception List

The exception list contains exceptions that might be thrown by IDL operations. They store a list of IDL `TypeCodes`. The IDL code for the `Exception-List` is shown here:

```
pseudo interface ExceptionList {
        readonly attribute unsigned long count;

        void add( in TypeCode exc );
        TypeCode item( in unsigned long index ) raises (CORBA::Bounds);
        void remove( in unsigned long index ) raises (CORBA:Bounds);
};
```

The resulting Java code is

```
package org.omg.CORBA;

public abstract class ExceptionList {
        int count;
        public abstract int count();

        public abstract void add( TypeCode exc );
        public abstract TypeCode item( int index )
                throws org.omg.CORBA.Bounds;
        public abstract void remove( int index )
                throws org.omg.CORBA.Bounds;
}
```

7.1.13 Future Types

The Java Development Kit (JDK) 1.0.2 specification does not support IDL `long double` and `fixed` types, although later versions of Java may do so. Table 7.2 lists these types and the logical corresponding mapping.

Table 7.2   Future Type Mappings

IDL Type	Java Type	Exceptions
fixed	java.math.BigDecimal	CORBA::DATA_CONVERSION
long double	undefined	

7.1.14   Interface

Interfaces in IDL map one-to-one with interfaces in Java. Along with the direct name mapping, a helper class is created, the name of which is simply the name of the interface with the suffix `Helper`.

The interface `org.omg.CORBA.Object` is extended by the Java interface. Also mapped to the Java interface is the signature of each operation defined in the IDL interface. This means that for every object that implements the generated Java interface, the methods that correspond to the IDL interface's operations can be invoked by any other object in the CORBA system.

The sole responsibility of the helper class is a static narrow method that allows any class of the `org.omg.CORBA.Object` type to narrow its own object reference so that it can determine its type. If the specific type of the object cannot be discerned, the exception `CORBA::BAD_PARAM` is thrown.

Attributes in an IDL module map directly to Java with the addition of accessor and modifier methods. When writing Java code it is common to prefix `get` and `set` to the name of an attribute's accessor and modifier methods, respectively. Since proper capitalization cannot be discerned every time, the Java code generated does not prefix `get` and `set` to these methods, thus avoiding ugly method names. Lastly, read-only attributes in IDL do not generate a corresponding modifier method.

For example, if the IDL code is

```
module InterfaceModuleExample {
        interface AnInterface {
                attribute long longValue;
                readonly attribute long longReadOnlyValue;
                long anInterfaceMethod( in long value )
                        raises( SomeException );
        };
};
```

the resulting Java code is

```
package InterfaceModuleExample;

public interface AnInterface extends org.omg.CORBA.Object {
        int longValue;
        int longReadOnlyValue;
```

```
        int longValue();
        void longValue( int i );
        int longReadOnlyValue();
        int anInterfaceMethod( int value ) throws
                InterfaceModuleExample.SomeException;
}

public class AnInterfaceHelper {
        ...  // Generated interface-related code

        public static AnInterface narrow( org.omg.CORBA.Object obj ) { ... }
}
```

7.1.15   Module Name

The name of an IDL module is mapped one-to-one to the corresponding Java package. For example, the Java package name `package Sample;` ... maps quite simply to `module Sample { ... }`.

7.1.16   NamedValue List

A `NamedValue` list is a container for a series of `NamedValue` classes. The IDL definition for `NVList` is as follows:

```
pseudo interface NVList {
        readonly attribute unsigned long count;

        NamedValue add( in Flags flags );
        NamedValue add_item( in Identifier item_name, in Flags flags );
        NamedValue add_value(       in Identifier item_name,
                                    in any value,
                                    in Flags flags );

        NamedValue item( in unsigned long index ) raises (CORBA::Bounds);
        void remove( in unsigned long index ) raises (CORBA::Bounds);
};
```

If an index supplied to the `item(...)` operation is negative, or more than the number of items contained in `NVList`, a `Bounds` exception is thrown. Similarly, the `remove(...)` operation throws a `Bounds` exception for an invalid index. The remaining methods allow an instance of `NamedValue` to be added to the list. The variables declared by the operation arguments provide information about the addition. The corresponding Java code is

```
package org.omg.CORBA;

public abstract class NVList {
        int count;
        public abstract int count();

        public abstract NamedValue add( int flags );
        public abstract NamedValue add_item( String item_name,
                int flags );
        public abstract NamedValue add_item( String item_name,
                org.omg.CORBA.Any value, int flags );
        public abstract NamedValue item( int index ) throws
                org.omg.CORBA.Bounds;
        public abstract void remove( int index ) throws
                org.omg.CORBA.Bounds;
}
```

The `typedef` known as `Identifier` is reduced to its equivalent `java.lang.String` component.

7.1.17   NamedValue

A `NamedValue` connects a name with a value. Operation arguments and return values can acquire additional information via a `NamedValue` instance. The IDL code for this pseudo-interface is shown here:

```
typedef unsigned long Flags;
typedef string Identifier;

const Flags ARG_IN = 1;
const Flags ARG_OUT = 2;
const Flags ARG_INOUT = 3;
const Flags CTX_RESTRICT_SCOPE = 15;

pseudo interface NamedValue {
        readonly attribute Identifier name;
        readonly attribute any value;
        readonly attribute Flags flags;
};
```

The resulting Java code is

```
package org.omg.CORBA;

public interface ARG_IN { public final static int value = 1; }
public interface ARG_OUT { public final static int value = 2; }
```

```
public interface ARG_INOUT { public final static int value = 3; }
public interface CTX_RESTRICT_SCOPE { public final static int value = 15; }

public abstract class NamedValue {
        public abstract String name();
        public abstract org.omg.CORBA.Any value();
        public abstract int flags();
}
```

7.1.18   Nested Type

With the exception of the `Inner` classes, Java classes cannot be declared within the scope of an interface. In IDL, type declarations can be declared within an interface, but they remain visible to that interface alone. To allow mapping to Java, `package` is appended to the IDL's type name.

For example, if the IDL code is

```
module AnExample {
        interface AnInterface {
                exception AnException { };
        };
};
```

the resulting Java code is

```
package AnExample.AnInterfacePackage;

public final class AnException extends org.omg.CORBA.UserException { ... }
```

7.1.19   Null

An object that has no valid reference anywhere in memory should be assigned the value `null`. The only exceptions to this rule are array and `string` objects. A Java-based array should have all its elements zeroed out (or assigned to `null`), but never set an array reference to `null` if it must be marshaled. A string should be assigned to the empty string (`" "`) if it is no longer valid.

7.1.20   Octet

Java's `byte` maps directly to `octet` in IDL.

7.1.21   Other Type Conversions

The type mappings for `ins`, `doubles`, `floats`, and such, were described in the subsection "Basic Types" on page 264.

7.1.22   Passing Parameters

In IDL, arguments are passed to an operation via the `in`, `out`, and `inout` keywords. An `in` parameter maps to a call-by-value parameter in Java; an `out` or `inout` parameter, to a call-by-result parameter, represented by a holder class for the parameter type. A holder class must be used for `out` and `inout` parameters because Java recognizes only parameters passed-by-value.

For example, the IDL

```
module A_Module {
        interface AnInterface {
                long aMethod( in long longIn,
                              out long longOut,
                              inout long longInout )
        };
};
```

maps to Java as

```
package A_Module;

public interface AnInterface {
        int aMethod( int longIn,
                     IntHolder longOut,
                     IntHolder longInout );
}
```

7.1.23   Pseudo-Interface Definition Language (PIDL) Exceptions

There are three standard exceptions of the type CORBA PIDL: `BadKind`, `Bounds`, and `InvalidName`. These classes have neither helper nor holder classes, nor are they listed in any Interface Repository. Since the exception `org.omg.CORBA.UserException` is their inherited base, they can be used similarly to normal User exceptions.

7.1.24 Pseudo-Objects

A pseudo-object in IDL becomes either a Java language construct or a pseudo-interface. A pseudo-interface is usually defined as a Java construct with the following rules:

- It is not a CORBA object.
- It becomes a `public abstract class`, with no inheritance.
- It is not listed in the Interface Repository.
- It lacks a helper class.
- It lacks a holder class.

One or more of these rules may be overridden by a definition declared in the PIDL. For example, a pseudo-interface maps to the `org.omg.CORBA` package.

7.1.25 Sequence

A Java array corresponds to the IDL `sequence` type. The names of both are the same. When the sequence's type is required, an array of the given type is declared. For example, a sequence of integers maps to an array of integers. Checking of boundary access is not performed until the sequence has been marshaled. If the array bounds are exceeded, the exception `CORBA::MARSHAL` is thrown.

7.1.26 String

Java's `String` object maps to IDL's `string` type. Range and bounds checking is performed if the `String` object is marshaled. If it contains a character that is out of range for the character set, a `CORBA::DATA_CONVERSION` exception is thrown. If one of its accessed elements lies outside the `String`'s length, a `CORBA::MARSHAL` exception is thrown. An IDL string differs from an IDL `wstring` in that no range checking is performed on a Java `String` that maps to a `wstring`. With `wstrings`, only a `CORBA::MARSHAL` exception may be thrown.

7.1.27 Structure

Java does not have a one-to-one mapping for the IDL structure type declaration. Instead, an IDL structure maps to a Java class of the same name with `public` variables of the same type as defined by structure. In addition, the equivalent Java class has two constructors. The first takes no parameters and allows the structure's values to be initialized to default values; the second takes in one argument per variable defined in the structure. There are no accessor methods in the mapped Java class, which helps to reduce the size and complexity of the code while increasing execution speed.

For example, if the IDL code is

```
struct AStructure {
       long aLong;
       string aString;
};
```

the resulting Java code is

```
public final class AStructure {
       public int aLong;
       public String aString;

       public AStructure() { }
       public AStructure ( int aLong1, String aString1 ) { ... }
}
```

7.1.28 System Exceptions

The class `org.omg.CORBA.SystemException` is used by all CORBA System exceptions. Each derived exception is declared `final`, which means that no subclass exceptions may be created. Also, no public constructors exist for `org.omg.CORBA.SystemException`, making it impossible to create an instance of that class. Table 7.3 shows all standard IDL exceptions and their corresponding Java classes.

Each exception houses a string, a minor code, and a completion code. The minor code is set to zero within the default constructor; `COMPLETE_NO` is the default value for the completion code; and an empty string is assigned to the string value. An additional constructor is available to create an

Table 7.3   IDL-to-Java Mapping: Exceptions

IDL Exception	Java Class
CORBA::BAD_CONTEXT	org.omg.CORBA.BAD_CONTEXT
CORBA::BAD_INV_ORDER	org.omg.CORBA.BAD_INV_ORDER
CORBA::BAD_OPERATION	org.omg.CORBA.BAD_OPERATION
CORBA::BAD_PARAM	org.omg.CORBA.BAD_PARAM
CORBA::BAD_TYPECODE	org.omg.CORBA.BAD_TYPECODE
CORBA::COMM_FAILURE	org.omg.CORBA.COMM_FAILURE
CORBA::DATA_CONVERSION	org.omg.CORBA.DATA_CONVERSION
CORBA::FREE_MEM	org.omg.CORBA.FREE_MEM
CORBA::IMP_LIMIT	org.omg.CORBA.IMP_LIMIT
CORBA::INITIALIZE	org.omg.CORBA.INITIALIZE
CORBA::INTERNAL	org.omg.CORBA.INTERNAL
CORBA::INTF_REPOS	org.omg.CORBA.INTF_REPOS
CORBA::INVALIDTRANSACTION	org.omg.CORBA.INVALIDTRANSACTION
CORBA::INV_IDENT	org.omg.CORBA.INV_IDENT
CORBA::INV_FLAG	org.omg.CORBA.INV_FLAG
CORBA::INV_OBJREF	org.omg.CORBA.INV_OBJREF
CORBA::MARSHAL	org.omg.CORBA.MARSHAL
CORBA::NO_IMPLEMENT	org.omg.CORBA.NO_IMPLEMENT
CORBA::NO_MEMORY	org.omg.CORBA.NO_MEMORY
CORBA::NO_PERMISSION	org.omg.CORBA.NO_PERMISSION
CORBA::NO_RESOURCES	org.omg.CORBA.NO_RESOURCES
CORBA::NO_RESPONSE	org.omg.CORBA.NO_RESPONSE
CORBA::OBJ_ADAPTER	org.omg.CORBA.OBJ_ADAPTER
CORBA::OBJECT_DOES_NOT_EXIST	org.omg.CORBA.OBJECT_DOES_NOT_EXIST
CORBA::PERSIST_STORE	org.omg.CORBA.PERSIST_STORE
CORBA::TRANSACTIONREQUIRED	org.omg.CORBA.TRANSACTIONREQUIRED
CORBA::TRANSACTIONROLLEDBACK	org.omg.CORBA.TRANSACTIONROLLEDBACK
CORBA::TRANSIENT	org.omg.CORBA.TRANSIENT
CORBA::UNKNOWN	org.omg.CORBA.UNKNOWN

instance of a particular exception with the three attributes, given the values of the constructor's parameters. A third constructor allows an exception to be created with a string containing a reason it was thrown.

7.1.29   Typedef

Java has no construct for declaring arbitrary type definitions (`typedefs`). In contrast, IDL offers two types of arbitrary type definitions: simple and complex. The simple IDL types that map to Java's basic types (`byte`, `char`, `int`, etc.) are immediately translated, as expected. The IDL `typedefs` that declare the simple types are translated into the corresponding basic type. As for complex `typedefs`, when a simple or user-defined type is found, the mapping stops breaking down the `typedef` into its simpler components.

7.1.30   Union

Once again, Java has no mechanism for creating a union. As with structures, the name of the union declared in IDL is mapped to the name of an equivalent Java class. Unions are emulated in Java by a class with the following properties:

- A default constructor.
- An accessor method for the discriminator, called `discriminator()`.
- One accessor method per branch.
- One modifier method per branch.
- A modifier method for each branch having two or more case labels.
- A default modifier (if required).

These properties assist the mapping of unions from IDL to Java. However, unions are slightly more complex than the sum of their properties and so must follow several rules:

- When there is a naming conflict, the conflicting name must be given an underscore prefix.
- When an expected branch has not been set, `CORBA::BAD_OPERATION` is thrown when any accessor methods are invoked.

- When a branch has at least two case labels, the simpler modifier for that branch sets the discriminant equal to the first case label. Then another modifier method for that branch is made. The additional modifier takes a unique discriminator parameter to differentiate it from the original.
- When a branch is the default case label, the modifier method assigns the discriminant a unique case label.
- When a set of case labels includes all possible values for the discriminant, the IDL-to-Java compiler must produce an error message to prevent erroneous Java code from being generated.
- `default()` (or `_default()` if the name clashes) is the default modifier when a default case label is unspecified and all possible discriminant values are unused.

For example, if the IDL code is

```
union A_Union switch( AnEnumeration ) {
        case first: short firstShort;
        case second: long secondLong;
        case third:
        case fourth: octet fourthOctet;
        default: boolean defaultBoolean;
};
```

the resulting Java code is

```
public final class A_Union {
        public A_Union() { … }

        public <switch-type> discriminator() { … }

        public short firstShort() { … }
        public void firstShort ( short value ) { … }

        public int secondLong() { … }
        public void secondLong ( int value ) { … }

        public byte fourthOctet() { … }
        public void fourthOctet ( byte value ) { … }
        public void fourthOctet ( int discriminator, byte value ) { … }

        public boolean defaultBoolean() { … }
        public void defaultBoolean ( boolean value ) { … }
}
```

7.2 Special Considerations

Portions of the IDL-to-Java specification do not deal (directly or otherwise) with the syntax mapping of either Java or IDL, yet they are an integral part of the specification and should be examined.

7.2.1 Creating and Defining Transient Object

A transient object is created by instantiating the `Servant` class.

The `Servant Base` class maps IDL interfaces to their Java-based implementations. For example, if an IDL interface is called `AnInterface`, the base class defined in Java is similar to:

```
public class _ AnInterfaceBaseImpl implements AnInterface {
        ...
}
```

Once the `Servant Base` class is written, a `Servant` class must be written, which extends the `_AnInterfaceBaseImpl` class, as shown in the preceding code. This means that the `Servant` class must implement all public methods declared in `_AnInterfaceBaseImpl`, including those declared in `AnInterface`, plus the public methods from the interfaces that `AnInterface` may have extended.

7.2.2 Connecting a Transient Object

To connect a transient object to an ORB, first a handle to an ORB must be obtained; then the ORB's `connect(...)` operation must be invoked; and finally the transient object to be connected must be passed. A call to an ORB's `connect(...)` method using the same transient object after a successful connection has been established will be ignored. A connection might occur without warning if a transient object has a nonlocal object as a parameter to one of its operations. Stated another way, vendors of ORBs may connect transient objects at their discretion, but they must perform a connection when the `connect(...)` operation is invoked.

7.2.3 Disconnecting a Transient Object

Disconnecting a transient object from an ORB requires first obtaining a handle to the ORB and then invoking the ORB's `disconnect(...)` operation and passing it to the transient object to be disconnected. A call to `disconnect(...)` using the same transient object after a disconnect has been achieved will be ignored. An attempt to invoke an operation on a disconnected object will result in the exception `CORBA::OBJECT_DOES_NOT_EXIST` being thrown, but requests received through communication paths outside the ORB may proceed.

7.2.4 Java Version

The Java Version reference is based on Sun Microsystems' JDK 1.0.2 specification as of February 1998. The OMG may provide developers with a fuller implementation of its IDL specification in the future.

7.2.5 Naming Conflicts

If variable, argument, or operation names come into conflict when IDL code is mapped into Java code, the IDL identifier name is prefixed with an underscore when translated into Java.

7.2.6 Proprietary Extensions

The ORB sets minimum requirements of its vendors in order to provide interoperable object communication mechanisms. However, ORB vendors may make additional (proprietary) extensions to the specification. If using an ORB with extensions that lie outside the standard set by the OMG, the system designer must choose between staying pure or using the extensions, realizing that objects might no longer be accessible by other ORBs, other hardware, or even other software platforms.

7.2.7 Reserved Names

Certain names used in IDL are in direct conflict with Java keywords, or they are used by CORBA internally. They are listed on page 282.

- `basicJavaTypeHolder`, where `basicJavaType` is a basic type in Java
- `interfacePackage`, where `interface` is an IDL interface name
- `typeHelper`, where `type` is an IDL user-defined type
- `typeHolder`, where `type` is an IDL predefined type
- Java's keywords:

abstract	default if	private	throw
boolean	do implements	protected	throws
break	double import	public	transient
byte	else instanceof	return	try
case	extends int	short	void
catch	final interface	static	volatile
char	finally long	super	while
class	float native	switch	
const	for new	synchronized	
continue	goto package	this	

If any of the listed keywords are used in IDL, the resulting Java code is mapped with an underscore (_) prefix, assuming, of course, that the IDL type, or interface, is a legitimate IDL type name.

7.3   CORBA Design Goals

The main criteria addressed by CORBA are as follows:

Fast Execution Speeds

The code generated from the mapping of IDL to Java must promote reasonably fast execution speeds. This means creating as few objects as possible, for two reasons: first, creating objects in Java is an expensive operation on its own; and second, the garbage collector must use some time to free up the memory used for objects that are no longer valid.

Small Size Constraints

Given that the main execution environment for Java bytecode exists within a Web browser, the resulting CORBA-compliant applet must be kept small. This means that the memory usage of the applet will be small as well, which presumes that most of the work for the applet will be performed by server objects on remote machines.

Upward Compatibility

The design specification deals adequately with future modifications by ensuring that new methods and user-defined types may be added without breaking old code. It also permits vendors to add proprietary interfaces and operations, with the stipulation that they support the full set of CORBA APIs.

7.4   CORBA Classes

7.4.1   Holder

Holder classes are often found in IDL code that has been mapped into Java. For that reason, the declaration for a typical holder class has its own section in the specification. For IDL `union`, `struct`, and `enum` types, in addition to a newly generated Java class, there exists two supporting classes (with the exception of the `Array` class). A holder class allows the type it represents (an object or basic type) to be either written to an output stream or read from an input stream. The following Java code illustrates the typical structure of a generated holder class:

```
public final class GeneralHolder implements
                org.omg.CORBA.portable.Serializable {
    … // Additional variables
    … // Additional methods

    public void _read( org.omg.CORBA.portable.InputStream i ) { … }
    public void _write( org.omg.CORBA.portable.OutputStream o ) { … }
    public org.omg.CORBA.TypeCode _type() { … }
}
```

An instance variable of the type being wrapped by `holder` can be found among the holder class's member variables. `CharHolder`, for example, has `char value` as a member variable declaration. The value for `value` is the value being held (in this case, a character).

7.4.2 Streaming APIs

A simple way to read and write an object over a network is to convert it into a stream and perform regular stream operations on its series of bytes. CORBA's streaming APIs are responsible for reading and writing an object over a network, which involves converting it to a stream of bytes and then sending that data to the destination machine. The streaming APIs also deal with basic types. The Java classes for CORBA's streaming APIs are shown here:

```
package org.omg.CORBA.portable;

public abstract class InputStream {
        public abstract boolean read_boolean();
        public abstract char read_char();
        public abstract char read_wchar();
        public abstract byte read_octet();
        public abstract short read_short();
        public abstract short read_ushort();
        public abstract int read_long();
        public abstract int read_ulong();
        public abstract long read_longlong();
        public abstract long read_ulonglong();
        public abstract float read_float();
        public abstract double read_double();
        public abstract String read_string();
        public abstract String read_wstring();

        public abstract void read_boolean_array( boolean[] value,
                int offset, int length );
        public abstract void read_char_array( char[] value,
                int offset, int length );
        public abstract void read_wchar_array( char[] value,
                int offset, int length );
        public abstract void read_octet_array( byte[] value,
                int offset, int length );
        public abstract void read_short_array( short[] value,
                int offset, int length );
```

```
          public abstract void read_ushort_array( short[] value,
                  int offset, int length );
          public abstract void read_long_array( int[] value,
                  int offset, int length );
          public abstract void read_ulong_array( int[] value,
                  int offset, int length );
          public abstract void read_longlong_array( long[] value,
                  int offset, int length );
          public abstract void read_ulonglong_array( long[] value,
                  int offset, int length );
          public abstract void read_float_array( float[] value,
                  int offset, int length );
          public abstract void read_double_array( double[] value,
                  int offset, int length );

          public abstract org.omg.CORBA.Object read_Object();
          public abstract org.omg.CORBA.TypeCode read_TypeCode();
          public abstract org.omg.CORBA.Any read_any();
          public abstract org.omg.CORBA.Principal read_Principal();
}
```

A CORBA input stream can be created only from an instance of CORBA's output stream. To further complicate matters, CORBA's output stream is created via an ORB's `create_output_stream()` operation. The Java code for both the CORBA output and input streams is shown here:

```
package org.omg.CORBA.portable;

public abstract class OutputStream {
          public abstract org.omg.CORBA.portable.InputStream
                  create_input_stream();

          public abstract write_boolean( boolean value );
          public abstract write_char( char value );
          public abstract write_wchar( char value );
          public abstract write_octet( byte value );
          public abstract write_short( short value );
          public abstract write_ushort( short value );
          public abstract write_long( int value );
          public abstract write_ulong( int value );
          public abstract write_longlong( long value );
          public abstract write_ulonglong( long value );
          public abstract write_float( float value );
          public abstract write_double( double value );
          public abstract write_string( String value );
          public abstract write_wstring( String value );
```

```
        public abstract void write_boolean_array( boolean[] value,
                int offset, int length );
        public abstract void write_char_array( char[] value,
                int offset, int length );
        public abstract void write_wchar_array( char[] value,
                int offset, int length );
        public abstract void write_octet_array( byte[] value,
                int offset, int length );
        public abstract void write_short_array( short[] value,
                int offset, int length );
        public abstract void write_ushort_array( short[] value,
                int offset, int length );
        public abstract void write_long_array( int[] value,
                int offset, int length );
        public abstract void write_ulong_array( int[] value,
                int offset, int length );
        public abstract void write_longlong_array( long[] value,
                int offset, int length );
        public abstract void write_ulonglong_array( long[] value,
                int offset, int length );
        public abstract void write_float_array( float[] value,
                int offset, int length );
        public abstract void write_double_array( double[] value,
                int offset, int length );

        public abstract void write_Object(
                org.omg.CORBA.Object value );
        public abstract void write_TypeCode(
                org.omg.CORBA.TypeCode value );
        public abstract void write_any( org.omg.CORBA.Any value );
        public abstract void write_Principal(
                org.omg.CORBA.Principal value );
}

package org.omg.CORBA.portable;

public abstract class InputStream {
        public abstract boolean read_boolean();
        public abstract char read_char();
        public abstract char read_wchar();
        public abstract byte read_octet();
        public abstract short read_short();
        public abstract short read_ushort();
        public abstract int read_long();
        public abstract int read_ulong();
        public abstract long read_longlong();
        public abstract long read_ulonglong();
```

```
public abstract float read_float();
public abstract double read_double();
public abstract String read_string();
public abstract String read_wstring();

public abstract void read_boolean_array( boolean[] value,
        int offset, int length );
public abstract void read_char_array( char[] value,
        int offset, int length );
public abstract void read_wchar_array( char[] value,
        int offset, int length );
public abstract void read_octet_array( byte[] value,
        int offset, int length );
public abstract void read_short_array( short[] value,
        int offset, int length );
public abstract void read_ushort_array( short[] value,
        int offset, int length );
public abstract void read_long_array( int[] value,
        int offset, int length );
public abstract void read_ulong_array( int[] value,
        int offset, int length );
public abstract void read_longlong_array( long[] value,
        int offset, int length );
public abstract void read_ulonglong_array( long[] value,
        int offset, int length );
public abstract void read_float_array( float[] value,
        int offset, int length );
public abstract void read_double_array( double[] value,
        int offset, int length );

public abstract org.omg.CORBA.Object read_Object();
public abstract org.omg.CORBA.TypeCode write read_TypeCode();
public abstract org.omg.CORBA.Any read_any();
public abstract org.omg.CORBA.Principal read_Principal();
}
```

CHAPTER 8

Enterprise JavaBeans to CORBA Specification Mapping

This chapter describes (1) how distribution is mapped, including the relationship between an EJB and a CORBA object and how Java's Remote Method Invocation (RMI) relates to the EJB specification of OMG IDL; (2) how the Common Object Services (COS) locates EJBHome objects; (3) how EJB transactions map to the OMG Object Transaction Service (OTS); and (4) how EJB security maps to CORBA security.

8.1 Enterprise JavaBeans

Enterprise JavaBeans (EJB) is an architecture for developing and deploying component software. The software developed via EJB is object-oriented, distributed, and tailored for enterprise-level Java applications. The applications developed are scalable, transactional, and secure with respect to multiple users. More information about EJB can be found at http://www.javasoft.com.

8.2   *Mapping for Distribution*

The Remote Method Invocation (RMI) is Java and JavaBeans' primary means of object distribution. RMI and the Internet Inter-ORB Protocol (IIOP) are both inter-object communications protocols. RMI is exclusively Java (hence EJB), whereas IIOP is cross-language, used by CORBA. RMI will eventually support IIOP. Thus, IIOP should be used in EJB applications using CORBA instead of RMI, at this time. Although CORBA does not explicitly state that IIOP must be used, CORBA and IIOP are becoming almost synonymous. Thus, we presume that applications using EJB with CORBA have IIOP as the underlying communications protocol.

8.2.1   Mapping Remote Interfaces to IDL

Every Enterprise JavaBean deployed by the EJB server has two remote interfaces: `EJBHome` and `EJBObject`. The Java-to-IDL Mapping (http://www.omg.org/docs/orbos/97-03-08.pdf) and Objects by Value (http://www.omg.org/docs/orbos/98-01-18.pdf) describe precisely how these two interfaces are mapped to IDL.

8.2.2   Mapping the Handle Object

An Interoperable Object Reference (IOR) defines the standard mapping of the `Handle` object. The IDL code for the mapping is as follows:

```
value Handle();
value StandardHandle : Handle {
        public string EJBObjectIOR:
};
```

8.2.3   Mapping the EJBMetaData Object

Like `Handle`, `EJBMetaData` is a value object. The IDL code for the mapping is

```
value EJBMetaData();
value StandardEJBMetaData : EJBMetaData {
        public string    EJBHomeIOR;
```

```
        public string      homeClassName;
        public string      remoteClassName;
        public string      keyClassName;
        public boolean     isSession;
};
```

8.2.4   Marking Transaction-Enabled EJB Objects

A transaction-enabled bean has its transaction attribute set to BEAN_MANAGED, SUPPORTS, REQUIRED, REQUIRES_NEW, or MANDATORY. It maps to CORBA according to the following rules:

- The transaction-enabled bean's remote interface must have its corresponding IDL interface inherit from the CosTransactions::TransactionalObject IDL interface.

- An Enterprise bean's home interface must have its corresponding IDL interface inherit from the CosTransactions::TransactionalObject IDL interface.

8.2.5   Client Stubs

The client type dictates the type of stub used for the communication path. Client stubs may be RMI/IIOP or regular IDL stubs, as specified by language-specific CORBA mappings.

8.2.6   CORBA Objects and EJBs

The CORBA runtime can use a servant that implements the Enterprise JavaBean's CORBA IDL. The servant delegates method invocation to the appropriate Enterprise JavaBean via TIE-based skeletons (defined in CORBA 2.x), which are created when the bean is instantiated.

8.3   *Mappings for Names*

A CORBA-based Enterprise JavaBean runtime is necessary to publish and resolve EJBHome interface objects via the OMG's COS NameService. The

`NameService` can be used via the Java Naming and Directory Interface (JNDI) API in coordination with the regular COS naming service provider, or it can be used directly via the COS Naming API.

8.3.1 COS Namespace Layout

The `BeanHomeName` property, which can be found in each bean's deployment descriptor, gives the pathname in the namespace where the Enterprise bean's container object is bound.

A sample Java archive (JAR) file contains the following names: `company/ payroll/receivable`, `company/payroll/payable`, and `company/ manager/president`. This sample archive contains five naming contexts:

- The root of the COS namespace (which is transparent). It can be retrieved by invoking the ORB's `resolve_initial_references` method with `NameService` as the parameter.
- The location (also transparent) of the JAR file (or where it is "installed"). There need not be a relationship between the first and second naming contexts. If they differ, the client must be told the path that lies between them.
- Context 1 with the name `company` bound to it.
- Context 2 with the name `payroll` bound to it.
- Context 2 with the name `manager` bound to it.

The following rules govern construction of an instance of `CosNaming::Name` (so that `CosNaming` APIs may be used) from a container path:

- The container path should be parsed from left to right.
- Each name separated with the forward slash (`/`) becomes an `id` field of type `CosNaming::NameComponent`.
- The `NameComponent` representing the `kind` field is always an empty string (`" "`).

8.4   *Transaction Mapping*

Use of the OMG Object Transaction Service (OTS) for transaction support requires a CORBA-based Enterprise JavaBean runtime. This section describes how Enterprise JavaBean transaction concepts are mapped to OTS.

8.4.1   Propagation of Transactions

EJB-to-IDL mapping guidelines ensure that a transaction-enabled EJB's remote interface will have its IDL interface inherit from the `CosTransactions::TransactionalObject` IDL interface. This makes certain that the ORB and the OMG OTS propagate the context of the client's transaction (presuming the client has a transaction context) to the appropriate EJB object.

8.4.2   Transaction Container Support

All client method invocations for an EJB are interposed by the container for that particular bean. Interposition assists the container in its declarative transaction management. Table 8.1 lists the actions taken by the Enterprise JavaBean runtime server in response to the EJB's transaction attribute.

Table 8.1   EJB Runtime Response to Transaction Attributes

Transaction Attribute	Client's Transaction	Server Operation on `TransactionCurrent`
TX_NOT_SUPPORTED	—	—
	Transaction 1 (T1)	Suspend T1 Invoke JavaBean Resume T1
TX_BEAN_MANAGED	—	Resume JavaBean Transaction Invoke JavaBean Pause JavaBean Transaction
TX_REQUIRED	—	Start Transaction 2 (T2) Invoke JavaBean Stop T2
	T1	Inherits T1

Table 8.1   EJB Runtime Response to Transaction Attributes   (Continued)

Transaction Attribute	Client's Transaction	Server Operation on `TransactionCurrent`
TX_SUPPORTS	—	—
	T1	Inherits T1
TX_REQUIRES_NEW	—	Start T2
		Invoke JavaBean
		Stop T2
	T1	Pause T1
		Start T2
		Invoke JavaBean
		Stop T2
		Resume T1
TX_MANDATORY	—	Throw TRANSACTION_REQUIRED exception
	T1	Inherit T1

Note that "Stop Transaction" indicates that either a commit or an abort will result depending on the respective success or failure of the operation invoked on the Enteprise bean.

Exception handling aside, the following pseudo-code shows the implementation of a CORBA-based container that has the necessary semantics of an Enterprise bean's transaction attribute:

TX_NOT_SUPPORTED

```
clientTransaction = Current.suspend();
result = bean.operation( arguments );
Current.resume( clientTransaction );
return result;
```

TX_BEAN_MANAGED

```
clientTransaction = Current.suspend();
Current.resume( transactionInstance );
result = bean.operation( arguments );
Current.suspend();
Current.resume( clientTransaction );
return result;
```

TX_REQUIRED

```
if( Current.getStatus() == StatusActive ) {
    return bean.operation( arguments );
} else {
    Current.begin();
    result = bean.operation( arguments );
    Current.commit();
    return result;
}
```

TX_SUPPORTS

```
return bean.operation( arguments );
```

TX_REQUIRES_NEW

```
clientTransaction = Current.suspend();
Current.begin();
result = bean.operation( arguments );
Current.commit();
Current.resume( clientTransaction );
return result;
```

TX_MANDATORY

```
if( Current.getStatus() == StatusActive ) {
    return bean.operation( arguments );
} else {
    throw org.omg.CORBA.TRANSACTION_REQUIRED( … );
}
```

8.4.3 Demarcation on the Client Side

It is not unusual for a CORBA client to demarcate transaction boundaries using the OTS `Current` interface. However, it is the CORBA-based EJB infrastructure's job to make sure that the client's transaction context is sent to the transaction-enabled Enterprise beans.

8.5 Security Mapping

The ORB must know the client's identity, or at least be able to determine it, for the proper access control to be administered. A JavaBean's deployment descriptor yields the bean's identity, which can then be checked against an

Access Control List (ACL) when one bean communicates with another (client/server scenario) or when a bean tries to obtain protected resources.

The identity of a client bean is based on an ORB's security and communication protocol. This protocol is typically one of the following:

- *IIOP.* Sent down the communication path is an instance of `CORBA::Principal`. The user identification, given by the operating system, can be mapped by the ORB to verify the client bean's identity.

- *Common Secure IIOP (CSI).* A specific security mechanism (GSSKerberos, SPKM, CSI-EMCA, etc.) is used in conjunction with Secure IIOP (SECIOP) to verify the client bean's identity.

- *IIOP over Secure Socket Layer (SSL).* The X.500 standard provides the client bean's identity using SSL authentication.

If CSI or IIOP over SSL is used, `CORBA::Principal` becomes deprecated. This means that the ORB should have implemented either the Common Secure IIOP specification or the CORBAsecurity/SLL to ensure reliable security.

8.6   Enterprise JavaBeans IDL

The IDL code for exceptions and other objects is given here: first, the source for Enterprise JavaBeans and then the source for the Exception IDL mapping.

```
// EBJ Source
#include "java.lang.ExceptionValue.idl"

module javax {
    module ejb {
        value CreateException : ::java:lang:Exception();
        exception CreateEx {
            CreateException the_value;
        };

        value DuplicateKeyException : ::java:lang:Exception();
        exception DuplicateKeyEx {
```

```
        DuplicateKeyException the_value;
};

value EJBException : ::java:lang:Exception();
exception EJBEx {
    EJBException the_value;
};

value FinderException : ::java:lang:Exception();
exception FinderEx {
    FinderException the_value;
};

value ObjectNotFoundException : ::java:lang:Exception();
exception ObjectNotFoundEx {
    ObjectNotFoundException the_value;
};

value RemoveException : ::java:lang:Exception();
exception RemoveEx {
    RemoveException the_value;
};

value Handle();
value StandardHandle : Handle {
    public string EJBObjectIOR;
};

value EJBMetaData();
value StandardEJBMetaData : EJBMetaData {
    public string     EJBHomeIOR;
    public string     homeClassName;
    public string     remoteClassName;
    public string     keyClassName;
    public boolean    isSession;
};

interface EJBObject {
    EJBHome getEJBHome();
    Any getPrimaryKey();
    void remove() raises( RemoveEx );
    Handle getHandle();
    boolean isIdentical( in EJBObject object );
};
```

```
        interface EJBHome {
            EJBMetaData getEJBMetaData();
            void remove( Any primaryKey ) raises( RemoveEx );
            void remove( Handle handle ) raises( RemoveEx );
        };
    };  // module ejb
};      // module javax


// Exception IDL source mapping
module java {
    module lang {
        value Exception {
            public ::CORBA::WstringValue detailMessage;
        };
    };  // Module lang
};      // Module java
```

CORBA Glossary

Activation   The steps taken to ready an object for executing a requested operation.

Active State   The state in which a Portable Object Adapter (POA) manager's associated POAs start receiving and processing requests. Even in the active state, a POA may need to queue requests, depending on the resource limits of its ORB.

Addressing   The Object Model specification of an object reference as the name of a CORBA-compliant object that uniquely identifies that object. An object reference must point to the same object each time that object is addressed. However, an object may have more than one reference, so that all references point only to that object for the object's lifetime.

Application Object   An object created by a single vendor that controls the vendor's interfaces. In this sense, Application object is basically another term for *application*. Application objects sit outside of CORBA and are not standardized by the OMG.

Application Programming Interface (API)   A predefined set of code (commonly software objects) that defines, or yields, a well-documented behavior. The documentation should tell programmers what functions are available to them as well as their location. Alternatively, an API can be a specification for behavior at the code level whose implementation is left to a vendor of that particular API.

Argument   In essence, a synonym for *parameter*. The variables passed to an operation are known as the arguments to the operation.

Attribute   An interface may define attributes. Attributes are simply variable declarations. Essentially, this means that the resulting object that implements the interface containing attributes will have two additional functions. One will allow the attribute to be set (changed), the other will allow the attribute to be retrieved.

Behavior   The observable effects of the object upon executing a requested operation.

C   A system programming language developed at Bell Laboratories to implement a new operating system on a DEP PDP-11 minicomputer. C is a terse language that includes data types, data separations, simple flow control, and the ability to directly modify memory addresses.

C++   A programming language developed at AT&T by Bjarne Stroustrup. It was originally implemented as a translator to normal C that would combine object-oriented techniques with efficiency and portability.

Character Set   The Latin alphabet, Japanese characters, characters specific to certain European languages (such as the German ß), and other characters. A character set has no notion of code, but rather is used to represent, organize, or control data.

Class   A software entity used primarily in object-oriented languages to define a set of attributes and/or behaviors that may be inherited by subclasses, instantiated in the form of objects, or used statically by themselves.

Client- and Implementation-Resident ORB   ORBs written to use the routines in clients and implementations via a communications mechanism, such as an IPC or location service.

Client Object A CORBA-compliant object that sends a request to another object (typically a server object) to invoke a particular operation.

Client Stub A means by which non-object-oriented languages may communicate with ORBs in order to use objects.

Comment In IDL, an English-based description of an interface. Block comments span multiple lines (starting with / * and ending with * /). Line comments are only a single line (starting with / /).

Common Data Representation (CDR) A transfer syntax for mapping OMG IDL data types to a bicanonical, low-level representation. As specified by CDR, this representation has three major features: variable byte ordering, aligned primitive types, and complete OMG IDL mapping, which ensures that the data is transferred from agent to agent without dependencies on the underlying hardware / software platform.

Common Facilities Common services that many applications use, but that are not as critical as object services themselves. An electronic mail service might be classified as a common facility.

Common Inter-ORB Protocol (CIOP) A CORBA protocol written to serve four main functions: (1) supporting multivendor, mission-critical ORB-based applications; (2) leveraging DCE services when possible; (3) allowing efficient implementations using public DCE APIs; and (4) preserving the freedom of an ORB's implementation.

Common Object Request Broker Architecture (CORBA) An umbrella term for the set of components that facilitate the language-, operating–system- and hardware-independent specification that allows objects to communicate with one another across heterogeneous and homogeneous networks.

Component Object Model (COM) A framework for integrating components developed by Microsoft Corporation. It maintains the interoperability and reusability of distributed objects by allowing developers to build systems by assembling reusable components from different vendors. Also, an API that allows the creation of components for use in integrating custom applications or to allow diverse components to interact.

Constant   An identifier whose value never changes throughout its lifetime. That value may be any literal.

Context Object   An object containing properties, each of which has a name and an associated string value. Context properties usually contain information about a client object, the environment, or the circumstances of a request that do not readily map to parameters.

CORBA Module   A module in which all names defined in CORBA are declared. This stops predefined CORBA names from clashing with names in programming languages and software applications.

Deactivation   The steps taken after an object has executed a requested operation.

Deferred Synchronous Operation   One of two ways in which a client may ask for an operation to be completed. The first is the regular invocation, which leaves the client object waiting for the server object to finish the request and return a value. The second is a deferred synchronous operation in which the client object asks a server object to perform an operation, but does not wait for a return value.

Delegation   The passing of a method invocation request from one object to another. When a client object requests an operation, the server object relays the request to an object (unknown to the client) that is capable of performing the operation. The server hands the result of the operation back to the client object (presuming the operation yielded a return value).

Discarding State   The state in which a POA manager's associated POAs disregard all incoming requests, and any client requests result in a `TRANSIENT` system exception indicating that the request must be resent.

Distributed Computing Environment (DCE)   An industry-standard, vendor-neutral collection of distributed computing technologies that has security services, name services, and a scalable model to help organize remote users, services, and data. DCE runs on all major computer systems, supporting distributed applications in heterogeneous environments, and is used in some of the most important areas of computing: security, the World Wide Web, and distributed objects.

Distributed Environment   A system of several interconnected computers whose means of connection is undefined. The machines themselves can be personal computers, Unix workstations, portable laptops, Cray supercomputers, or any other device capable of executing the code for a CORBA-compliant object. The network through which the machines communicate (via CORBA) can be anything from a local area network to the Internet.

Domain   In the CORBA architecture, a collection of objects that have a particular characteristic in common, used as a means of partitioning components. A domain can be recursed—that is, any given domain may contain other domains.

Dynamic Invocation Interface (DII)   The CORBA interface that allows client objects to invoke an operation at runtime by specifying the object, the name of the operation, and the operation's parameters. Unlike the predefined stub operation, here the name of a stub is known at compile time.

Dynamic Skeleton Interface   Like the Dynamic Invocation Interface, this is an interface that allows an ORB to invoke methods on objects without knowing an operation's name and parameters until runtime. A static knowledge (such as a string representation) of the operation's name may be used, or the name may be looked up at runtime via an Interface Repository.

Environment-Specific Inter-ORB Protocol (ESIOP)   Within a specific networking infrastructure, essentially a set of instructions for bridging the communications gap between ORBs. All ESIOP specifications must conform to the general ORB interoperability architecture.

Exception   A means to indicate that an error occurred during an operation. Not only do exceptions release the client object from knowing the exact value of an error, but they also allow the server object to give the client additional exception-specific information.

Externalized Object Reference   A reference to an object converted to an ORB-specific string representation. This allows the reference to be stored in files, displayed for debugging purposes, and such.

First In, First Out (FIFO)   The ordering of data in a queue such that it will be read out in the exact order that it was written in.

Function   A named sequence of instructions to be carried out by either a client object or a server object. *Operation* and *method* are sometimes used synonymously with *function*. Functions differ from procedures in that they return a value to the client.

General Inter-ORB Protocol (GIOP)   A standard transfer syntax for transferring low-level data between ORBs. The GIOP is built for ORB-to-ORB communications and designed to work with connection-oriented transport protocols (such as TCP/IP) that comply with a minimal set of assumptions.

Holding State   The state in which a POA manager's associated POAs queue all incoming requests. The maximum number of requests that can be queued depends on the resource limits of a POA's ORB. If the limit is reached, any additional client requests will result in a TRANSIENT system exception indicating the request must be resent.

Identifier   In IDL, a sequence of alphanumeric characters and the underscore (_) of any length. Identifiers must start with either an underscore or an alphabetic character, and are case insensitive.

Implementation   The actual software code that conforms to a given interface. An object being coded to a particular interface must respond to all of the operations as defined by the given interface, and have accessor methods for all declared attributes.

Implementation Repository   Usually, the location for installation of implementations and control of policies that deal with the activation and execution of object implementations. It contains information that assists the ORB in finding and activating objects.

Inactive State   The state in which a POA manager's associate POAs are shut down. This state is not temporary, so all new client requests are rejected. The client is informed of this rejection in a vendor-specific manner.

Inheritance   The means by which one interface derives the attributes and behaviors of a base interface. The derived interface may add new attributes and behaviors, and it may use the attributes and behaviors of the base interface as though they were declared in the same scope.

Interceptor An implementation of a service (such as security) that may be inserted in the invocation path—that is, small pieces of software that automatically run after a client object requests an operation, but before that operation is invoked. Interceptors are not a required extension to ORBs.

Interface A description (for other objects) of the set of operations an object is capable of performing. Client objects may invoke the methods described by an object's interface only if they provide proper information (parameters, return value, etc.) as dictated by the interface.

Interface Definition Language (IDL) A universal mapping language to describe the operations particular objects understand. IDL allows for objects written in different computer languages to communicate with one another over heterogeneous networking environments. Thus, for example, an object written in object-oriented COBOL can execute on a Macintosh. The Macintosh object can receive a request to invoke a given method from, say, a C++ object executing on an IBM clone. The C++ object can use the COBOL object transparently, as though it were running on the clone itself.

Interface Repository A service that holds IDL information (in the form of persistent objects) for use by objects at runtime. It is through this service that the dynamic invocation becomes extremely useful.

Internet Inter-ORB Protocol (IIOP) The specification for transmission of GIOP messages over a TCP/IP-based network. IIOP permits ORBs to be interoperable in Internet protocol domains.

Interoperability The capability of objects to communicate within a heterogeneous environment. The objects are interoperable in that they can send and receive requests transparent to the underlying system.

Interoperable Object Reference (IOR) A reference to a data structure that contains information about the communication bridges between ORBs. This information answers questions such as "Is the object null," "What type of object is it," "What protocols are supported," and "What ORB services are available?"

Inter-ORB Bridge Support The APIs and conventions that facilitate the necessary interoperability bridges between ORB domains.

Inter-Process Communication (IPC) A means for creating a distributed program, in which a single application may have many subprocesses executing on different machines. IPC is used for communication between processes on the same network.

Keyword Words that may not be used for names of variables, objects, or interfaces. There are many reserved keywords in IDL. Keywords must not mix case, but be used as they are shown in the following table.

any	double	interface	readonly	unsigned
attribute	enum	long	sequence	union
boolean	exception	module	short	void
case	FALSE	Object	string	wchar
char	fixed	octet	struct	wstring
const	float	oneway	switch	
context	in	out	TRUE	
default	inout	raises	typedef	

Library-Based ORB An ORB in which light-weight objects with sharable implementations may reside. With this type of ORB, stubs may be the methods themselves. The data for the objects is made available to the clients, but the implementation insists that the client not damage it.

Literal A constant value assigned to an identifier. IDL has five literals: integers, characters, floating-point numbers, strings, and fixed-point numbers. A sequence of digits 1–9 is treated as an integer. A character enclosed in single quotes is treated as a character. A floating-point number is an integer, followed by a decimal, a fractional component, then an e or E. A string is a sequence of characters enclosed in double quotes. A fixed-point number is the same as a floating-point number ending in d or D, and either the integer or fractional component may be missing (but not both).

Mapping The specification of an IDL object's operations that have a one-to-one correlation with those of an object written in another computer language (Java, C++, Smalltalk, etc.). All operations for an IDL object must be implemented as methods in the implementation language. However, not all the methods of an implementation language object must be mapped into IDL.

Marshaling The transparent sending of requests, and possibly objects, from one place to another. The request may be sent over the Internet to and from a distant machine or to and from the same machine. (A smart ORB recognizes the source and destination machine as the same and avoids the marshaling process.) In marshaling the request, or object, is broken down into a sequence of bytes, which are then sent to the destination that assembles them and completes the request.

Method In object-oriented terminology, a function or procedure encapsulated by an object. In CORBA, methods are called *operations*. The difference between a method and an operation is that a method can be exclusive to an object, whereas an operation may be invoked by any client object at any time.

Multiplexing Connection A client's ability to send requests to many server objects over the same connection, so long as the server side of the connection supports multiple-request response. This eases the load on the server; however, the client is entitled to open a new connection for each server object it wishes to send the request.

Narrow Character Typically an 8-bit character, which is enough information to represent all the characters used in western European languages.

Object A unique entity that provides at least one service that can be invoked by a client. A client, in this case, is usually another object unrestricted in terms of its software, hardware, or location within the distributed environment.

Object Adapter A CORBA entity reponsible for generating and interpreting object references, invoking operations, ensuring security, activating and deactivating implementations, mapping object references to implementations, registering implementations, and so forth. It is also known simply as an *adapter*.

Object Creation An event that signals a new object unique to the entire system. It has at least one object reference, also one of a kind, that refers to that object only.

Object Destruction An event that indicates that an object is no longer accessible from an ORB. All object references to it become invalid.

Object Linking and Embedding (OLE) A Microsoft Windows facility that allows the use of several Windows applications to produce a single document.

With OLE, the original data becomes an object within the application using the data. It can appear as an icon, a Windows metafile, or ordinary text. OLE allows the user to start another Windows application and edit its data from within the application using the data.

Object Management Group (OMG)   The organization responsible for the creation of the CORBA specification. The OMG's goal for CORBA is the development of object-oriented software that is reusable, portable, and interoperable within heterogeneous networked environments.

Object Model   An organized way of presenting the terminology and concepts behind objects. The OMG object model is abstract, as it does not tie itself exclusively to any one field of technology.

Object Reference   The information that specifies a unique object within an ORB. Object references are transparent to the application objects communicating with other objects through the ORB, but the object reference given to a particular client object can be used only while that object exists. Finally, the OMG specifies there must be a unique object reference that does not point to any object (i.e., there must always be at least one valid object reference whose value is undefined).

Object Request Broker (ORB)   The CORBA component that gives objects the ability to send and receive requests and responses within a distributed runtime environment. It is essentially a small software program that awaits requests from a CORBA-compliant object on one machine to send a request or response to a CORBA-compliant object on another machine.

Object Request Broker Interface   An ORB interface provides some functions that are outside the realm of stubs or dynamic invocation (such as copying object references). Since most of an ORB's functionality is given through the object adapter, stubs, skeletons, and dynamic invocation, the ORB interface is a small specification.

Object Services   A collection of interfaces and objects that support the implementation and use of other objects. Services run independently of the application domain and are required to build any distributed application.

Operation   A unique entity to indicate a service that can be requested by client objects. Operations may be generic in that a single operation can be requested on different objects, which might implement it differently. This may result in different behavior than expected.

ORB Boundaries   The partitioning of an environment into multiple ORBs. Security is a good reason for specifying ORB boundaries. An Internet ORB, for example, might allow public information to be widely accessible, whereas a Company ORB might place restrictions on the information made available.

ORB Interoperability Architecture   A conceptual framework that specifies the main components of interoperability and identifies compliance issues. The ORB Interoperability Architecture specifies conventions to insure that independently produced ORBs can be used with each other in a seamless fashion.

Parameters   A value passed into (or out of) an operation. Parameters have both a mode and a type. The mode dictates whether the parameter is sent from the client object to the server object (specified by the keyword in), from the server to the client (keyword out), or both (keyword inout). The type of the parameter restricts what variable type may be passed to the operation.

Pipe   A special communications path through which data passes between unrelated processes. One process (or more) writes to it, while another process reads from it.

Pointer   A programming convention whereby a variable references a location in memory at which data of that variable's type can be found. Pointers abound in C and C++, but are hidden in languages like Java and Smalltalk.

Policy Domain   The collection of roles and criteria that govern the objects within a particular domain. When an object is created, the ORB implicitly associates it with at least one policy domain. Policy domains allow problems to be attacked at the policy management level, rather than at the individual object level.

Policy Domain Manager   A unique object within each policy that records the membership of objects within a particular domain and facilitates their addition and removal from their domains. By virtue of being an object, a domain manager is a member of a domain, usually the domain it manages.

Policy Object   An object that encapsulates a specific type of policy. The policy itself becomes associated with a particular domain indirectly. The policy object is associated with a domain manager, which is in turn associated with a given policy domain.

Portable Object Adapter (POA)   A software entity defined by a standard set of interfaces that gives programmers the ability to write object implementations that can be ported across different ORB products. There are several other goals that a POA is designed to meet: support for objects that have persistent identities, support for the transparent activation of objects, support for multiple distinct instances of a POA on a server, and so forth.

Preprocessing   The stage of compiling where macros are substituted and source files are combined. Directives that provide line numbering control in diagnostics and debugging are also evaluated at this point.

Procedure   A named sequence of instructions to be carried out by either a client or server object. The terms *operation* and *method* are sometimes used synonymously with *procedure*. Procedures differ from functions in that they do not return a value to the client.

Protocol   A predefined set of messages (or data) that defines how software entities can exchange information. The client knows what information the server is waiting to receive, in the format specified by the protocol. Similarly, the server knows what responses the client can reasonably expect (and hence respond to).

Pseudo-Object   An object that does not have any object references and that cannot have any of its operations invoked via the Dynamic Invocation Interface. Most pseudo-objects cannot be used as arguments to operations.

Remote Procedure Call (RPC)   A communications layer above the layer that provides access from one procedure (method, function, or operation) to another. It is much like a local procedure call. This type of communication is point to point and synchronous; however, there are ways to make RPC asynchronous.

Reply Message   The return values from request messages. Replies encompass `inout` and `out` parameters and the results of operations, and may also include exception values and object location information.

Request A client object invocation of a method (either a procedure or function) on another object. The request dictates the operation, target object, any number of optional parameters, and a request context.

Return Result The value returned to the client by the server after the client requests an operation to be executed.

Scope The visibility of an object or identifier (collectively "variable"). A variable may be declared global to a module, global to an interface, or used within a structure, a union, an operation, or an exception. Types, constants, enumerations, exceptions, interfaces, attributes, and operations also are scoped.

Server An entity that implements at least one operation on at least one object. Server objects execute operations requested by clients.

Server Object A CORBA-compliant object that receives a request from another object to have a particular operation invoked.

Server-Based ORB A software entity whose job is to route requests from clients to the implementations. Clients and implementations can establish communication paths with one another via one or more servers. The operating system would view the ORB as a regular software entity, leaving the clients the freedom to use regular IPC to communicate with the ORB.

Skeleton When a particular language is mapped to IDL, the interface to the methods that implement each type of object. Via the skeleton, the ORB calls the methods on an object that implements a given interface.

Smalltalk A computer language first written in 1972 (Smalltalk 72) by Alan Kay and others. A later version, Smalltalk 76, was completely object-oriented. In 1980, Smalltalk 80, a uniformly object-oriented programming environment, became the first Smalltalk version to be commercially released.

System-Based ORB An ORB used chiefly to increase security, enhance robustness, and augment performance. The ORB itself becomes a service offered by the operating system, which allows many optimizations to occur—for example, having the ORB detect object communications on the same machine and using simple IPC as opposed to marshaling.

Thread The code that is running within its own execution space. Threads run concurrently with other threads, allowing multiple tasks to be completed nearly simultaneously. For example, a program may calculate digits of pi indefinitely in one thread while awaiting input from the user in another thread.

Tokens In IDL, any identifier, keyword, literal, operator, or separator. White space in IDL refers to comments, horizontal and vertical tabs, newlines, and formfeeds. It is ignored, serving only to separate tokens.

Transient Object An object that exists only during the lifetime of the thread or process that created it. This is the opposite of a *persistent object*, which outlives its creator thread (or process) and exists until it is explicitly deleted.

Type An entity that defines results and parameters. Types include 16-, 32-, and 64-bit unsigned 2's complement integers, fixed-point decimal numbers up to 31 significant digits, single- and multibyte characters, booleans indicating TRUE or FALSE, enumerated types (ordered sequences), strings, and the any type, which represents any basic or constructed type.

Wide Character A 16- or 32-bit character used to represent a character in languages such as Japanese, Chinese, and Korean.

X/Open An organization comprising information system suppliers, software user organizations, and software companies. In order to enhance the portability of programs at the level of source code, X/Open has combined existing and emerging standards into a vast systems environment known as the Common Applications Environment (CAE).

Index

Index

About the Author

Reaz Hoque

Reaz Hoque is an author, speaker, and consultant currently working as a technical evangelist for EcCubed, Inc., an electronic commerce company that provides mission-critical electronic commerce components for the enterprise. Prior to joining EcCubed, Reaz worked as a technology evangelist for Netscape Communications Corp., where he wrote sample code and technical articles on Netscape technologies. Recently he spoke at Internet World, SIGS Java Expo, SIGS XML conference, and the Eighth International World Wide Web. His books include *Practical JavaScript Programming* (IDG Books, 1997), *Programming Web Components* (McGraw-Hill, 1998), *CORBA 3* (IDG Books, 1998), *JavaBeans 1.1 Handbook* (McGraw-Hill, 1998), and *InfoBus Programming* (Wiley, 1998).

About the Contributing Authors

Gabriel Minton

Gabriel Minton is Chief Technology Officer for Husky Labs, Inc., a software and systems integration company based in Shepherdstown, West Virginia. He also teaches courses on distributed programming and Java at George Washington University. Gabriel has authored several papers on CORBA and has spoken about Java and ActiveX.

Dave Jarvis

Dave Jarvis is a software architect. His current focus is object-oriented analysis and design as it relates to Java-related technologies. Dave works in the telecommunications industry and welcomes the challenge of staying abreast of the latest computer technologies.

Sukanta Ganguly

Sukanta Ganguly has been involved with distributed computing for the past three years. His passions are compilers, interpreters, programming languages, and the like. He has been spent many long hours studying different distributed development environments and platforms and is strongly attracted to operating systems and databases.

Vishal Anand

Vishal Anand is a software engineer and object-oriented design consultant who specializes in NT and C++ programming. He maintains a developer's forum on the Internet where he answers questions on C++, NT, and MFC/SDK. Vishal also consults on Web technologies and often helps friends and foes develop Web sites.

System Requirements

Windows 95/98 and NT

Pentium 100 or better

100 MB HD space(minimum)

32MB of Ram(minimum)